What Others Are Saying...

"We truly thought – and I actually said - it was impossible for anyone to add that much value in a two–day strategy offsite. Then Scott offered to do the work for free - paying him only if we succeeded. It was "an offer we couldn't refuse". One month later, his invoice was one of the easiest I've ever approved, and we gladly paid him. He did a truly amazing job of helping us collectively understand how our internal networks and external supply chain actually worked as a whole system. We used our common insight to leverage critical control points to achieve our own seemingly impossible goal."

– Ike Harris, Vice President
HP Global Notebook Supply Chain
Taipei, Taiwan

"Scott Spann has developed a unique and powerful systemic approach for enabling key decision makers and stakeholders to understand perceived problems in a larger context. It is one that weaves human relationships in ways that mirror the conceptual relationships in the system — but with an end in mind. Out of those interwoven relationships (both human and conceptual) emerge the leveraged responses we need to successfully deal with the complex, wicked problems confronting us today."

Fritjof Capra,
author of *The Tao of Physics* and
The Hidden Connections,
coauthor of *The Systems View of Life*

"Scott Spann often accomplishes the impossible. He has a rare talent for helping multi-stakeholder groups see a unified picture of something that is beyond any single person's point of view. He works his 'magic' through a deep understanding of complexity, systems thinking, and human discovery. He brings the right tools to the table so that people can not only 'see' together, but they can also think and act together in powerful new ways. As anyone in the Systems Thinking world will attest, this is no small feat and is a necessary step in solving the intractable problems we face today."

– Anne Murray Allen, Faculty
The Academy for Systems Change

"I think that among the most important jobs of a business leader is to make sound judgments regarding strategic priorities and allocation of resources. Regrettably, most of these judgments are made without practical, accurate understanding of the real leverage points for change in any given business system. Scott's work makes interdependencies and leverage points visible and causes these great results - inspiring insight; reduced risk; better, more confident decisions; a method for explaining big decisions. It is only through Scott that "system thinking" came alive for me and for our clients. It is no longer a slippery concept and has become real through his thinking and his tools. For me, he provides safer, smarter, more confident judgments that fuel the agile execution of strategy. Thank you, Scott, for that."

– Mickey Connolly,
CEO, Conversant & author,
The Communication Catalyst

"I worked with Scott during a time of significant and holistic transformation of a $25B high technology business. Scott's in-depth understanding of strategy, organizational dynamics and what it takes to drive sustainable business success is outstanding. And, when you couple that with his amazing ability to put the business strategy into a context that brings the people of the organization into *the center of the development and implementation of the strategy, the outcome is that it drives results quicker and more effectively than anything I've experienced before. Working with someone with Scott's expertise along with his high integrity, willingness to challenge the management team to rise to its highest potential, along with his wonderful personality was truly a joy."*

— Mary E. Peery, Senior Vice President
Hewlett Packard, IPG

"Scott is the best strategy consultant I've ever met. I formerly worked at McKinsey & Company doing corporate strategy, and subsequently worked with most of the top tier consulting firms as a private equity investor and now as a hedge fund manager. In all of my experiences with the best in the fields, Scott Spann stands out as a singular exception for having the ability to not only identify the core issues facing a client and develop a clear strategy to address those issues, but also formulate that strategy within the broader context of social, environmental, and cultural dimensions that are required to really make a strategy work. He has the highest professional and ethical standards. To work with Scott is to have the opportunity to grow as a person."

— Ray Conley, Partner,
Palo Alto Investors, LLC

"Extremely intelligent, strategic, and trustworthy"

— John Dukellis, Director,
Product Management at Google

"Literally, an unbelievable ability to simplify, clarify and make actionable the complexity of our business"

— David Taylor, Chief of Staff,
HP Global PC Notebook Supply Chain

"We had Scott assist us with highly substantial changes to our entire operational construct. He comes to a project with the intent to make a real and positive difference. Sorting out complex situations is his specialty. His keen intellect, critical thinking capability and disciplined logic would be very tough to match. His thoughtful, open-minded approach allowed us to see things that were right under our noses. He made an incredibly positive difference. If I had one person to go to for my toughest issues, I would seek help from Scott."

**– Doug White, Vice President
Lockheed Martin's Fleet Ballistic Missile Portfolio**

"Scott Spann has a unique and uncanny ability to help executives articulate business strategies and plans. It is as if he reaches down into their minds and hearts to help these executives extract the essence of their expertise to address current critical business challenges."

**– Frank Rogers-Witte, Director,
HP IPG Executive Staff Effectiveness**

"Scott knows more about strategic systems thinking and systems analysis than anyone else I know. He's poured a lot of his magic into this book; if you're trying to tackle big, complex, wicked problems, this book is absolutely essential. Leaders who believe they can rely on traditional strategic planning in today's world are living in the past."

**– Tim Kelley, global change agent and
author of *True Purpose***

I don't believe more of the same will result in different outcomes... Scott Spann is a very interesting and gifted consultant who specializes in working with diverse community groups on "wicked problems"--messy, circular and aggressive issues. He has been successful in helping groups with seemingly different objectives and approaches find common ground to enable [them] to work together in new ways. Scott's efforts created the necessary break-though for REAMP to really take off.

Prior to his involvement, great well-intended folks were so wedded to their own agenda we couldn't effectively move forward boldly to game-changing strategies.

– Becky Erdahl, Executive Director,
Carolyn Foundation

"The most powerful and effective leadership offsite of my career"

– Erle Nye, CEO,
TXU

Scott Spann is a systems thinker and problem solver.... Scott was an incredibly positive force in Midwest energy politics and policy, helping the REAMP collaboration of NGOs and funders at its most critical juncture--the formative year. Through his efforts, REAMP players thought deeply about the system of electric industry and clean energy advocacy.... Scott [built] a dynamic systems model that every NGO player accepted as "the way things work". He helped NGOs see how to push on the system to effect change--and since then, our influence and efficacy has dramatically increased. Since that time, REAMP has built a chaordic network of NGOs that have dramatically changed the power relations and changed the debate on energy independence and global warming solutions. Many new resources in philanthropy have come to the Midwest as a result, and high transparency and high trust has characterized the REAMP network's efforts.

– Michael Noble, Executive Director,
Fresh Energy

Solving for the

Impossible...

*Harnessing Chaos & Complexity to
Heal Business, Society & the Earth*

*An Evolutionary
Strategic Method & Mindset*

by
R Scott Spann

Solving for the Impossible
Harnessing Chaos & Complexity to Heal Business, Society & the Earth
An Evolutionary Strategic Method & Mindset

ISBN: 978-0-578-98607-4

A Quick, Essential Preface

(Open me first!)

A funny thing happened on the way to the printer…

I'm told that the problem with not *immediately* publishing a finished manuscript is that one's thinking continues to evolve—sometimes at an even quicker pace—tempting one to engage in endless loops of rewrites. I'm no different.

When I was in the software world, we dealt with this by mandating a "code freeze"—no more changes allowed. Again, I'm no different.

I'm there—and, along with that, this edition of the book is already behind. So even though my experience in solving "impossible" problems continues to evolve, this book won't—not for now.

But I hadn't yet written this preface. So I have a bit of wiggle room to share something vital about what this book—what this strategic method and mindset—is fundamentally all about—and how that came to be. Briefly…

I jumped back into the "business" world from what I'll call the "healing" world—my time as a Rolfer®, a trauma and a developmental psychotherapist—with the specific intention of bringing what I'd learned about being more fully Human[1] into the Business world. But admittedly, I had no real idea how that would play out. Luckily…

---

[1] Given the significance of being Human in today's World, I've chosen to adopt the German custom of capitalizing certain nouns from time to time to call out their vital importance in this way of working—even of being.

Though I re-entered the Business world in the domains of culture change (in Mergers & Acquisitions) and leadership development (with Fortune 100 CxO's), I was eventually asked to do strategy work for corporations and NGO's operating at a global level—something that, given the emerging complexity of the space, demanded that I train in systems thinking and system dynamics.

It was then that I discovered the implicit fit between how we can become more fully Human and how we can bring that to bear on creating a step-change in a system's performance, especially in the midst of chaos & complexity—be it a business, social, or natural system. I also discovered how, rather than trying to change mindsets first (an all-too-common error), allowing clients to experience the *methods* employed by doing real work would bring about the *mindset* shift— rather than the other way around. As these methods cumulatively evolved into a methodology, I eventually reached a state where my clients—in addition to acknowledging and appreciating the strategic and performance results we achieved—were using words like "bliss", "compassion" and even "love" to describe the end state of our work together (yes, it surprised me, too).

When I started this book, I envisioned it as a straightforward take on strategy—admittedly in a radically different way—but still within the domain of strategy as we normally think of it. But then (I was writing during the pandemic), as our economic, social, and environmental struggles continued to increase—even accelerate—I came to realize (after I'd handed the manuscript over to my editors) that a very different, much more explicit mindset was needed—that of Healing.

Despite the audacity of applying such a concept to my work, the need for healing so deeply resonated with me that I was compelled—no matter how naïve it may seem at first glance (but only at first glance)— to call out Healing for the following reasons…

First, the time for speaking about strategy in terms of sales revenue, net profit margin, gross margin, MMR (monthly recurring revenue),

This is it ♡♡♡ _for my book_

NPS (net promoter score), etc., has run its course. Don't get me wrong—they are still necessary—i.e., "necessary but not sufficient". But, given what's confronting us today, we _must_ do better. We are now called upon to evolve within our lifetime(s)—to evolve relative to what's emerging (and emerging at an increasing rate). Hence, further prompting me to declare the result of this Work to be, in addition to Healing, Evolutionary.

For me (and I hope for you), approaching today's issues/opportunities as if we're practicing the art and science of Healing fulfills both of those "promises"—that of Healing and that of Evolving. In my years in the healing professions with my colleagues in Boulder, CO (physicians, chiropractors, acupuncturists, etc.), we were continually exploring what we were about—what was our Purpose. What did it mean to heal[2]? At its root, it means "to make whole"[3]—something that rang true for us then—as it does for me now—especially as applied to the need for wholeness in our relationship with Business, Society, and the Earth + _our selves + our role with each of these_

So imagine if one adopts the concept—the mindset—of healing _(Self)_ Business, Society, and the Earth—and, through that, the possibility of evolving in real-time. What shifts? What new ways of seeing or sensing become available to you? What changes in your tone of voice, or your way of looking at an issue/opportunity? Even in the way you experience your physical body? The way you move? Even your gestures, facial expressions, and body language?

Most importantly, what changes in the way we are at Work? In what we choose to work on with whom and how? The way we lead? What happens to those metrics—and even to our creativity—individually and collectively—and our rates of innovation—when we orient ourselves around Healing and Evolving? My experience is that the standard metrics improve–in service to something even more

key for my book

---

[2] BTW, in my practice, the role of "healer" applied to the client. I was simply the "guide".
[3] https://www.etymonline.com/word/heal

valuable. But the answer to those questions has greatest significance, not with me, but with you—an answer I hope that, when you're ready, you'll share with me—and with others.

I call out Healing and Evolution here because, though it's an indispensable component of the evolving work, I didn't specifically call it out in the book. I wasn't writing from that "state of being" at the time. I was much more attentive to getting the specifics right—those of the stories and the structure—the methods—trusting that those would bring about the shift in mindset. But…

My post-manuscript epiphany was that, for this way of working to live into its potential—and have its much-needed impact—especially now, I need to be explicit about it from the beginning—in the hopes that you, too, will be aware of it as you step into this—and throughout.

So as you read this book—exploring this way of working—you might want to experiment (or not) with immersing your Self in the Healing and/or Evolving perspective—just to see what you can then bring—what *we* can then bring—to Business, Society, and the Earth.

Either way, I trust you'll find value here—and look forward to hearing from you. In the meantime…

Hope this finds you & yours thriving today,

Scott

August 7th, 2021
Aboard *Vivant Pleinement*
Sausalito, CA, USA

Table of Contents

Introduction: Part 1

...in the beginning...

"That's impossible"...

...said David, Chief of Staff for a global notebook supply chain (GNSC)—the supply chain responsible for producing and delivering the #1 laptop in the world.

"Okay," I said. "Tell him I'll do it for free. Pay me only if I succeed."

One month later, we were paid.

So what happened? How were we able to take on a challenge that some of the smartest supply chain professionals in the world thought was impossible—and succeed? How does one do it having never seen—or even read about—a supply chain? More importantly, how have we consistently developed high leverage strategies for nearly two decades now, across cultures, across industries, across issues? From working with former guerrilla leaders and the military in Guatemala to energy companies in the United States; from strategies for restoring the Great Lakes Fisheries with The Nature Conservancy to the U.S. Navy's Fleet Ballistic Missile System; from Vermont's Education System to Sustainable Food and Agricultural Systems in California?

As I hope the above examples illustrate, while this particular example played out in a global business corporation, the same successful outcomes have emerged in multi-sectoral and multi-stakeholder issues in communities (e.g., around affordable housing); entire regions (e.g., solving multi-sectorally to preserve 250MM acres of forest land); at the state level (e.g., addressing child protection or EPA compliance); and more, many of which you'll learn about later in the book.

More on "how" in a bit. For now, back to David and his supply chain...

David and I, along with my friend and colleague, Julie Naster of Conversant,[4] had been exploring how David and the GNSC were going to solve their currently overwhelming challenge: that is, tripling the output of the GNSC over the next three years. Moreover, do it at a time when they were struggling to meet production quotas as it was. Our conversation went like this...

I asked David what they'd tried so far. He shared that they'd asked the organizational staff what was needed to respond to this growing demand for their laptops. What came back? Requests for 127 initiatives. Far too many to manage, much less fund.

Me: "Okay, have you narrowed that down?"

David: "Yes, the Executive Team (ET) reduced the 127 to 25."

Me: "Would you bet your 401k on that?"

David: "Hell no! That decision was the result of who was the most insistent, the loudest, the best lobbyist..." etc.

Me: "What if we could get that list down to 5–7 initiatives that every member of the Executive Team agrees would enable them to accomplish their goal?"

David: "Can you do that?"

I went on to explain, in clear, simple, straightforward terms, how it could be accomplished. He was in!

A few days later, David came back with "impossible."

It turns out that, while the team as a whole was willing to engage in this approach, the truly capable, talented leader of the Shanghai-based Supply Chain, Ike, sincerely thought that it was impossible—that

---

[4] For more on this insightful and impactful body of work, see www.conservant.com or, better yet, read *The Communication Catalyst* by Mickey Connolly, Richard Rianoshek (2002).

no one could add that much value in their upcoming 2-day offsite to design their strategy for tripling their supply chain throughout.

That's when I heard someone say the words "Fine. Tell him I'll do it for free. Pay me only if we succeed." Turns out that someone was me–something that was completely unfair to my partner, Julie, given that we'd never even imagined such an offer—ever.

Still, having applied these principles in other extremely challenging settings, I was confident enough to place a substantial bet that they would hold here, too.

My offer prompted (understandably) a long pause from David…

"Well, that's a bold offer," he eventually managed.

"Well, it should be! If I'm telling you it's doable, I should literally put my money where my mouth is."

After a few more brief conversations scattered over the week— most notably with Ike—we dove into the project on what was now (given the time spent going back and forth) a tight one-month timeline. Here's how that played out, in four acts, how they got to their 5–7 initiatives (and how we got paid) …

Act #1: a 360° View

If I couldn't see the supply chain and understand how it functioned as its own organism in its own competitive ecosystem, then there was no way I could help Ike and his team hold an inclusive, rigorous, productive conversation about how the GNSC currently functioned and, most importantly, what it would take to make it perform better— significantly better—i.e., three times better. I had to first get my own head around the complexity of the global supply chain.

For that, I needed a 360° view of the supply chain from the perspectives of the key actors and stakeholders in the system—i.e., from marketing, sales, designers, component suppliers, original design manufacturers, data systems, logistics, government relations, etc.—12 interviews/perspectives in all. For each of them, I asked two simple questions: "What are you trying to cause?" and "What's required for you to be successful?" And wherever possible, I asked them to tell me that based upon their favorite success stories, their best real-world examples of how they had previously achieved such goals (remember, these folks are really smart, so they know this stuff).

And I dove in deep here. If there was something I didn't understand—something I couldn't see in my mind's eye, something that just didn't make sense to me—I asked for an example or for more information or for reference to a document or to another person or…. My basic assumption was that I wasn't the stupidest person in the room and that, if I didn't understand something—if it wasn't crystal clear to me, then possibly others hadn't thought deeply enough about it to express it in its simplest, most fundamental terms.

From that came a set of clear, sufficiently rigorous stories about what makes for a successful supply chain. The only problem was that these stories, as they stood, didn't naturally fit together—they were diverse, independent, isolated, often conflicting views—a bit like the all-too-oft cited (and, sadly, all-too-oft true) tale of "The Blind Men and the Elephant".[5]

---

[5] Source: Himmelfarb et al 2002: 1526 (artist: G. Renee Guzlas). All rights reserved ©. J. Himmelfarb, P. Stenvinkel, T.A. Ikizler and R. M. Hakim. Reproduced with permission.

Act #2: *Integrated Map of the GNSC's Ecosystem*

Still, I knew that the stories did, somehow, physically fit together in the real world. After all, the supply chain did exist—and it did work. The only question was, "How do these various bits and pieces fit together"?. And in such a way that describes both how the GNSC currently functions and how it needs to function to achieve the executive team's goal.

But I was in luck. I had a starting point. Their goal was 30MM units in 3 years. And I knew that, by applying the rules from systems thinking/system dynamics along with McKinsey's[6] concept of MECE[7] (mutually exclusive and collectively exhaustive), I should be able to at least begin the chore of rigorously, actionably describing their ecosystem.

[NOTE: Feel free to now skip to Act #3 if you're not interested in a bit of the detail about the "how" of this mapping.[8]]

So I asked myself, based on the conversations I'd had, is there a finite set of 5–7 or so abilities (generically called "resources") required to accomplish that goal? It turns out that there were 6. And I can share them here, as they're generic enough that I'm not violating our non-disclosure agreement (NDA). They were the ability(s) to:

- Make timely determination of present and future regional demand
- Secure quality supply in alignment with demand on time and below market cost, sustainably
- Produce high volume, low cost, on time quality product at peak efficiency, scalably
- Deliver 30MM units on time at low cost through year 3 and beyond

---

[6] See https://en.wikipedia.org/wiki/MECE_principle

[7] With all due respect to General Stanley McChrystal and his critique of MECE, there are valid, insightful applications of the concept as we'll demonstrate in the section on "Clarity with Another."

[8] Now's a good time to remind us all of the wisdom of that admonition that "all models [maps] are wrong, some are useful." This one was quite useful. ☺

- Achieve and extend notebook market leadership
- Influence the future structure and function of the Notebook Supply Chain ecosystem

Once those 6 were clear, it was then simply a matter of applying the same ruleset (i.e., what is the next level of "5–7"?) to each of those 6—which enabled me to see what, how and why these original 6 were, themselves, caused by anywhere from 2–7 additional elements/resources, and so on.

As these unfolded, I was able to discriminate and relate (from their individual stories) the larger, inclusive, integrated story encompassing the shared view of the reality of their Supply Chain as a whole.[9]

In the end, what emerged was a "causal diagram"[10]—a map of the 175 elements—175 resources linked: 1) to one another, 2) to those original 6 abilities and, ultimately, 3) to the overall goal in a way that clearly and completely explained, at an actionable level, how their supply chain functioned in physical reality.

Act #3 Exploring their Map:

Okay, now I had MY head around it, but THEY didn't. Nor was I (yet) convinced that the map would hold up to the scrutiny of an Executive Team deeply (and legitimately) concerned about the success of their supply chain—in short, the success of their business, their careers and those of their staffs—at their needed 3X level. They had already been through several feisty conversations about how to proceed and, understandably, had valuable opinions about how things worked and, therefore, what should be done. But despite that, they still didn't align.

So I'd be lying if I said that I wasn't a bit nervous about what would happen when these really smart people attacked this representation of

---

[9] While I can't share their map (that NDA thing), you can see an example of such a map later on in the book in the section entitled *"The Real World: Consilient, a startup"*

[10] For more on this, search "causal loop diagram." But please, not without seeing George P. Richardson's _Problems with Causal Loop Diagrams_, System Dynamics Review, (1986).

their "impossibly" complex supply chain challenge (yes, I wanted and needed them to literally attack this —it had to be rock solid!).

What arose, though, was a rich, thoughtful, informed and informing conversation about how their supply chain actually worked, down on the ground. The map served as a rigorous storyboard that could literally hold their exploration–their conversation–about their ecosystem. When someone was concerned about the impact of an aspect currently under consideration on another part of the supply chain, we were able to either immediately point out that impact elsewhere in their ecosystem or incorporate it by changing their map in real time. When someone's attention suddenly shifted from the topic under discussion to another part of the system, we were able to literally point out where it was covered, then agree to complete the current conversation—knowing that we would eventually get to that bit—even better, get to it in the proper sequence.

In the end, the map turned out to be 95% accurate, with one exception. As Ike framed it, it turns out that none of us really understood how logistics functioned—well, at the very least, hadn't articulated it clearly enough. So he tasked us with clarifying and reworking that one section. Despite that, we had enough shared clarity to move on to identifying the systemic levers. (And we did clean up—and finally understood—logistics immediately following our 2-day offsite.)

TIMEOUT: About Math

While the leaders I work with don't need to be mathematicians to benefit from this, I'd be doing you a disservice here if I didn't call out that I relied on a form of math in developing their map—literally— in the spirit of the aforementioned MECE. This way of working is half-rooted in that under-appreciated and underutilized body of knowledge: systems thinking and its rigorous counterpart, system dynamics. It really is math—seriously, calculus and algebra. (Hey, these are complex systems and you'd better come at them with the right tools for the job.)

But I also have to share what accounts for the failure to use these tools for the job. We've too often failed to humanize these tools, failed to make them accessible in more human ways. We've not previously understood how to deploy them in ways that humans can literally, innately and, therefore, willingly internalize. That's where a fundamental understanding of what it means to be human comes in handy (back to my days as a psychotherapist). The inclusion of this critical missing perspective is a large part of what accounts for the consistent success of this specific approach.

Bottom line, we have a responsibility, as leaders, to call out the "math" of our proposed solution or strategy—not just our hope or hunch or opinion. Without the ability to clearly articulate both what we think and how we know that to be true, we're relying on, well, this cartoon[11] says it best...

---

[11] Creator Sidney Harris; Copyright© ScienceCartoonsPlus.com ;Reproduced with permission.

Act #4: Levers

Oh yeah, those 5–7 levers that I promised David (and Ike). We were fortunate here. While I normally would insist on a formal analysis of their now validated map (that math thing, again), the ET had already gained enough understanding of the possible levers (remember, they previously had 127 initiatives to choose from) to move forward without such an analysis. Using their now shared view of reality—i.e., their map—to guide their thinking and reflection, they were each able to create, as a starting point, a list of what they *individually* believed were the 5–7 levers.

They then shared those with one another and (again, using the map to ground their explorations), refined those to a list of THE 7 levers that everyone on the ET *collectively* agreed would, if successfully implemented, enable them to achieve their goal.

In addition to discovering their 7 levers, the map exploration triggered a series of insightful learnings along the way. Just a couple of quick examples (btw, these hold true for any manufacturer so, again, nothing confidential here).

Logistics left holding the bag:

When Sales (in good faith) conservatively estimates volume for the year, Logistics buys container space for future shipping at both net present value and volume discounted prices. But when those conservative sales numbers are (as hoped) exceeded at year's end, Logistics has to tank either: 1) margins (by buying shipping space on the spot market at the now highest price, thereby eroding already slim margins) or 2) customer satisfaction (by protecting margins and delivering late). This insight opened the way for some great conversations with Sales.

Any color—so long as it's Black?

When Marketing legitimately wanted to offer a wide array of models to attract customers, Design went to work developing them. But when it came time for the ODM (original design manufacturer) to make their initial manufacturing runs in China, when a problem arose on the line, they had to call in the Design Team to help troubleshoot it. So if you have double or triple your normal designs, suddenly you find that: 1) your design teams are pulled into 2-3 times the troubleshooting sessions (pulling them away from next generation design work) and/ or 2) should you have more than one line go down, you're now bottlenecked by your Design Team having to troubleshoot multiple lines. So reducing the number of designs eases your ODM risk.

The first night of the offsite, over dinner, as members of the ET bemusedly shook their heads—still wondering how we'd accomplished this "impossible" task, Ike graciously directed that we be paid, even before the offsite formally completed (we still had one more day, during which we planned to detail the strategies for each of the levers).

Whew!

I don't say "whew!" lightly. One of the things that I and the leaders I work with have had to become (un)comfortable with is that, in complex systems, the solutions are emergent[12]—you can't dictate or predict them. They arise from within the ecosystem itself, often in surprising, counterintuitive ways. Said another way, if we attempt to force solutions on a complex issue/opportunity/system, we run the serious risk of oversimplifying them and driving the system into chaos (more on this in a bit when we explore Dave Snowden's Cynefin framework).

As a result, this way of working is inevitably *un*comfortable. I know THAT we will come up with the solution. I know HOW and WHY we'll arrive at the solution. I simply can't guarantee A SPECIFIC solution, or even rough it out in general terms. It has to emerge.

I can say that each time, the result has met or exceeded the original expectations of the leader(s), usually including and transcending what

---

[12] See Dave Snowden's Cynefin framework below in "Context #4"

they're seeking. As a result, I'm always delightfully surprised (and, admittedly, relieved) at what emerges.

Speaking of…

Offsite Epilogue:

It turns out that no one had ever actually "seen" the entire Supply Chain—something now made possible by their map. Each actor in the system was operating and making critical decisions based on their own individual, incomplete perspective (it's complex, right?). Now, however, their shared ability to see and understand the impacts and interdependencies across the Supply Chain gave them, as an ET, a whole new level[13] of insight about the importance of the relationships between and among the Supply Chain staff, suppliers, and other partners.

So Ike did something that was to have even deeper and broader impact. He insisted that each member of the ET share their portion of the map with their staffs. A few weeks later, I received a call from David enthusiastically describing that the map of the Supply Chain now decorated the halls and walls of the facility. Not only was it being used as a tool for shared understanding and decision making, it was even being used by Human Resources to recruit new hires, demonstrating how the Supply Chain leadership's grasp of their domain was far more advanced than that of other business units.

A Promise

Doing the "impossible" requires, among other things, compelling inspiration. For the last 30+ years, I've found such inspiration in a quote I've attributed to Gilles Pajou (CEO of the French pharmaceutical

---

[13] Using higher order labels to "tag" groups of more complex interactions enables a higher order conversation. See the link between ethology and language evolution in the work of Frans de Waal cited in *Bonobos: Unique in Mind, Brain and Behavior*, edited by Brian Hare, Shinya Yamamoto, (2017), p.119.

company Pharmacia) that goes something like, "A leader is someone who makes a promise they know *must* be made, then has to change in order to keep it".[14]

And this attitude—this spirit—has shaped much of my life, as a trauma psychotherapist, as a businessman, as a parent, as an internationally competitive athlete, even before I ran across Gilles words. The trick, of course, is figuring out *what* to change and *how* to do that.

So it's in that spirit that ***this book—this conversation—is a promise to you to help you understand that it's possible to harness your own chaos and complexity in the midst of your own "impossible" issue/ opportunity.*** It's a promise I want to—I need to—be held accountable to,[15] if only because we have an increasing number of "impossible" issues/opportunities to deal with, and decreasing time in which to do that, something we'll explore together when we get to Context #2 & #3 below.

TIMEOUT: Our Opportunity(s)

You'll notice throughout that I frequently, repeatedly use the term "issue/opportunity". I do so for two reasons. First, as my friend Fritjof Capra (a strong supporter of this way of working) first made popular in his book *The Tao of Physics*, the Chinese symbol for danger is made up of the symbols for both crisis and opportunity. If we inhabit this perspective, we can choose to use such moments to make significant leaps forward, to resolve fundamental causes vs. simply applying symptomatic (i.e., temporary) relief. I've repeatedly found this to be true—that the human energy/motivation available in crisis—when

---

[14] It turns out that I was close here. The actual quote (by way of Robert Dilts in his book *Visionary Leadership* (1996)) is "in order to 'grow as a leader' a person must feel a strong will to modify the environment to make it better, then create challenging situations that (he or she) can't get out of except by changing".

[15] Seriously—if anything I offer here doesn't seem like it's in line with my promise, email me (scott@innatestrategies.com) and let's get back on track.

thoughtfully channeled—calls to our deeper, typically untapped human potential.[16] Hence, the now popular often misused phrase, "Let no good crisis go to waste."

Secondly, on the repeatedly part, we seem too often concerned/consumed by the sense of loss that a crisis represents, vs. its flip side: potential gain. And gain has in many ways been the steady path of humanity as we've continued to evolve our understanding and our potential for an increasingly—but not yet sufficiently—shared, significantly higher quality of life.[17]

By choosing to make such a promise, by choosing not to approach this as "business-as-usual", I hope to call out that what's required here is nothing less than a paradigm shift and, with that, a shift in both mindset and behavior—one that will enable us to answer the question:

must quote for my book

"Now that we know what's possible, what's stopping us? What's stopping me?"

for my book

Such a shift—and my accompanying promise—is, given who I choose to believe you to be as a leader, a two-way promise. That is, this book is making the promise to support you, but in a shift of paradigm/mindset that only you can generate for yourself. And I'm doing so for reasons that will become clear before you and I are done with the "context" portion of the next chapter.

---

[16] This is a positive twist on that "never let a good crisis go to waste" insight.

[17] I'm speaking here of the general upward trend of what's possible while, at the same time, aware of the cost too many have paid for much of that gain—i.e., the atrocities visited on indigenous peoples, colonialization, environmental destruction–things we now have to begin to heal.

So if this is a promise you'd like to engage in, then I invite you to join me in more deeply exploring just how the "impossible" isn't. Here's hoping you'll join me in the next section where I lay out:

- The 4 fundamental questions
- The 2 fundamental domains
- The 4 Critical Contexts
- The 6 organic levels of the Body of Knowledge.

Critical musts for 1st paradigm mindshifts + behavioral change

Introduction: Part 2

Your "Impossible" Problem

This book is driven by 3 fundamental elements:

- You
- Reality
- What you're seeking to cause.

So why you...?

...because I'm choosing to believe *three things* about you.

First, when I jumped into writing this, I reflected on my "ideal" reader/leader. On the one hand, my ideal leader(s) have, in fact, run the gamut from: former guerilla leaders in Guatemala still struggling for the freedom of their people; to social workers in Minnesota overcoming structural barriers enabling the neglect and outright abuse of vulnerable children; to business, government, NGO and social leaders in whole communities recovering from devasting natural disaster—and more. Each of them (and I'm betting this includes you) expresses the qualities I'm about to call out. Still, I needed (just to be able to focus) to bring up a single individual to hold in my mind's eye as I began to write.

What (actually, who) sprang to mind was the head of strategy for a well-respected, global company I've worked with recently, one whose leadership I admire—as do those around him—one who "gets" it, who's highly intelligent, passionate (and compassionate), experienced, creative, and transparent. He has a set of essential qualities[18] that I choose to believe also apply to you. He is/you are a good leader, embodying:

- Commitment to achieving worthy goals, no matter what
- Awareness of the need to think systemically, to see and act on behalf of the "whole"
- Authenticity—what we see/hear is what we get in your behaviors and in your actions
- Self-awareness of your strengths and weaknesses—always learning, always improving
- Relational intelligence and ability—understanding the critical importance of engaging others …

… in short, s/he is/you are creative vs. reactive, balancing both the task and the relationship sides of the evolving leadership equation.[19]

Second, I believe that you wouldn't have opened this book or considered this option if you weren't facing a significant issue/opportunity, one that is:

- Complex—has lots of moving parts that are hard to get your head around
- Challenging—requiring a step-change in direction and magnitude in both the "what" and the "how" needed to cause change
- Urgent—has a tight, seemingly impossible timeframe
- Collaborative—requiring ongoing alignment and action with others, at scale…and…

…that you've made your own promise you know *must* be made, and now have to change (yourself) in order to keep it.

---

[18] For more on the rich, comprehensive, leading edge these come from, see Bob Anderson's "The Leadership Circle" 360 profile (www.theleadershipcircle.com)
[19] Ibid

Finally, and as importantly, I choose to believe that you're in a position of relative power—either locally or globally, or somewhere in between. That you're able to have a significant positive impact on your world, whether you're in a legacy organization or an entrepreneurial one—in business or society—shaped more by the 20th or by the 21st century. At this moment in time, what you do, why you do it, and how are literally critical to our survival as a species, now like never before.

So why Reality?

Yes, I'm deliberately using capital "R" Reality, as I'm speaking to THE reality, not "your" reality, as in "Well, that's *your* reality;" or "my" reality, as in "Well, that's not *my* reality." Once we open that can of worms, we're lost in opinions and ideologies—in our theories about what is or isn't—what works and what doesn't. (As Daniel Patrick Moynihan famously clarified, "Everyone is entitled to their own opinion, but not their own facts.")

I'm speaking about the Reality that we have created—that we have literally *caused*. The systems that produce Reality(s) like income inequity, out-of-control prison populations, climate change, political polarization, etc. I'm speaking of objectively verifiable Reality[20]—those things that confront us in our World today—issues that are seemingly impossible to resolve.

That Reality is not only the measure—the standard—to which we can hold Society, our leaders and even ourselves to account, but ultimately, it is, itself, the change agent that determines what our goals need to be vs. what seems (comfortably) achievable or practical or reasonable. It is Reality that determines what we simply *must* accomplish if so much of what we care about is to thrive. Reality, not ideology. And (luckily?) this Reality that we've by and large caused has a structure that determines its/our behavior—whether via legal

---

[20] For example, as defined by Jordan Peterson and/or Sam Harris

systems, tax policies, transportation systems, educational institutions, economic policies, etc.

And because we've caused these structures, we can "un-cause" what's harmful and, instead, design for more of what's most mutually beneficial—beneficial for ourselves and for Life itself.

TIMEOUT: COVID-19 Clarity

As I'm writing this book, COVID-19 and the November 2020 and January 2021 politicization of Reality have only increased my own sense of urgency here, so much so that I was tempted to do yet another (God help me—and you) edit of the manuscript from that perspective. However, that would: 1) only delay yet again publication and the chance to share this with you, 2) be in competition with the plethora of other such offerings and, most of all, 3) belie the significance of this as both pre-existing and, if we're not responsive/awakened, "post-existing" COVID-19.

That is, we would be re-examining and re-assessing the conventional, suboptimal, symptomatic approaches that got us here in the first place. Instead, we need to dig deep into the root cause, and through that, embrace the foundational paradigm shift in understanding both the causes and our responses that COVID-19 simply and tragically illuminates—at scale. Though I likely don't need to, I'll remind us of Einstein's insight that "We cannot solve our problems with the same level of consciousness that created them." Hence, our needed shift.

So why what you're seeking to cause?

Out of the literally hundreds of leaders I've been privileged to work with, I can only think of three who I would consider "bad" leaders. And even for those, the ultimate "what" they were seeking was admirable. It was their "how" that was destructive.

So like the leader who sprang to mind as I sat down to write this, I trust that you, too, are seeking to do the right thing—that either I or my children or my grandchildren will be better off because of what you're up to—what you're seeking to cause. That's what systems (and Systems Thinking/System Dynamics) are all about—that the structures you put in place are intended to produce the positive outcomes we seek to experience.

Lastly, as you may have gathered by now, I use that word "cause" deliberately. That is, *by our action or—too often—inaction*, we do collectively (and individually) create the world around us. At this point in our evolution as a Species, and as a Society(s), we are causing massive changes: to our oceans, to our landscapes, to our climate, to our economy(s), our legal and political system(s), to the lives of our children, of families, of our communities, our nations, and ethnicities. To one another and, thereby, to ourselves.

So my choosing to believe that you're seeking to cause good in our world serves me as I write this. Besides, if you choose to work in this way, you can't help but do the right thing, can't help but align with Reality. Those are, in the end, the only decisions, the only actions that eventually—if not immediately—truly work.

Your own "impossible" problem?

So "impossible". What arises in you—in your body, your mind, your heart (literally—does it beat faster?) even in your nervous system—when you confront the Reality, your own Reality, of "impossible?"

When David posed GNSC's "impossible" challenge to me, I found myself more alive, if that makes any sense—simultaneously both excited and scared, on the edge of my capabilities and really having to increase my awareness, stay fully present and bring my best—and more. I was excited at the prospect of making such a significant contribution to such a committed team taking on such a seemingly impossible problem.

"Scared" (the best word I can come up with, and not a bad thing in my experience) in that some truly smart people didn't see how it could be done—yet I'd promised them that it could.

That doubt on the part of smart leaders that the "impossible" is possible is a recurring theme in this work. It's part of why this book, to say nothing of this work, is essential. Just as there are little-known ways to improve one's performance through the way we eat or train or _____ (fill in your own word here) in order to improve performance,[21] here we're exploring a little-known way to lead in an age of wicked problems.

But I wasn't at all overwhelmed by my excitement and/or my fear. Instead, it was simply a healthy state of being to inhabit a source of energy to keep me on my toes—alert, curious, responsive, and engaged with each and every leader I worked with throughout the project. It's no different from the state of being an athlete or any performer inhabits when engaged in meaningful, healthy competition.[22]

What determines whether a leader is overwhelmed by an issue/opportunity[23] or proactively engages with it is a function of whether or not they're sufficiently resourced, both attitudinally and technically, to be able to deal with it. At the beginning of the GNSC story, I promised you "more on 'how' in a bit".[24] And as I hope you've gathered from the bet I made with David and Ike, I'm committed to keeping my word. Keeping that promise is the design intention that guides this book and this evolving conversation with you—one that I hope continues beyond this tome.

---

[21] If you're into performance, Tim Ferris' book Tools of Titans (2016) is an excellent portal into practices of a host of high performers in business, art, sport and more.

[22] Just search for athletes or stand-up comedians who get "ill" before games/performances.

[23] I often refer to a "problem" as an "issue/opportunity" in the spirit of my friend Fritjof Capra's book, The Turning Point (1984) in which the Chinese symbol for crisis is a blend of danger & opportunity.

[24] We'll also explore the "why" of this in Chapter 5 on Scalability.

TIMEOUT: "Conversation?"

I use the term "conversation" here because I want you—actually, we collectively need you— to confront this way of thinking and working, even this way of feeling and being. I need you to test for yourself whether this way of solving such complex, multi-stakeholder—even or especially, multi-sectoral issues/opportunities—actually works.

What I'm specifically seeking to avoid is that too often cited throwaway of "trust the process", a convenient way of avoiding responsibility for either: 1) clearly designing, explaining, and executing what we're up to—whether as the leader or the consultant or...whomever, or 2) rigorously exploring and assessing the process/approach for ourselves. So DON'T trust me (not that I'm not trustworthy, quite the opposite). Rather, you need to gauge this for yourself—to decide whether or not one should adopt, even embody, this work.

So we'll begin our exploration at a 30,000-foot level with some useful questions that frame this way of working. From there, we'll work from the ground up, building understanding and ability level by level.

30,000 feet: 4 Fundamental Questions

At the highest level, there are 4 fundamental questions, explored at 3+ fundamental levels, enabling action at a 4th, as follows:

- How do we come to shared understanding and alignment about:
  1. the state of Reality[25]?

---

[25] I'll repeat: When I use the term "Reality", I mean it in the physical, scientific sense—vs. the too often misguided notion of "your reality" and "my reality". If we default to the latter (around climate change or poverty or racism or...) we come untethered from our ability to align—to find an intersection of common interest and/or mutual benefit—we cast ourselves adrift.

- past, present & future

2. the structure causing that Reality?

- via our map of our ecosystem

3. where to intervene in that Reality?

- via our leverage point analysis of that map,

4. then (& only then), how to make the structural then behavioral changes?

- via our integrated, high leverage strategy & action based on those levers.

In this fourth one, I say "then and only then" as I've seen far too many change processes that begin with reorganizations or mergers or behavioral change trainings or (pick your own) flavor of the month trainings at the individual level without understanding the overriding system/structure that's producing our behavior in the first place. Yes, structure overwhelmingly overrides behavior.[26]

3 Emergent Levels +1

While we're exploring these questions, we're *deliberately* building emergent leadership, relationship & clarity at:

1. The individual level

- via individual interviews and individual systems maps

2. The subgroup level

- via affinity group explorations of Reality

3. The whole group level

- via strategic design & action...

---

[26] We need little more evidence of this than the recent explosion of awareness about structural racism and/or structural income & wealth inequity.

…enabling collaborative strategic action at:

4. The ecosystem level

- via decentralized, self-managing, scalable execution/ organizational design.

Why THIS conversation—THIS book

There's one critical distinction here that speaks to why, given all the varied and often conflicting places you could go to explore this topic, you might choose this book, this way of working, of thinking—even of Being. It is out of an uncommon fusion of business experience, practice as a psychotherapist, and development as a complexity/systems thinker that this way of working has emerged and evolved—and continues to.

It's the internalization of these unique, diverse, but ultimately intimately related disciplines that enables the weaving of what it means to be truly human into each step—every act—of this process. Doing so enables you, if you so choose, to create the initial conditions capable of evoking: 1) the best of what it means to be human (that "attitudinal" bit I spoke of earlier) 2) working in complex systems.

This way emerges at a time when we most need it, at time when the emergence of complex (even chaotic) issues/opportunities is increasing—and increasing at an increasing rate— issues/opportunities that we simply *must* solve for. And we can! You can! Despite what "they" say, it's NOT impossible.

So if you're ready to go deeper on the 4 fundamental questions that you'll need to explore, along with the 3+ fundamental levels for exploring them, read on...

About the structure and style of the Book

Since you've decided to go at least a bit deeper here, now is a good time/place to speak to the structure and style of this book…

The work has a structure of its own, one that keeps me in check, one you'll discover in just a moment. And in keeping with the spirit of a conversation, I want to come as close as we can to an authentic, in-the-present-moment conversation/relationship—with you, with your promise (and me with mine), with one another and, especially, with Reality. With that intention in mind, know that I deliberately speak spontaneously within that structure, wanting to ensure that this way of thinking, being, and even feeling/sensing flows for you as it does for me.

One minor note: Most of the illustrations herein, though they're printed in black and white, are much better viewed in color. If you'd like to see them in color, go to scottspann.com/impossible where you can either view them and/or download them as a pdf.

With that in mind, let's give you a framework within which to sort things as we go, along with a few of the idiosyncrasies I employ here.

Our Conversational framework & the 6 Organic Levels

Basically, we'll go (as the work does) level by level, from Individual to Team to Organization to ... and so on. And we'll cover these 6 levels imagining Relationship & Clarity to be like the double helix of DNA, both symbiotically dependent on and contributing to the other. That is, a deepened relationship typically yields more clarity just as greater clarity bolsters relationship. This means the path of our first six chapters delve into Relationship & Clarity at the 6 Organic Levels of:

- The Individual
- One Another
- Our Team
- Our Organization
- Our Market
- Our Ecosystem

...with the final chapter coalescing our learnings from "impossible" into:

- Possible!—that eye of the needle through which our journey with our wicked problems simply MUST pass.

I'll lay out some of the understanding of *what* this work does from this 6–level view so you know that it *can* be done. I'll also share real-world examples of *where* it's been done, to demonstrate for you that the "impossible" is actually *possible*.

Those idiosyncrasies

I'll admit that I've struggled a bit with the use of personal pronouns here—a struggle that belies a philosophy about Life. I don't like the use of the word "I"—except in those cases where, like a captain at sea, I need to accept full responsibility for the well-being of the crew, the vessel[27] and the journey.

I don't like it because, in many ways, "I" didn't create this work—not I alone. Oh yes, I'm the chronicler of this particular path. But this work could not have been birthed without the relationship I enjoyed with my teachers and mentors and, especially, with the hundreds of clients, leaders, colleagues and now friends I've been lucky enough to work with. And to work with them within the context of their own "impossible" reality(s) that they—not I—chose to take on. In fact, as I edit this, the COVID-19 pandemic unequivocally demonstrates one superordinate fact/reality (among so many): We're in this together! Similarly, I can't take undue credit here. So when you encounter the word "I", please know that, from my perspective and lived experience, we are creating and evolving this together.

Second among my idiosyncrasies is the occasional use of capitals when I speak of what I consider to be intrinsic elements that deserve to be called out. For example, "Reality" or "Life". When you come across those oddities, my intention is that we pay special attention to these elements as having almost their own personality, deserving of reflection—of paying attention to what is, at their essence their true

---

[27] A fitting simile since I live and work on my Beneteau 42s7 sailboat here in Sausalito, a delightfully simple & satisfying way to live, work & play.

purpose—as my friend Tim Kelley[28] would likely (and wisely) insist. Given that, I've chosen to adopt the German custom of capitalizing certain nouns from time to time to call out their vital importance in this way of working—even of Being.

One thing that really troubled me was my desire to be as transparent, authentic, and real as I could in my case examples. That works in the non-profit world, largely because those projects were transparent to many different, multi-sectoral actors—often including the public. But it doesn't operate that way in the corporate world where they typically use NDA's. Given that, working my way through a myriad of legal departments just didn't seem to pay off in the work/reward equation. So in those instances, I've either fictionalized some of the names and/or genericized the companies. Having reread them from that perspective, I think they still make their point. Again, that's for you to decide. Let me know if it doesn't.

One more idiosyncrasy: URLs. There are so many busted URLs out there that, though I try to take you directly to the source, if, for some reason, you land on a bad one, my apologies—I did my best. In those cases, I suggest you simply google it and you'll likely find, if not that specific reference, something good. But if not, let me know and I'll turn you on to my source.

Now that our conversational framework is in place…

Initial Conditions

So what had me say that to David? That "pay me only if we succeed" bit? I wasn't being reckless or irresponsible or unrealistic. Quite the contrary.

That spontaneous and, yes, confident response was the result of two domains.

One domain was contextual—four contexts, listed below, that have evolved over time. The second is the body of knowledge about

---

[28] True Purpose: 12 Strategies for Discovering the Differences You Are Meant to Make, Tim Kelley (2009).

working in this way—knowledge about what it means: ① to be more fully human and ② operate in complex-adaptive systems. The result is a set of principles, practices, and processes that blends the two into a durable, flexible, adaptive alloy[29]. But first, a bit about the initial conditions that birthed this distinctive approach…

Domain #1: 4 Contexts

Context #1: The irrefutable one. Reality

The first context is the most inarguable one. For the GNSC—and for most of us—the problem simply HAD to be solved. It was the Reality, the truth of the situation. There simply wasn't another choice—unless one chooses failure. And there was no better group of people with whom to solve this than Ike and his GNSC team.

The same was true with the U.S. Navy on their complex problem: maintaining the reliability, credibility, and cost effectiveness of the Submarine Fleet's Ballistic Missile System—the third leg of our National Defense Triad—critical to keeping us safe in an increasingly unstable, insecure global dynamic. It simply HAD to get done.

And the same with The Nature Conservancy, the USDA, indigenous peoples, fishermen, farmers, local economies, and subsistence fishermen with their complex, multi-stakeholder/sectoral problem: figuring out how to restore the fisheries in the Great Lakes—the largest collective body of fresh water on our Earth—once a rich, reliable, bountiful source of much-needed, low-cost protein. And so on…

Like so much of what we face today, the *physical Reality* is that we simply *MUST* figure out how to solve these complex, multi-stakeholder/sectoral business and social issues/opportunities—not unlike your own (if you're reading this book) complex issue/opportunity that simply HAS to be solved.

---

[29] In its almost literal sense, i.e., made by combining two or more elements, especially to give greater strength or resistance to corrosion.

Context #2: Our Emerging Gap
A little less obvious, until you think about it…

For more than 15 years now, I've been speaking to and responding to a real-world hypothesis that looks like this. (BTW, you be the judge about whether it's a hypothesis or just obviously true):

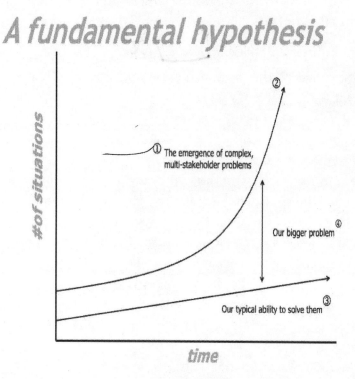

Though you've likely figured this out already, what I'm positing here goes like this[30]…

The ① rate of emergence of complex multi-stakeholder problems (think climate change, economic inequity, water shortages, housing shortages, poverty, undocumented immigration, transportation congestion, political stalemates) are increasing, and at an increasing rate ②. And these will

---

[30] If you'd like me to walk you through this, feel free to go to scottspann.com/impossible for the video.

continue to increase as: 1) our degrees of global interdependence continue to rise, 2) the buffers we've relied on continue to decline (e.g., clean air, clean abundant water, ecologically viable land, bountiful fisheries, fossil fuel reserves, soil fertility, ecosystem services, climate stability, etc.), and 3) especially relative to increasing demand (e.g., population growth, increasing expectations regarding equity and quality of life, greater life expectancy, migration due to conflict & climate, etc.).

I've explored this aspect with folks from management consulting firms like McKinsey[31], Bain[32] and Monitor[33], and we see this as largely true. It's also true that we couldn't build a consulting company large enough to close this gap. Hence, the need to share this way of working with you—at scale.

Our existing abilities to solve such problems ③, while they may have been adequate, never truly worked in the first place—at least not for the broad base of stakeholders impacted by the issues. Just look at the externalized costs/consequences of so many sectors of our economy, society, and environment[34]. The gap between the rate of emergence of complex, multi-stakeholder problems and our typical ability to solve them is increasing at an increasing rate. It's that growing gap that is, in fact, our larger problem ④.

Keeping those externalizations and unintended consequences in mind, many of my colleagues and clients conclude that our existing ways of "solving" such problems actually makes things worse. In reality I should redraw line ③, taking it down, not up. To that point...

---

[31] www.mckinsey.com
[32] www.bain.com
[33] Now Monitor Deloitte found here: https://www2.deloitte.com/us/en/pages/strategy/solutions/monitor-deloitte-strategy-consulting.html
[34] For more on this, google "cost externalization"

Context #3: Something's fundamentally broken...

For the last four years, I've been exploring a related, but more deeply troubling, dynamic that looks like this:

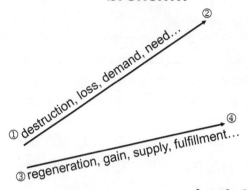

I've posited this fundamental dynamic to just about every leader I've interviewed over the last four years across a variety of issues and industries, and each has confirmed it. And again, you probably already grok this. But, just in case...

The ① rate of:

- Destruction—of ecosystems/ecosystem services, homes/ buildings from fire or storm, ..., or
- Loss—of farmland, forestland, coral reefs, wealth due to failed finance regulation, or
- Demand —for housing, education, living-wage jobs, or
- Need—for healthcare, mental health services, real-world political solutions, broad-based economic recovery

...is increasing, as approximated by the slope of that top line ②.

At the same time, while we *may* be making some progress, the rate of regeneration, gain, supply, or fulfillment ③ is growing at a lesser rate—roughly represented by the slope of that bottom line ④. Now, regardless of whether or not the specific slope of these two lines is precise, the general dynamic is troublingly clear—*these two lines are NOT converging*. And the time we have to address this is a primary, reality-based constraint.

It's critical here that I point out the danger in that bottom line. It gives us the false impression that we are making progress. And in absolute terms, that's true. That bottom line is moving up.

However, *in relative terms*—relative to the need—*it's false*. That experience of progress is subtly misleading as it belies the fact that we are not really—relative to Reality—progressing. Said another way, *our current rate of "progress" ④ will never close our gap*.

The insight this has generated for those I've worked with, though simple and obvious once you think about it, is in every case, startling. To be confronted with the fact that we are on a path that simply isn't working—especially when seen in such simple terms—prompts us to question *"What the hell is going on?"*. And to a person, each leader has agreed that something deeply fundamental about our approach to Life, to Nature and to One Another simply must change ⑤, not only in the "what" we're striving for (more on this reality in a bit[35]) but in addition, in the "how" we accomplish it (more ahead on this, too[36]).

Context #4: Putting the Contexts in, well, context—Complexity

I wasn't aware of this fourth and final context until much later in the development of the body of knowledge described here. But when it did appear, it readily explained, in retrospect, why the specific approach we're exploring here had been so consistently successful.

---

[35] See "What must shift" in Chapter 5
[36] See "How this shift" in Chapter 5

As importantly, it revealed how the work can, even must, continue to evolve. I found it so clear and compelling that I actually spent time training with Dave Snowden (the source for this[37]) and his group, Cognitive Edge, in what he calls the Cynefin framework. This is well-captured in his award-winning *Harvard Business Review* article[38] in the following illustration (I've added the Q1-Q4 and ①-④ labels to clarify the walk-through below):

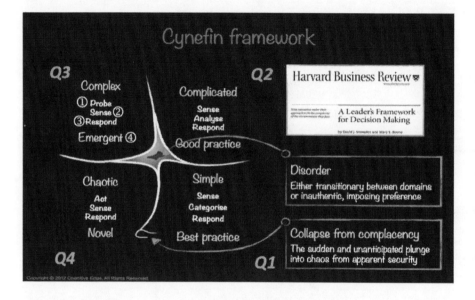

So why did this make so much sense to me?

First a bit of explanation about how I immediately recognized Dave Snowden's original insight and meaning based on my experience in complex settings.

---

[37] For a quick orientation to Dave's thinking here, see his two short (8-min & 2-min) YouTube videos: his explanation and his tongue-in-cheek example.

[38] *A Leaders Framework for Decision Making*, David J. Snowden & Mary E. Boone, Harvard Business Review, November 2007.

This rang true based initially on my experience as a trauma psychotherapist[39]. It had to do with the Cynefin "probe" when applied to a trauma session, as follows…

In my practice, I occasionally had to work with psychotics—those who, by definition, had lost touch with reality. Their "worlds" or internal systems were subject to rapid, unpredictable (for them and for me) change. So I couldn't respond to them with a "best practice" (the Simple system of Q1) or even a suite of "good practices" (the Complicated quadrant—Q2). My responses with them, if we were to navigate our way out of their Chaos (Q4), had to by definition be original and emergent (embracing the Complexity of Q3). Our interactions had to arise out of their own, unique ecosystem—the dynamic complexity of their individually complex (sometimes even chaotic) psyche.

The resonance between Cynefin's understanding of complexity and that of the framework for working with trauma had to do with the recognition of the critical nature of "probes".

In trauma, true healing only arises through the careful, thoughtful, even strategic use of probes. For example, I couldn't ask a client directly about their traumatic episode—only indirectly. I had to avoid re-triggering their traumatic event—commonly called a "flashback"—which would cause a client to relive the experience uncontrollably. Such an episode would actually make things much worse, not better, by activating and reinforcing their chaos/trauma, thereby deepening their negatively habituated neural pathway.

So I'd ask a (hopefully) innocuous question (a "probe") such as, "Was it hot or cold that day?" or "Were there leaves on the trees or not?" or "Was the sun shining or was it dark?" etc. Referring back to the Cynefin framework, that probe ①—that foray into their complex world—allowed me to sense ② their reaction.

---

[39] For those interested in a unique and highly effective approach to resolving trauma, I worked with and studied for 3 years with Peter Levine in his Somatic Experiencing methodology for addressing trauma where it literally "lives"—in the body and the nervous system(s). More at https://traumahealing.org/

I was looking for a change in their breathing pattern or the set of their eyes or the tightening of some part of their body—anything that indicated their autonomic nervous system was reacting to the probe. Based on their reaction to that probe, I would then respond ③ by shaping the next probe and the next and so on as we navigated their traumatic landscape—their world. Together, we did so in an emergent ④ manner, enabling them to renegotiate their trauma and ultimately, heal themselves.

Such probes, both in psychotherapy and in other complex systems, are designed as "safe-to-fail" probes. That is, experiments that, if they fail, won't crash the system. What was most appealing about this way of viewing complexity was that it more closely aligned with, in my experience, how Life itself operates in the case of trauma.

Based on this way of interpreting and appreciating the Cynefin framework—and as a way of applying this to harnessing the complex issues/opportunities I was encountering (i.e., solving for "impossible" problems)—I've adapted[40] Dave's framework as follows...

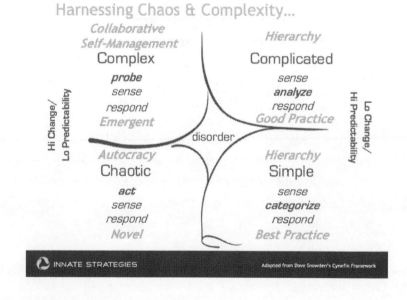

---

[40] Adapted with permission.

I find it useful to explicitly call out three things.

First, the circumstances that refocus our attention *from* the Simple and Complicated systems *to* the Complex and Chaotic—i.e., the rates of increasing change and decreasing predictability now arising in our world.

Second, the governance system needed in the Complex domain: Self-Organizing/Managing. This self-governance (something that's an accepted practice in Agile software development) is essential if we're to scale at a level that can respond to the elements I shared in Context #1. Those are: 1) the increasing rate of emergence of issues/opportunities in our larger ecosystem(s), and 2) their multi-stakeholder/sectoral nature.

The elegance of this framework (both the original and the adapted) is its ability to illuminate the "why" of this way of working (i.e., why it works) while simultaneously speaking to some of the "how", as follows:

Said most simply, in four parts:

1. In today's rapidly changing world
   - for the reasons described above re: decreasing buffers, increasing demands, etc.,

2. our most pressing issues/opportunities are in the Complex domain where solutions are Emergent,
   - i.e., they arise from the perspectives of a 360° set of the multiple stakeholders[41], who are either experts themselves or partnered with experts.

3. Governance is Self-Organizing/Self-Managing
   - via well designed networks made up of the multiple stakeholders and experts following the loose coupling of well-designed network protocols[42]

---

[41] BTW, even things like Nature and Life itself are stakeholders—or, for our own sakes, they better be.

[42] There's much to be learned about this from Stanley McChrystal's book Team of Teams, Fredric Laloux's Reinventing Organizations, Brian Robertson's Holacracy, Rachel Conerly's Collaborative Operating System, and Sociocracy 3.0. More on this later on in "Coordinating Complexity at Scale" below.

4. and strategies are best piloted in the form of probes

- known as "safe-to-fail"[43] probes—treated as opportunities to both rapidly advance solutions (as in the Agile software and design—even trauma therapy—worlds) while, at the same time, learning about the "unknown unknowns" in the ecosystem as the basis for adjusting our strategies.

- All the while moving from "uninformed optimism" through "uninformed pessimism" and "informed pessimism" to finally reach "informed optimism."

Though we'll go deeper on the specifics of this beginning in Chapter 4, I need to point out one pivotal insight here, one that also made tremendous sense to me—and another reason Dave's framework resonated.

That fold at the bottom of the vertical axis is meant to remind us that *attempting to solve a complex problem by oversimplifying it will drive the system into chaos.* Such oversimplifications often arise from attempting to replace our factual understanding about reality with an ideology. As I suggested earlier, please don't take my word for this—think through your own examples. Some starters include "Just say no" and the negative consequences in drug abuse[44]; "No new taxes" and the degradation of public infrastructure, now rated at D+[45]; or "Three strikes and you're out" and the explosion—and inequity—of our prison populations[46]; as well as current anti-immigration responses, and their negative economic and other impacts[47]. The near knee-jerk impulse to engage with our increasingly complex World via such

---

[43] This accords with John Doerr's OKR's described in his book Measure What Matters (2018)
[44] https://www.theguardian.com/society/2016/mar/08/nancy-reagan-drugs-just-say-no-dare-program-opioid-epidemic
[45] https://www.infrastructurereportcard.org/
[46] https://www.bbc.com/news/world-us-canada-33545971
[47] https://www.nytimes.com/2019/10/11/business/immigration-cuts-economy.html & https://knowledge.wharton.upenn.edu/article/us-immigration-policy/

oversimplified misconceptions—and the fact that they consistently worsen the situation(s)—largely makes the case for…

That Mindset/Paradigm Shift...

So it's this context—this/our Reality—that's driving the need for you and me to internalize, to embody—in the fullest, most human sense of that word—a literal "felt sense" of the environment within which we're operating.

And beyond that, to grok just how out of alignment our typical mindsets and methodologies are with Reality. Such shifts don't typically happen spontaneously. Just like any performance skill, we won't master them without some serious practice.

So what you'll experience in the remainder of our conversation here is two things.

First, I'll lay out the principles that underlie how this work works—often using bits and pieces of client work to illustrate the point. To ground those, I'll dive deeper into those principles with real-world examples of the practices and processes used to help leaders harness complexity and chaos.

The intention here is to ensure that these elements land in you to enable you, through some minimal repetition, to inhabit the needed mindsets. Mastery, however, requires practice. So let's have these stories serve as our practice for now.

Secondly, though much of what you learn here can be applied immediately, that's not the specific intention of this book. **This is not primarily an in-depth "how to" book**—that's my next one, the practitioner's manual. **This book is specifically designed to overcome a fundamental problem—the fact that so many leaders think that what they're facing is "impossible"**.

We need to disrupt the notion that doing more of the same—that "one definition of insanity" cliché—will somehow produce a different, better result. So while you may well have enough drive that you'll quickly convert these into your own principles, practices, and processes, if these don't immediately become clear to you, know that this didn't immediately become clear for me, either. *That said, if your need is urgent, let me know and we'll figure out how to get you what you need—now!*

Domain #2: A body of knowledge

Okay. So the domain of contexts was the first thing that I relied on in my spontaneous offer to David and Ike. What was the second domain?

I was actually being responsible in the true sense of the word—that I had the ability to respond—meaning that I knew, in very clear terms (ones I shared with David in our initial call), specifically how to respond to the GNSC's challenge. I had developed a proven set of principles, practices, and processes that gave me the confidence to know, with reasonable certainty, that I could help them solve for what they thought was impossible.

It's this understanding—this working, actionable knowledge of the framework for responding to the "impossibility" of chaos and complexity that makes up the rest of this book. I'm sharing this with you—and with as many people as I can (and, if you'll spread the word, as many as you can) because it's essential to closing those gaps posited earlier in Contexts #2 and #3.

So sharing this...

When you and I are successful here, by the time you finish this book, you'll have a clear, actionable grasp of how your own "impossible" issue/opportunity can be approached. And if you don't have enough of a grasp to actually do it on your own, you'll at least know that it can be done—that it's been done across industries, across issues, and across cultures. Through that, you'll know where to go for resources. So let's get started—those gaps aren't getting any smaller...

Some years back, I wrote a whitepaper entitled, *Some things are impossible—until they're not: Solving 'wicked' Business and Social problems.* It was a title designed to lighten the seeming hurdle of adopting this approach and this mindset. Much of what I said then (unfortunately) is still relevant today—actually, even more so. So I'm going to borrow just a bit of that earlier writing to get this rolling...

Some Things are impossible—Until They're Not:
Solving "wicked" business & social problems

by R Scott Spann, Founder & Strategist,
Innate Strategies

Some things seem impossible. For us in our work, it especially seemed impossible to get a variety of stakeholders—all with different perspectives, different goals, different constituencies, different measures of success—to come to shared understanding and alignment about how to work together to achieve something completely new, something that would advance both the needs of each of the individuals and the collective as a whole. It seemed impossible in corporations, in communities, in non-profits, and in whole societies. And it was...until it wasn't.

An example: What if we were to tell you that, in Guatemala, we[48] engaged leaders of the national intelligence service and the military policy and leadership institutes, on one hand, and members of the former guerrilla movement on the other; leaders of the Catholic Church, on one end of the spectrum, and the leading Mayan philosophers and shamans, on the other; the leader of the President's commission on local economic development, from one end of the hierarchy, and the leaders of local villages, from the other; and so on: 30 different perspectives in all?

And then created a simple (well, relatively simple), one-page systemic representation—a map—of their combined world views, one that they all understood and agreed represented their

---

[48] The "we" refers to Jim Ritchie-Dunham (my good friend and work partner in the early days of this kind of work and my original mentor in the field of system dynamics/systems thinking) and myself.

world—all of its parts and pieces, and all of their interactions. And then came to shared alignment about the overall goal of their collective world.

Then, finally, identified the handful of critical resources (6 in all, out of 140+) that would enable them to move their world in the direction they all wanted it to go. And they did it by investing just 7 days of their time[49]. Some thought it would be impossible. And it was…until it wasn't.

Or let's harken back to that mention of the U.S. Navy and their complex problem—one that's essential to our national security and that of our allies—that of maintaining the reliability, credibility, safety, and cost effectiveness of the Fleet Ballistic Missile System. To give you a sense of the challenge they faced, they were tasked with ensuring a safe, secure, credible, and sustainable deterrent while maintaining or exceeding incredibly high-performance levels. And they were doing so in a context of increasing threat from China and Russia coupled with decreasing funding within an increasingly competitive military budget.

Despite that complexity—and despite a dynamic, increasingly uncertain environment—they simply HAD to get this done. As a result of this way of working, out of the 193 (at a high level) geographically diverse, interrelated segments that made up the Fleet Ballistic Missile System, they were able to unanimously identify the 7 highest leverage elements that would enable them to achieve their mission.

And before one starts down the path of choosing to believe that this won't work in the private sector, we[50] just recently did the same thing for a legacy technology company as they confronted pivoting their $30B, 66,000-person legacy computer hardware company to an "everything as a service" "edge-to-cloud" company over an 18-month

---

[49] Admittedly, 7 days spread over several quarterly visits.
[50] With my friends at Conversant: Mickey Connolly, Richard McDonald & Kell Delaney

timeframe. And that was done in just 6 weeks while investing just 2 days of group time.

Again, many in this instance thought that eliciting, designing, and assessing their strategic ecosystem was impossible—until they did it. So while I'll explicitly cite Guatemala and other non-profits as examples (primarily because they're public processes and therefore shareable), I'll offer up evidence of how and why this works in the private sector— to the degree that our NDA's (non-disclosure agreements)—permit). And I'll ask you to use your own judgment (and imagination) about how this applies in your world.

So naturally, a few questions arise: "How did they do that?" "Can it be repeated?" "Can others be taught how to do it?" The answer to all of these questions, borrowing from Peter Block, must be (and, by the way, is) "Yes".[51] We have to begin to do the impossible to successfully contain and resolve complex, multi-stakeholder (even multi-sectoral) problems—to tame wicked problems[52]. That's what's up for us today—that is the work of our World—now and, likely, for the next several decades to come, if our children and grandchildren are to have a world worth living in. And as this becomes clearer for you, then you'll be left with your own question: "Now that I know this is possible, what's stopping me?"

Solving these is a collective, collaborative endeavor—requiring a 360° view and a 360° conversation. And it's aided—actually, made possible—by integrating principles and practices from system dynamics,[53] systems thinking,[54] and complexity science with recent developments in trauma psychotherapy,[55] somatic developmental

[51] Block, Peter; *The Answer to How is Yes*; Berrett-Koehler, 2003.
[52] For more on "tame" vs. "wicked problems", see the work of Horst Rittel.
[53] See Forrester, Jay; *Industrial Dynamics*; 1958 and Sterman, John, *Business Dynamics*, 2000.
[54] See TheSystemsThinker.com for a range of resources courtesy of the Omidyar group and my friends Mike and Jeff Mohr.
[55] Again, via Peter Levine's Somatic Experiencing.

psychology,[56] and systems-centered group dynamics.[57] Systems thinking and systems dynamics,[58] as we've adapted and further developed them here, provide the structure that enables meaningful, fact-based, productive conversations about complex, often highly-charged issues.

But historically, systems thinking alone hasn't been enough. For us, it's been the combination of a systems-thinking structure with a psychologically-informed collaborative process that has made these complex, difficult conversations simple, meaningful, human events— yielding human solutions. And as you will see below, not just any collaborative process but one that acknowledges and leverages the complementary significance, contributions, and genius of both the individual and the collective—rigorous multi-stakeholder/sectoral collaboration.

So let's get to it. How does one do that? Said most simply, we continually focus on two things: 1) creating Relationship and 2) creating Clarity. And we do these two things at six organic levels: i) with oneself, ii) with another, iii) with one's team, iv) one's organization (or network), v) one's market (or constituents or beneficiaries), and vi) one's ecosystem (be it a business, social or environmental ecosystem). By focusing on Relationship & Clarity at these six discrete levels, leaders develop six critical, level-specific competencies as summarized in the table below and explained and illustrated (with case studies) in the remainder of this book. (Incidentally, please don't try to make too much sense of the table—yet. We'll go deeper, level by level, and it'll become clearer as we go.)

---

[56] See Bodynamics and [Marianne's work here]. For 3 years, I ran the Bodynamic practitioners Boulder practice and trainings while training with them and managing my own psychotherapy practice.

[57] See Agazarian, Yvonne; *Systems-centered Therapy for Groups*; Guilford Press, 1997.

[58] You'll notice we frequently use the terms "system dynamics" and "systems thinking" together. Without detailing our rationale here (but contact us if you really want to hear it), just know that when we use the term "systems thinking," we're referring to learnings, mindsets, and tools from both domains.

Emergent Impact Principles

creating:	Relationship	Clarity	
@ the level of:			**evoking:**
Self	Grounding in your context, experiencing your system and choosing your role	Internalizing a systemic point of view and taking a personal stand	**Leadership**
Another	Engaging with others in their passion, their work goal & a success story, and adding value to them	Creating an individual causal map of their goal, their top 3-5 core competencies and their story	**Trust**
Team	Gathering around shared passions, discovering a positive goal, and exploring your shared reality	Discovering & assessing your team goal; understanding that goal's behavior over time; mapping your system as a whole	**Innovation**
Organization	Aligning around your global goal; inventing & cross-pollinating your strategies and confronting your reality	Analyzing your map & discovering your levers; designing & testing specific strategies; taking 1-next step	**Execution**
Market(s)/ Constituents	Probing your 'market'; engaging in emergence; collaborating across your system	Designing a networked structure & strategy for execution at the market/ constituent level	**Scalability**
Ecosystem	Giving critical stakeholders a Voice, demonstrating your strategic understanding and adding value	Integrating stakeholder goals, needs and value exchange via a thoughtful, balanced stakeholder assessment	**Sustainability**

INNATE STRATEGIES

Some explanation…

Relationship...

…is that ability to come to know one with a degree of intimacy—oneself, another person, a team, an organization, a population, an ecosystem—to come to a deep, internalized appreciation of what another is attempting, regardless of whether or not they succeed or fail at it, regardless of how it impacts me or my agenda. I'll admit that I find it far easier to do this by starting from a place of assuming positive intent, as I did with you. From this place of seeking intimate, personal understanding, seeking with a near fierce curiosity. From this connection—from the center of one world ("mine") to the center of another ("theirs")—360 degrees of possibility come into view—a view that is unattainable when one simply stands outside a circle looking in.

Bottom line, if we are to truly lead our system, we have to be able to establish relationship with ourselves, with others and, most importantly, with Reality itself—to simultaneously hold those perspectives as the place from which our leadership emerges.

Clarity…

… emerges when real-world complexity has been explored, discriminated, re-integrated, and simplified down to its fundamental, most essential components and interactions. What emerges from this is a set of simple, clear, complete conversations that, when taken as a whole, combine to explain 360 degrees of experience, yielding a complete and meaningful explanation of the world as the collective "we" of the system see it, know it, and even feel it.

About the levels…

They're not rocket science. They're obvious, actually. But then, that's the goal of this work—to make the heretofore obscure obvious. And yet, it is this practice of consciously (and somewhat artificially) compartmentalizing them that the levels enable us to harness complexity remarkably well.

In keeping with the needed style of this, they're very simple, very intuitive, very easy to understand and talk about.[59] They represent a nested, interrelated, and natural set of building blocks for creating connections between people, their ideas, their experiences—even their oft-ignored feelings—our *most* Human of elements/assets.[60] And we recognize that these levels are an abstraction and use them accordingly.

---

[59] By the way, being easy to talk about is often underrated, yet it's really important when you're trying to create relationships in large, complex systems or scale an idea across an organization, market, or society.

[60] See, for example, Justin Fox, *From "Economic Man" to Behavioral Economics*, HBR, (May 2015).

For example, to the degree that an individual has a strong sense of self (i.e., relationship with self) and knows what they are trying to accomplish in the world and how (i.e., clarity about self), they are in a much better position to interact with, contribute to and/or influence others—other people, teams, organizations, etc. And oddly enough, we've seen that getting clear—especially on one's own—is often problematic. It's as if, for many of us, that it's through interacting with others that we become clearer about ourselves.[61]

Correspondingly, for others it is often in their interactions with us that they—people, teams, organizations—in turn become clearer. This iterative process of ideation, creation, and re-ideation is, like simple language, highly underrated—often seen and admonished as a waste of time. And, if done in an unstructured or unfocused way, it is.

But with the right focus, structure, and system-based, collaborative process, this organic way of building relationship & clarity can be incredibly effective and efficient—preparing a team or organization to move and adapt organically to changes in their environment with striking speed—a critical capability in a rapidly changing, increasingly unpredictable world. (Remember, the team in Guatemala established such a level of relationship & clarity with an investment of only 7 days, a $30 billion tech company in just 2 days.)

Bottom line here: as leaders we need to be able to traverse each of these abilities and at the same time, weave them together to ensure that we, our partners, teams, and organizations manifest the levels of leadership, trust, innovation, execution, scalability, and sustainability essential to our mission's success. This conscious, careful design and delivery of this self-reinforcing "weave" from individuals through to organizations and the larger ecosystem

---

[61] Alan Watts demonstrates this using fundamental physics—see below at "Self"

is essential if we're going to come out of this process with the relationships needed to act on the high-leverage strategies that emerge from this way of working.

While the prior matrix lays out "what" we're going for, there's a corresponding set of tools used that enables the "how", as follows:

Emergent Practices

creating:	Relationship	Clarity	evolving :
@ the level of:			
Self	Individual Interview Goal Discovery	Designing an Individual System Goal & Map	Leadership
Another	Individual Interviewer Success Story	Validating an Individual System Goal & Map	Trust
Team	Functional Subgrouping	Behavior Over Time Graph, Map Validation & Stakeholder Analysis	Innovation
Organization/ Network	Whole Group Strategic Summit	Integrated Map Analysis & Strategy	Execution
Market/ Constituents	90 Day Teams	90 Day Projects/ Probes	Scalability
Ecosystem	Self-Organizing/ Managing Network	Flight Manual's Awareness, Alignment & Action	Sustainability

 INNATE STRATEGIES

I'm sharing this here because I'll be speaking to each of these practices as we move through the levels. And I'd rather you have the framework *before* diving in versus after. I want you to have a place to anchor what's coming. So again, don't worry too much about this framework at the moment. Its value will become evident as we proceed, level by level. That said, let's dive in…

Chapter 1: At the level of the Individual

Individual Relationship x Individual Clarity = Leadership

Our Formula...

TIMEOUT: What's with the "equation"?

Okay, what's with the "formula" here? Just how geeky is this going to get?

This is actually critical. I'm not putting this in here just to be clever. And I'm going to repeat this at every one of these organic levels, for this reason—and check me on this.

There's a math to working in this way—not just at the level of a rigorous systems map or the analyses we'll talk about at the organizational level—but even (or especially) at the human level. What I'm saying with this equation is that my leadership ability is a product of both my *relationship and* my *clarity*—they impact one another. And that impact is a true product (as in multiplication) not simply a sum (as in addition). For example, if my relationship with you is strong (say, at 1 on a scale of 0.0-1.0) but my clarity is weak (say, 0.5), I'll actually damage/bring down my leadership ability to the degree that I'm not being clear (e.g., 1.0 x 0.5 = 0.5). Think about this for a moment, seriously. How has your sense of connection to a leader been influenced when they say something that doesn't make sense? If you're like most sane, healthy people, if they say something that doesn't fit with Reality (even if you initially have a high opinion of them) their overall credibility (and, therefore, effectiveness) falls.

A deeper look. Now a dip into the nitty-gritty—not the whole thing, not yet. You'll see plenty of that in the next chapters via real-world examples from client cases. First, let's make sure you have a clear overview.

The 6 levels in the previous section are laid out in the order they are because, ideally/optimally (and in keeping with Snowden's principle of "emergence"), it works best this way—allowing the insight to arise from within the ecosystem itself—from the individual actors, starting with you, and then with other individuals—through to the team level and eventually, the organizational level and beyond. In a complex adaptive system, even a top-down process must be fed from the bottom up.

As I've said, this process isn't linear. It mirrors the non-linearity of the issues we deal with. All of this is interrelated and iterative as one system. It exists as a whole, not as a bunch of parts. Still, we have the greatest success when we enter the system by building individual relationship *first*, then proceed to evoking individual clarity, using that as the basis for building relationship & clarity with another, then with a team, and so on.

Self. Hmmm? Well, this is about seeing yourself in an almost impersonal way, a paradoxical concept, but then, "selves" are. The Buddhist Alan Watts[62] spoke to this challenge in his series of lectures to IBM executives aboard the converted ferryboat Vallejo (just up the channel here in Sausalito), using an anthropomorphized metaphor of physics. He pointed out that neither a single object in space nor two objects alone could accurately assess their actions—their position in space, their "state of being". Meaning, in the spirit of anthropomorphizing, I can't tell if: a) I'm spinning on my own axis while observing you as stationary or b) I'm stationary with you rapidly orbiting around me. It's only with the presence of a third object that either one of us can begin to orient ourselves.

---

[62] Alan Watts, *Out of Your Mind 03: The Web of Life (Part 1)*, 19:10.

Our positions and actions are relative—to one another and a 3rd thing. Translating this here—to our work in the real World—we must first orient ourselves relative to our own 3rd thing, often taking the form of our shared goal, mission, or purpose. This process begins with "me", literally. It begins when I (or you) engage with a new group of people or place or issue/opportunity—a new company, community, organization, network, challenge, any new system. "I" have to get "myself" into relationship with this system, to orient myself relative to others and to Reality in order to get clear about my Self in the context of this system as follows…

Relationship with Oneself

We see getting into relationship with ourselves as having three parts:[63] *grounding ourselves in our context, experiencing our system, and choosing our role.* The first, *grounding in our context*, means locating myself/yourself in Reality—identifying the boundaries of the system with which I'm engaging—of the problem or opportunity I'm beginning to work on/care about. Then getting clear about its purpose[64] and even its goal—all of this within the Reality of physical time and space.

The Town of Vail, for example, was caring about how the town "achieves and sustains Vail as the premier international resort and resort community, able to provide premier service at its current size sustainably over the next 5–10 years". Here, if we wanted to, we could literally walk the boundaries of this system—Vail, Colorado—reach out and touch each of the members of the system, the merchants, the resort workers, the citizens, the guests—then step back and see and hear their interactions within their system. And we could hazard a guess about how the system would unfold over time, given certain

---

[63] These three, and some of the other understandings and techniques we've found successful, are borrowed from SCT—Systems Centered Therapy—birthed by Yvonne Agazarian and developed by a community of group therapists—work that's in the process of being ported to the organizational world.

[64] As elegantly articulated and supported in Collins & Porras' *Built to Last* (1994)

initial conditions and likely future events. And we could measure, year by year over the next 5–10 years, whether or not they were achieving their goal in pursuit of their purpose. Such processes tether us to Reality—to our promise.

We humans are experiential creatures. So there needs to be some way to actually *experience* our system, to become authentically curious about the passions, goals, and worldviews of others in the system, to literally walk around in it, seeing, hearing, and feeling what serves the system and what doesn't.

In work with my friends at Stone Yamashita Partners, executives of a Global20 company, for example, were paired with customers on the lowest rung of the economic and social ladder (undocumented immigrants). These executives were exploring an emerging market possibility—specifically, financial services for this market segment. They shadowed these immigrants through their day as they tried to engage in what, for most of us, are everyday economic transactions: cashing checks or transferring funds and remittances or repaying loans.

These executives experienced how a population with a strong work ethic, strong sense of family and community, and strong moral values were consistently misled—lied to, cheated at every opportunity—by that part of the business community that currently "served" them. This ability to experience another human being epitomized the current system and gave each of the executives both a cognitive and an emotional, uniquely human, point of reference from which to make decisions—as well as a passion for making the best decisions.

What emerged from this deeply human experience of the system's Reality was an individual and collective ability to innovate in ways that would not have been possible from simply analyzing the data (which they also did). Each decision they made was examined in the light of "How/would this benefit Miguel or Juan or Isabel?" "How will this help us keep our promise to each of them?"

Finally, from this grounding in Reality, I/you then need to decide—to choose, actually—what role to play in this/our/my system.

Or said in a more systemic way, what role does this system that I've come to be interested in—or care about or be committed to—*need* me to play if it's to accomplish its goal. This role is the "impersonal" part.[65] And once this is clear, the question/challenge then becomes "Do I have the behavioral flexibility required to fulfill that needed role?"[66]

For CARE Guatemala, it became clear to Jim and me, for example, after experiencing a bit of their system, that poverty was not just CARE's problem. It was *our* problem. And that it wasn't our role to "help" CARE resolve poverty. We chose that it's one of our roles to resolve poverty—and that our work with CARE is simply a vehicle for that. It's this level of immersion in a system—this level of relationship— that lies at the heart (literally) of working in this way.

Clarity with Oneself

These relational elements—context, experience, and role—create the initial conditions for internalizing a systemic point of view and taking a personal stand. This comes into clarity when you successfully internalize enough of these points of view to literally hold the system in your awareness, in your consciousness, in your nervous system—in both your mind and your body. And, from this awareness, to take a stand for whatever it is that optimizes the system, whatever creates the greatest mutual benefit—a mutual benefit that (let's don't forget) benefits "me", too.

Only from such a point of clarity can we help others to see and understand why, where, and how the system needs to evolve. And it's essential to understand that, while this is a personal stand, it's not a *personalized* one. It's a *systemic* one—one that sees and appreciates the passions, goals, and worldviews of each of the stakeholders, both

---

[65] Something I learned from Yvonne Agazarian and Systems-Centered Training.

[66] One of my early mentors in leadership and organizational change, Gary Koyen, would consistently challenge us with the question "Do you have the behavioral flexibility needed to evoke the needed change?".

individually and collectively—including "me" but not exclusive to "me". Without such clarity (that of holding both the individual and the collective concerns) I'm/you're/we're simply one more voice among many opting for my opinion or special interest or bright idea. That's usually the last thing the system needs.

Leadership

Leaders (as defined by the term "lead") go first, right? That's implicit in the job title. So this stand, this point of view, this commitment—rooted in your own personal relationship with and clarity about yourself and the system—provides the perspective you need to engage with the system as a leader.

Most importantly, by doing so you discover a source of energy—energy that is all too often overlooked in most systems-thinking efforts. There's an energy that emerges from creating relationship & clarity at the level of the self that spawns innovation and fuels the work required to move the system. And you'll need to call on this energy, this clarity, to awaken a room full—or an organization full—of people.

You also need the requisite variety[67] of a group—the diversity required to create a 360° approach to understanding, innovating, and evolving the system. Finally when you've sat with this, really soaked in it, you emerge with a distinctly different state of being[68]— something that's essential to how you show up from here on out—something that constructively—in a responsive, responsible, reality-based

---

[67] http://requisitevariety.co.uk/what-is-requisite-variety/

[68] Philosopher Martin Heidegger is one who spoke at length about the importance of this—that all human action (even "being") takes place in the context of a "for the sake of what"—some overriding purpose or reason for doing—and that the power of the individual is directly related to the power of this FTSOW. We've definitely found this to be true in our work—that the power of an individual leader is directly related to both the power of what they're "about" and how they are in relationship (Heidegger's "social nature" of humankind) with their colleagues and constituents and, especially, reality. (Or, if you prefer Nietzsche, State of Becoming.)

way—informs and influences each of the other individuals in the system and, through that, the system as a whole.

Speaking of reality-based…

The Real World - Ken Brooks[69], EVP of a top 3 publishing company:

Ken was keen on discovering, exploring, and employing leading-edge tools in business and in life. In keeping with that, he'd obtained three degrees—Bachelor's in Industrial Engineering, Master's in Applied Statistics and Master's in Computer Science. He'd studied Embodied Leadership, an Aikido-based model pioneered by Richard Strozzi--Heckler. He was quite familiar with Systems Thinking and Systems Dynamics, and much more. So when faced with a complex challenge—that of being one of the first major publishers to transition from the prevailing manual, analog production processes to digital—we looked at how best to align his team on their strategy.

Interestingly, while his team found value in the initial map—one that emphasized the essential role of people and talent in the transition—Ken wasn't satisfied, seeing that as necessary but not sufficient. So I offered—pro bono (part of keeping my promise)—to continue to go deeper with Ken until we landed on something that he agreed represented a breakthrough in understanding and insight for him and his goal.

I jumped on a plane, flew from San Francisco to New Jersey, and spent a day exploring with him what he was truly seeking. It's worth calling out here that often leaders are so consumed—tending to operational and organizational brush fires—that they rarely have time to step back and consider the forest vs. simply tending to the trees. With that in mind, I opened our conversation by asking Ken what he *really* wanted to cause in his current leadership role.

He reflexively came back with "increase shareholder value", an all-too-common response, even now. "Ken," I inquired "did you

---

[69] This story is shared with Ken's permission. Thanks, Ken.

really spend all those years getting degrees in engineering, statistics, and computer science simply to increase shareholder value? Is that what you're *really* going for here?"

What followed was a much deeper, much more personal revelation about what truly, fundamentally excited him: rekindling a source of energy that had the potential to fuel, not only "shareholder value", but also his creativity and leadership in forging a new path for the publishing company, the publishing industry, and their market as a whole. It turns out that Ken truly wanted to revolutionize the publishing industry by pioneering the promise of fully digitizing content. What emerged then was a much more insightful, valuable, and actionable systemic understanding of that process that showed up like this:[70]

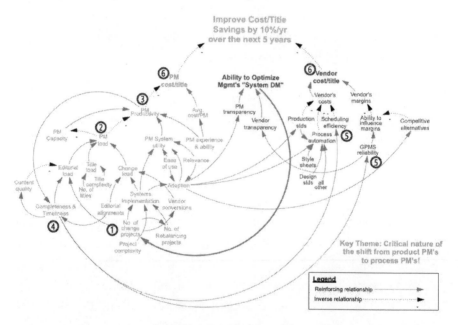

The breakthrough insight, obvious once you've systemically mapped it (that "forest vs. trees" bit), was that the key to transitioning from a

---

[70] For a detailed video walkthrough of this one, go to (scottspann.com/impossible).

manually managed *product* approach to a digitally driven *process* approach was to:

1. Slow down the number of change projects underway
2. Thereby decreasing the PM (Project Manager) Load
3. Which increases PM Productivity
4. Which leads to ensuring Completeness and Timeliness
5. Impacting the quality of the handoff to the vendor in the form of both GPMS reliability and scheduling efficiency
6. Which, in combination, lowers both PM and vendor cost/title

This represented a potential breakthrough, not only in understanding, but also in relationship—especially with vendors. It recognized the need for a shift from simply continuing to force vendor pricing down (thereby reducing their margins and their economic viability) to maintaining vendor margins by increasing the quality of PM product to the vendors—thereby reducing vendor costs while maintaining vendor margins.

Your Positive, Reality–Based, Measurable, Time–Specific Goal (+RBMTSG)

TIMEOUT: +RBMTSG?

While I say much more about this in the Organizational section (Chapter 4), I need to speak to something here that is critically important throughout this way of working—something I'm always on the lookout for, if it doesn't already exist. The goal. And by "goal" I mean a positive, reality-based, measurable, time-specific goal (+RBMTSG). In the GNSC case, it was a given: 30MM units in 3 years—sustainably, as determined by the math of market demand (the "reality-based" bit).

But in Ken's case, we had to discover it. We had to enable him to get crystal clear about precisely what he was seeking to cause by when—to achieve a level of understanding about the direction and magnitude of his goal—and that it represented a significant, seismic shift. Only then were we able to begin to design a map/system that would work for him. Such a goal not only serves as an ideal starting point for a map, it also serves to test the final map. Meaning: Would this system accomplish that goal? It clarifies, for each of the actors in the system, precisely what the direction and magnitude of the challenge is. It gauges what the relative ramp rates will need to be for the various resources. And so on…

I need to make one more vital distinction here about goals—right up front—as it has relevance throughout.

While an Individual (or Team or Organization) comes up with the goal, ultimately, the goal derives from physical Reality itself— whether it's about market share, units produced, percentage of affordable housing, carbon in the atmosphere, etc. It's NOT about whether the goal is achievable or practical in the way goals are (too) often talked about. ***This latter approach is a critical, serious, and even life-threatening error.***

And lest you think I'm being too extreme here, let's take climate change as a very clear example. Climate change could care less whether or not we can achieve the requisite ppm of carbon by a certain point in time. Regardless of whether it's achievable or practical, if we don't align with Reality by a certain point in time, the climate will cross a threshold from which recovery will become exponentially increasingly difficult.

And this same thing is true in companies concerned about market share or NGOs concerned about their causes or governments about their citizens. Goals need to be based not on our opinion or our ideologies about Reality—be they conservative or liberal. Such non-reality-based approaches are increasingly the case when we seek to oversimplify (even deny) complexity—vs. engage with it. Goals need to be based on the Reality of either what will occur if we don't respond at a certain order of magnitude by a certain point in time and/or what benefit could be gained. Again, think Climate or even COVID-19.

Back to Ken…

The map that emerged in response to Ken's goal, when coupled with the insight regarding talent management from the earlier map, offered a comprehensive approach to achieving his true goal, one that created the opportunity for greater trust and openness—with PM's and, especially, vendors. It offered a partnership that lent itself to greater transparency and an increased ability to optimize for the ecosystem as a whole—for both the publisher and vendors—capable of ensuring the sustainability of the ecosystem as a whole.

Internalization: Your own +RBMTSG

As a part of keeping my promise to you, I want to be sure that I explore with you the things you can actually do to embody this way of working, this way of thinking and, perhaps especially, of being/becoming.

So at this first level, I invite you to ask yourself, "What would enable me to get crystal clear—to develop a felt sense—about my own positive, measurable, time-specific goal—one that's reflective of the Reality of what's needed—vs. a "safe" goal—vs. one that's achievable or practical or…?"

This isn't necessarily easy. In my own case and for my clients, it usually requires quite a bit of experiential research to really understand the scope and scale of what's required. In Guatemala, for example, I knew that—without at least a bit of the Reality, of felt sense of what the K'iche and Mam Peoples were confronting—I wouldn't be able to design for them in a way that would have a meaningful impact on their issue/opportunity. So I asked one of the former Guerrilla leaders, Benjamin, to take me out and make me weep. He did and, from that experience, I was infinitely more valuable to CARE going forward.

You, too (I hope), will find over time that embodying—internalizing a felt sense (as did our G20 leaders with undocumented immigrants) is an invaluable investment as it anchors everything else—in something externally tangible and objective—and in something subjective—something internally, personally meaningful.

Now that you've got a sense of the Individual, we're ready for the next level …

Chapter 2: At the Level of Another

Partner Relationship x Partner Clarity = Trust

While, for simplicity's sake, I always start out talking about this as the level of "another", what I don't like about that word is that it sounds too much like what my friend, John Powell,[71] describes as "othering"—an artificial state—vs. belonging, our natural/innate state of relationship. Holding someone literally as an "other" is not reflective of the level of relationship required to overcome the challenges before us—challenges that, more often than not, involve true multi–stakeholder collaboration.

My experience has been that what is essential (if we're to solve our "impossible" problems) is that we partner with one another in the true sense of the word—i.e., that we share risk. That's what true partners do in business and in relationships. That's what Ike and I did with the work on the GNSC's supply chain when I offered that he pay me only if we succeed.

Forging authentic relationship with another at the level of intimacy needed to evoke shared clarity is an incredibly rich experience for both the interviewer and the interviewee.[72] For the vast majority of those we've worked with (with the exception of "Bullies"—see below), from CEOs of F100 corporations to police and firemen in

---

[71] Search John Powell, Othering & Belonging Institute, UC Berkeley.
[72] You have no idea how much fun working this way can be—or maybe you do!

local communities to leaders of governments and NGOs alike, we've found what they deeply care about isn't actually "personal" at all. It isn't simply about them. They aren't ultimately selfish. They almost always care about something much bigger than themselves or their families or their friends or even their organizations. They care about something that benefits the whole—whatever that whole, that larger context—is.

TIMEOUT: Bullies

Let's not be naïve here—there are "bullies" in systems. They are usually emotionally and psychologically, if not physically and spiritually, damaged individuals who are very rarely concerned about others, much less the whole. And dealing with them is something we'll speak to when we get to the Organizational level. I simply want to acknowledge them here, since I'll largely speak as if everyone has the potential to care about the whole. Sadly, not quite everyone does.

Most often the reason it doesn't look like a leader has that deep level of caring is that they're trying to solve a fairly complex problem for a set of diverse stakeholders with unique, complex needs. And they simply don't have the right toolset for doing that. They don't even know that it's possible.

Hence, some of the really awkward, ultimately foolish, and even damaging decisions we see from time to time. It is, however, not only possible but essential that we, as leaders in systems, learn to sit with another human being and really understand them deeply. To listen at a level that enables us to speak from their place in the system—from their perspective—while not losing track of our own perspective, experience, and expectations/needs.

TIMEOUT: State of Being/Becoming

I need, at this point, to bring something into sharp relief. Remember that "state of being/becoming" element we touched on earlier? State-of-being/becoming lives at the heart of all of this. My/your ability to enter into a relationship with genuine curiosity about another—to generate authentic, transparent presence—is essential to the success of this. We sometimes shift into this state by asking ourselves "How can I become fiercely curious about what this person is interested in and good at?" or "How can I 'fall in love' with what this person cares most deeply about and spends their life doing?" When Jim and I were working in Guatemala I learned a seminal lesson about this, one that impacts me to this day.

We needed to interview a leader in Guatemala's Intelligence Service, something I'll (reluctantly) admit that I wasn't looking forward to. I was aware of some of what had gone on in the Guatemalan Civil War, of the "disappearance" of thousands of Guatemalans at the hands of the Government. I was also aware of the complicity of my own government in these atrocities. So I had some preconceptions about, especially, the Intelligence Service.

It didn't help that, as Jim and I were being escorted to the interview on the top floor of their headquarters in downtown Guatemala City, we passed through several airlocks manned, on each side, by soldiers with automatic rifles. Yet when we arrived and I sat before this leader, I suddenly realized that, if anyone on the planet could recognize insincerity, it was this guy—*that was his job.*

I realized that if I wanted to be of service to the whole, If I wanted to truly understand, even internalize this leader's perspective, I had to shift my state of being from one of pre-judgment to one of authentic, unbiased, present-moment curiosity. For me that translated into— for the next 60 minutes, anyway—"falling in love" with this guy, caring about what he most deeply, truly cared about. It was my job to assume a positive intent at the root of his work. I could always fall out of love in an hour. But for now, I had to go there.

What unfolded was a very clear picture of how he, too, struggled to get the right information to the President and other key decision makers in an effort to save lives. And how that was too often overruled by the will of those concerned about something other than the whole. There is this place, this attitude, this chosen belief that the person in front of me (Bullies excepted) is operating from a place of intelligence and positive intent—that is, if one is to do this work. It's a place from which meaningful, generative conversations emerge and shared understanding—even alignment across the system—begins. Achieving this state of being and maintaining it throughout the work with the system, has become a practice that I doubt I'll ever outgrow or ever fully master.

Relationship with Another

We've found four things to be particularly valuable and efficient in getting to quickly know another person in a system: *Engaging with others in their passion, their work goal, and their success stories, and adding value to them*. Every time we do this, we evoke a level of personal and professional clarity they've rarely experienced before. And we leave the conversation with mutual respect and a strong, trusting—often caring —Relationship.

Engaging with their passion

Again, Guatemala. After setting the context with a leader for our 1-on-1 interviews, we simply asked them—this representative of a particular stakeholder group, an aspect of the ecosystem—what they most wanted to see happen for their fellow citizens in Guatemala. The answers—from military leaders, from educators, from businesspeople, from former government ministers, from across the spectrum—were thoughtful, compassionate, authentic hopes for the well-being of all of Guatemala's citizens. And they were clearly passionate about their hopes as they described for whom these dreams were important and why, as they described what must happen if Guatemala is to fulfill her potential.

Once we've gotten clear about this together—once they've recalled it and shared it and we've heard it—we've established the foundation for our shared relationship to the system—a point of reference we will, together, work toward—an aspect that must be included if we are to work collectively to improve the system—the "whole".

Understanding their current work, their goal, and how they succeed...

...is just plain fun to do, especially if you come to understand it through *their success stories*. People love to tell these stories and they're almost always meaningful, even delightful, to listen to—especially when you enter into them with a sense of deep, authentic curiosity.

One thing about success stories that's absolutely and pragmatically essential is that you're assembling your understanding of the system based on real-world examples—things that have actually been proven out in physical reality—based on things they know how to do—vs. people's fantasies. And success stories are an ideal way to ensure this.

There are two other factors that lie at the heart of approaching this through the lens of success stories. One comes from Jerry Sternin's concept of "Positive Deviance"[73]—i.e., learning from successful outliers rather than discarding them as irrelevant anomalies. Another is from David Cooperrider's "Appreciative Inquiry"[74] work, where deliberately adopting a positive (vs. negative) bias focuses us on what we are *for* versus what we are *against*. Doing so shifts our mood (and, therefore, our physiology) in the direction needed to tackle "impossible" problems. Done in this way, you learn an incredible amount about

---

[73] See *The Power of Positive Deviance: How Unlikely Innovators Solve the World's Toughest Problems*, by Richard Pascale, Jerry Sternin, Monique Sternin (2010)

[74] *Appreciative Inquiry: A Positive Revolution in Change*, by David Cooperrider and Diana D. Whitney (2005)

how they do what they do—if you listen from a systems-thinking perspective. So an essential bit about systems-thinking…

Clarity with Another

This takes the form of creating an individual causal map of their goal, their top 3-5+ core competencies and their story in the form of a causal diagram. Systems-thinking has a lot to teach us about achieving clarity. We (the system-dynamics/systems-thinking community) know, from building thousands of system models that, by and large, there are usually only 3-5+ things that directly cause a goal to be achieved. This aligns with that helpful application of MECE (mutually exclusive and collectively exhaustive) that we referred to earlier. There may be 20 or 50 or 100 things that, taken all together, cause it—but those other 15 or 45 or 95 things aren't *directly* responsible—they drive the 3-5+ things that are. Here's an example of a relatively simple causal diagram that captures Michael Noble's story[75]—at the time, the Executive Director of Minnesota's ME3. To recall how one develops this, refer back to GNSC's Act #1 above:

Causal Diagram – a sample

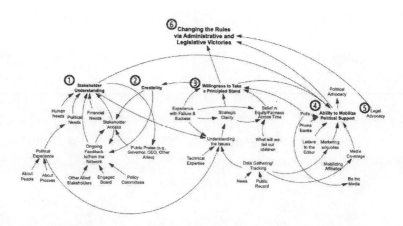

---

[75] For a detailed walkthrough of this one, go to scottspann.com/impossible.

Here's a quick primer on how to make some sense of this. (Don't worry, we won't walk through the whole thing—just enough to get you started[76].) It turns out that, though this wasn't what their vision or mission statement said, Michael's goal and that of his organization (based on their best success stories) was actually "changing the rules via administrative and legislative victories" ⑥. This is accomplished—or caused by—at the highest level, five critical resources or abilities:

1. **Stakeholder understanding**—i.e., the level of understanding of the stakeholders involved in the issue

2. **Credibility** — i.e., the organization and leadership team's credibility

3. **Willingness to take a principled stand** — i.e., not taking a stand on each and every issue but only on those issues where a principle of fundamental importance to their purpose/mission is at stake, and to take that stand based on principles—not a vitriolic stand based in an isolated ideology

4. **Ability to mobilize political support** — i.e., when such principles are at stake, to draw on that stakeholder understanding, credibility, and principled stand to get people out and engaged to change the administrative or legislative outcome, and, finally,

5. **Legal advocacy** — i.e., the use of the laws and regulations to enforce both the spirit and the letter of already established precedent to bolster their position on a principled issue.

All the other items on the map are critical, i.e., they must be there for their "system" to function, but they are supportive of (or cause) these top five which, in turn, cause the goal ⑥.

---

[76] Again, for resources, search "causal loop diagram". But please, not without taking a look at George P. Richardson's *Problems with Causal Loop Diagrams*, System Dynamics Review, (1986).

The significance of this is twofold. First, it makes understanding complex things much simpler when you can sort them based on their degree of influence—are they primary or secondary or tertiary, etc.[77]

Secondly, if you're to influence a system, understanding *causality* in the system is particularly useful. Knowing what pushes on what and in which direction, and what other things are then affected, helps you see where you should intervene in a system—if you are to have the desired result with a minimum of negative unintended consequences—and a minimum of time, money, and stress.[78]

This requires some skill in thinking systemically and dynamically—in actually building models that really work—because as you're asking these questions about their success story, you're doing so either from the model you're actively building in your head as they speak or from the blank spaces in that model that you need to fill in. And you're reflecting your thinking back to them, first, to validate (or not) your emerging model of how they do what they do and, secondly, to let them know that you do truly hear and understand them.

When you're done with your initial conversation, you'll be able to summarize their success story in a few simple sentences that capture the depth and breadth of what they do with an understanding and clarity that usually hasn't existed for them before. And you can do it in a way that captures and clarifies just how much value they add. ***And, in doing so, you add value to them***, thereby deepening relationship.

Based on their interview and success story(s), we come back with a small, clear, complete map of their unique system: their goal, their top 3-5+ core competencies and the finite set of other elements that make

---

[77] Many leaders we work with—even at the G100 level—simply can't clearly articulate (initially) their primary goal, much less the top 3 - 5+ things that make that happen. Oh, they can tell me that it's market share or shareholder return or profit, but these are usually abstractions of their true goal—necessary but related metrics—not their true goal. Simply helping leaders get clear about this is a tremendous *value add* to them, and to your relationship with them through your demonstrated ability to engage them in a brief conversation that helps them get clearer at both a strategic and even tactical level.

[78] As my good friend and colleague, Mickey Connolly of Conversant, is fond of saying.

up their success model. It's one they can understand, modify, validate, and actually use to move their enterprise forward, as Michael did with his, using it to reorient his board and his staff and to inform his strategic rebranding/marketing campaign.

Summoning this degree of clarity accomplishes five things:

- It adds value to how they think, something we must do at every touch if we're to continue to deepen relationship and trust

- It demonstrates to them, in their own context, that this approach is anything but "business-as-usual"

- Each interview/map increases our overall understanding of the ecosystem, better informing us about the ecosystem as a whole and thereby better preparing us for the subsequent interviews

- By doing so we've actually given them their own, personalized, customized primer on systems-thinking

- And finally (and perhaps most valuably), we've in essence created an implied contract to support this leader in holding true to their purpose and what's required to achieve it—one we can call on as the work proceeds.

For most leaders, this is the first time—often in a 20-year history of doing what they do so well—that they've clearly articulated what they do and how they do it. (For example, see Porter Wharton's story below.) It's a tremendous value add for them—and for your relationship.

Trust

This ability to clearly see, understand, and restate what another person is about in a way that adds value, is the evidence that your curiosity—even your caring—is authentic—that you actively listened—that you really "get" them and their work, their world, even their purpose. And in the process of deliberately causing this level of relationship & clarity, you build trust—the kind of trust that comes from caring enough to really understand—even internalize—someone else's perspective—to really live in it, if just for a bit. But this "bit", constructed in this way, stays with you—both of you.

Building trust at this level is particularly important because: 1) it's so essential to successful teamwork—truly to any work with others, and 2) it's often difficult to initiate trust-building at the team/group level because of the competition between goals, ideas, and action—and sometimes status— that exists at the level of the group—where group dynamics kick in. The complexity of the dynamic at the group level is an order of magnitude greater than the dynamic that exists at the individual level. Doing this Individual part well at this 1-on-1 level builds a resource of trust—an individual's trust in both the process and in you. Such trust is a resource to be drawn on when we begin the work with the team—and beyond.

TIMEOUT: Increasing readiness

So where are we (and the others) now in the process? Well, each individual has experienced being interviewed and mapped. They're each in a clearer and stronger relationship: 1) with themselves, the level of self, and 2) with what's important to them—what motivates them as an individual and what they're good at. They're also now in a strong, appreciative[79] relationship with you. Now each member of the group can speak with both clarity and passion and can actually engage in meaningful, well-structured, precise conversations about what they care about, what they do and how they do it—from this rigorous foundation. They're ready—you're ready—to engage as a team.

The Real World—Porter Wharton III:

My friend and colleague, Hal Rabbino, and I met Porter for lunch to explore what he'd taken on in his role at one of the world's top resort companies.

---

[79] Again, see David Cooperrider and "Appreciative Inquiry"

I was fascinated by Porter. He began his career as Director of the Colorado Public Interest Research Group advocating for, as the title says, the public interest. He had evolved into a masterful blend of public servant, political consultant, and public relations professional—someone for whom I quickly developed a deep level of respect and appreciation. When I first sat with Porter in his office, I discovered a wide, rich range of books on philosophy, political science, religion, and other non-business topics on the shelves ringing his office. He truly cared about, believed in, and devoted his career to optimizing for the public good—from wherever he was positioned in business and society. In his role at the resort company, his chosen purpose was to optimize the blend of economic value and quality of life for the communities in which the company was engaged.

During our lunch, I asked Porter what he was working on. His response was a bit staggering as he listed off the diverse, often conflicting, stakeholder needs he was trying to balance. It turns out that his role as VP of Public Affairs was a strategic imperative for the company. He was responsible for the company's relationship with the various communities the company was active in. And that determined whether or not (and how and when) they could expand and/or improve their resort facilities, develop their surrounding real estate holdings, and plan and build out the supporting retail and recreational offerings. Failure to create a mutual understanding and appreciation of the essential needs and aspirations of the various diverse community stakeholders (of which the company was but one) would mean, at the very least, significant delays (if not denials) in permitting, development, and, subsequently, operation and revenue.

At one point in our conversation, I asked Porter, "How do you get your head around all that?[80] He replied along the lines of, "I don't. I wake up at 3 a.m. running through the list in my

---

[80] Given the "brand" too often (and unfairly) associated with systems thinking/system dynamics (i.e., "been there, done that"), this phrase has been one of the ways I introduce the concept that *it is possible to harness complexity*—i.e., I rarely ever use the terms systems thinking or dynamics.

head, trying to make sure I'm not missing anything." As we dove a bit deeper, we discovered that Porter spent the better portion of each Monday with his team running down their lists of active projects (77 at the time), their current status, advances, setbacks, and next steps. Even with that investment of his and his team's scarce time, he didn't feel he had as solid a grasp on their portfolio as he needed. Nor did he feel his team was reliably clear on how to handle the interdependencies that existed between each element—interdependencies that impacted one another as they invariably morphed from week-to-week.

So we set a goal for Porter of not waking up at 3 a.m. each morning—of so clearly and crisply delineating not only what he did but how he did it, even how he set priorities—that both he and his team could reliably, predictably, confidently act knowing that they were moving forward in alignment across their strategic portfolio.

The first step was making sure that Porter was in relationship with and clear about his own individual leadership role. This was something he'd found nearly impossible to articulate in a way that his team could grasp—much less internalize and consistently operationalize. The most straightforward way to get there was for me to interview him about his toughest success story(s) about what it looks like when he's working at his best—and then systemically map that.

He described, in detail, how he'd been able to ensure the development of two controversial projects in Denver, Colorado: the new Broncos Stadium and the Denver International Airport. For each of these, there was a strong case to be made for the benefits that such developments would bring to the area. And there was a strong case for opposition to both as well. For Porter, these stories were an easy way for him to do a deep dive on how he acted on his commitment to creating mutually beneficial outcomes. What emerged were the following systemic representations.

TIMEOUT: My Bad!

Early in my "mapping" career, my mapping abilities were quite crude (see below). Still even these imperfect initial skills added significant value to Porter. I share this in the hopes that you're encouraged, based on what you're learning here, to begin to experiment with this way of thinking/seeing—without the need to be "perfect" before adding value.

The first one was a graphical representation of Porter's strategic vision Illuminating the resort's ability to contribute to community well-being[81]:

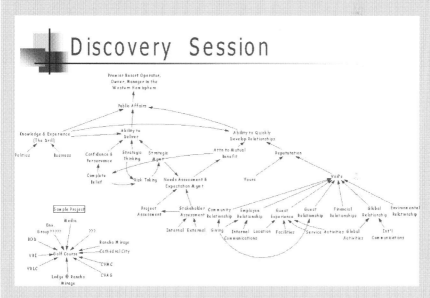

The second, bit more rigorous, map was a systemic view of what his team needed to accomplish in order to achieve those stakeholder benefits, thereby gaining project approval:

---

[81] I'm not going to walk you through these here as what they reveal isn't the point. What's important is *that* they revealed value to Porter. For a detailed walkthrough of these two, go to scottspann.com/impossible.

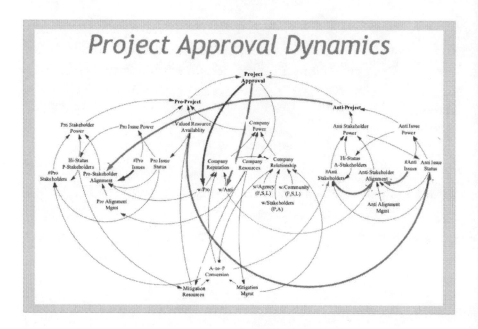

From there, we were able to accomplish two essential next steps.

First, we could align his team around both the "why" and the "what" of their work by sharing a comprehensive, integrated and reality-based/success-based framework. This served as the consistent basis for exploring and assessing the relative health of each project relative to stakeholder needs and expectations.

Secondly, we used this insight to design an at-a-glance project management system[82] capable of displaying Porter's 3 a.m. list of 77 active projects along four dimensions: strategic impact, strategic risk, level of investment (indicated by the size of each project on the bubble chart) and current status (indicated by bubble color: green/good, yellow/fair, red/poor). This visual could finally offer him the level of confidence he needed to assure that he really did have his head around the moving parts for which he was responsible. And in the process, position him to more productively repurpose his (and his staff's) Mondays.

---

[82] This doesn't show up well at all in black & white—especially the inverse relationships. So if you want to see it in color, you'll find it at scottspann.com/impossible

Our work together was so successful that, years later, after Porter had reignited his consulting practice, I got a call from him asking for his individual map—citing it as the best way he'd yet come across to explore and explain for his clients what he did, how, and why.

Internalization: Your Own Individual Map

Extending our promise to this level, take some time to re-inhabit your own favorite success stories—those experiences, projects, or moments when you were performing at your best—when you were your fuller Self. This is critical to your ability to both inventory your abilities and, given the rate of change in our world, to continue to develop them—to evolve your Self. Once there—once you're back in that "state of being/becoming"—distill out of those experiences first your goal and then the 3-5+ resources/abilities that enabled you to be so successful.

If you care to take it farther, refer back to the GNSC example of how to such maps are constructed. Or check out the DIY section[83] of my website for a short course on how to do it.

Then boundary test your 3-5+ (or your map). Pull up other successes. Does this set explain those, too? Then pull up a failure or two and ask whether or not a weakness in one of 3-5+ explains how or why that happened. Ask yourself: If that weak element had been healthy, would you have succeeded?

I periodically revisit the design/development of my own success model—both for my work and for the continued evolution of my business (and my Self). I find it a consistently reliable source of insight—especially relevant when I get too far into the trenches of meeting project deadlines—when I most need to remind myself (when I come up for air) of where I'm headed, why and how.

Now that you've got a sense of the level with "another", we're ready for the next one...

---

[83] https://www.scottspann.com/diy/

Chapter 3: At the level of the Team/SubGroup[84]

Team Relationship x Team Clarity = Innovation

TIMEOUT: Dampening vs. Amplifying Confusion

Okay, that formula again. It's important to call out here just one of the many reasons for getting into relationship and getting clear at the earlier levels. And it's easier to understand specifically what we're going for here when we speak about it in the negative. Meaning if I bring someone who is not clear into the room with others who, similarly, aren't clear, I'll simply amplify confusion.

Additionally, if I bring them into the room without some common basis of relationship, I risk amplifying discord. So to have any chance at all of creating value for those in the room, I must ensure that we're strong on one or the other: relationship or clarity and, ideally, both. I can strengthen them 1-on-1 through the processes previously described in Levels 1 and 2, and port that strength, that resource state, into the room.

Done properly, the clarity, relationship, and trust thus birthed is transferable. Still, to the degree that either one is lacking, the principles and processes below will strengthen both.

---

[84] Within an existing organization, we use the term Team; within a newly forming network, the term Subgroup—until such time as Teams form.

Team

In a complex–adaptive system, when we move beyond 1-on-1—whether with an existing team or newly forming small group—we lose "control"—as if we ever had it! This is due in part to moving from an *interpersonal* dynamic to the significantly more complex *group* dynamic.

Groups are smart—as long as we've been smart. That is, if we've set them up to be smart—the subject of this chapter, btw. We can't tell a team what to do or even how to do it—not if we want to access their fuller potential. We can lead a team, but we can't really push or drive a team—not sustainably. Teams have to form their own relationships—with themselves and, through that, with reality. They have to find their own way[85] toward their own purpose and goal—admittedly, within the goal of the larger system.

But what you can do is design a good process—a good structure, a good container—within which a team can find themselves and their way. And that's precisely what good systems-thinking tools, coupled with good collaboration processes, do. If we do our job well, the team itself will begin to guide the process. They will become those emergent actors so essential to harnessing complexity. They will become a force of their own—course-correcting us when we drift off point and monitoring both individual and group behavior[86]—continually orienting toward their chosen, reality-based goal. At this level, the lines between purely relational work and purely clarifying work begin to blur a bit. So from time to time now, we'll talk about them almost

---

[85] The two best sources I know on dealing with really smart, really challenging teams are the SCT (Systems Centered Therapy) work developed by Yvonne Agazarian & her colleagues and a self–governance system christened Holacracy—developed by my friend Brian Robertson & his colleagues.

[86] It continually amazes me how a group can handle difficult personalities (even bullies) once the group is clear and aligned. Time after time, we see a group—originally intimidated by a dominant personality—bond around a compelling shared purpose and an internalized comprehension of their shared reality to such a degree that they simply won't let themselves be distracted by anyone attempting to deter them. Once the group has reached alignment, it's fascinating to see a formerly dominant member begin to self-manage in order to remain a part of (or re-join) the group.

as if they are a continuous whole—which, if we're doing our job well, they are.

Team Relationship

A word here about something critical to good relationships: choice. While we offer authentic choice at each level of our work, we do so much more explicitly now. We allow people choice, not just choice for the sake of choice, but choice about things that they are truly, deeply interested in, even passionate about. Most people we work with are deeply passionate about what they do—even if the systems they operate in have stymied their ability to act on it—even dulled their enthusiasm. We offer them choice by allowing them to…

…gather around their shared passions, discover a positive goal, and explore their shared reality.

There is a lot at play...

…at this level—so much so that it would be easy to overwhelm ourselves with detail. So I'm going to limit the team part of our conversation to five critical, interrelated practices/tools, as follows:

- SCT's (Yvonne Agazarian's) Functional Subgrouping
- Conversant's "Cycle of Value"
- A Shared Goal
- The Behavior Over Time graph (BOT)
- The Integrated Map

…leaving the rest for the practitioner's manual (the next book). Let's break that down.

Functional Subgrouping

A largely unknown but absolutely critical part of building relationship at the team level—and, from there, throughout the organization, network, or ecosystem—is allowing individual members choice in *gathering around shared passions*. This is distinctly different from what I used to do/believe, which was to gather cross-functional teams. There are times when the latter is highly valuable, but not at this stage of harnessing complexity—for reasons that will soon become apparent.

I'm using the word "passion" here for a reason (feel free to substitute your word: concern, interest, desire...). Accomplishing anything of significant meaning/importance—especially anything "impossible"— requires that we not rely solely on what's rational.

It requires that we engage with our fuller Self, with one another and with Reality from an embodied felt sense of commitment, one that I'm choosing to call "passion". It's been the failure to tap into this fundamental source of renewable[87] human energy that accounts for the failure of so many strategies—the failure to forge the link between internal motivation and external action. Said another way, we have to design the means for transferring the impulse for action from *outside* the individual—which is often the case in a typical management hierarchy—to *inside* the individual—which occurs in a well-designed self-organizing/managing network.

Functional subgrouping is a practice that derives from Yvonne Agazarian's Systems-Centered Therapy.[88] Yvonne's insight goes something like this (well, my paraphrase of it does—forgive me, Yvonne):

"You'll never get a diverse group of individuals to have an authentic conversation since most people are too concerned about being seen, heard, understood, appreciated and included. You must: 1) first

---

[87] As you'll see, we can successfully renew this source of energy by revisiting the artifacts produced in this section whenever the group—or individual members—begin to doubt themselves, one another, or the project.

[88] Properly structured and led, functional subgrouping, when coupled with system dynamics tools, enables a team to experience and learn collaboration as they do valuable, productive work. In the end, people know how to collaborate without our even needing to mention the word, outline the steps or "teach" them collaboration. Having them experience first, then understand it cognitively anchors much better than doing it the other way around.

discriminate and understand the differences among the apparently similar before you can 2) appreciate and integrate the similarities among the apparently different." [89]

Feel free to read that twice, as most people have to hear it twice when first introduced to this insight. And it's worth saying twice as my study with Yvonne (and other SCT practitioners) radically changed my approach to group work—for the better. For example, I used to begin with cross-functional teams, with varying degrees of success (or not), for reasons I now clearly understand–there were too many inherently competing interests and obligations.

All too often, I inadvertently embedded degrees of conflict that couldn't be resolved within the process—the container—I had designed. I now approach every engagement seeking to ferret out those members who are most closely aligned with one another, allowing them to first gather and get clear with one another—before bringing together all the diverse and often conflicting viewpoints from each/all of the other subgroups.

The Real World: Re-Amp:

The Backstory. One of the most successful down-on-the-ground climate change projects in the U.S. is Re-Amp (an acronym for Renewable Energy Alignment and Mapping Project), a project conceived of by Rick Reed and Jennie Curtis of the Garfield Foundation. They were curious about how one might go about successfully applying systems-thinking to an issue/opportunity as "impossible" as climate change.

Though it began as an effort to simply increase wind energy in the Midwest, by the time we harnessed people's passion, it evolved into a ground-breaking climate change network—one that's still going strong today, 16 years later—one whose core goal evolved and crystalized as reducing greenhouse gas (GHG) emissions 80% by 2030—a remarkable and, at the time, radical insight.

---

[89] Yvonne Agazarian, *Systems-Centered Therapy for Groups*, (1994), p. 20 has the precise wording.

For about three months, Rick and I had conversations about how to design such a project/process. Our conversations consistently stressed the essential nature of giving the humanistic elements (an early label for "relationship") equal footing with the systems-thinking side—what I'm here calling "clarity". And we made good progress in aligning on what a good consulting team—one capable of addressing both ends of that spectrum—would look like.

In the next call with Rick, he shared that they'd selected their consulting firm—and it wasn't me! Though disappointed, I couldn't disagree with his choice. The group they'd contracted with were my heroes in the world of systems-thinking and system-dynamics. How could I be anything other than congratulatory?

The next call from Rick, six months later, was to share that the process was in trouble—asking me to meet with him to diagnose what had gone wrong and how one might salvage it.

It turns out that, though the consulting team was comprised of skilled professionals with the right expertise, they'd over-emphasized the technical, systems-thinking side—paying only scant attention to the relational side. It gave even less weight to the need for emergence from the individual level up to and through the other levels. As a result, there was even an active conversation among key leaders in the group about dropping out, something that would doom the project.

This crisis (back to Fritjof's insight) created the opportunity—actually, the imperative—to build even deeper relationship with each leader. To do that, I personally visited with each one face-to-face—sharing our redesigned process with each, soliciting their feedback (again, emergence), and individually interviewing them. Then, in keeping with the Individual level described earlier, we mapped what each was seeking—independent of the project.

We did this "independent of the project" bit for two reasons. First, we needed to make sure that the project was actually a strategic fit for each leader. Anything else would ultimately be a waste of their time—and ours. And we explicitly called this out—this integrity check—as one of the ways of rebuilding lost trust and deepening relationship.

Lest one think that this only applies to cross-sectoral network building, I've encountered precisely the same dynamic in small and large organizations. If what a divisional lead or business unit head cares about isn't accounted for, the likelihood that they will authentically engage is remote.

Secondly, given the emergent nature of the problem/project, we didn't want our initial assumptions to inadvertently omit any of the leader's/organization's abilities, resources, and/or relationships—ones that, once we'd collectively aligned on a goal, might well be indispensable to our success. We then used these learnings as the basis for constructing a project that would serve both their individual needs and those of the group as a whole.

It was because of the individual interviews and maps that we were able to then identify the various passions—the diverse themes or affinity groups, if you prefer—vying for expression within the larger group.

Four subgroups emerged: 1) local economic energy development, 2) environmental sustainability, 3) energy policy, and 4) the utility industry. It was the awareness of these competing interests that helped to explain why the prior approach had been stymied. That is, bringing 24 strong, committed leaders into the room together without the requisite levels of relationship & clarity only served to amplify first confusion, then conflict. Our new awareness of differing passions also explained how functional subgrouping could resolve both—adding significant value to the overall project.

So how did functional subgrouping as a relationship-building tool fit in here? Well, I knew, based on the levels of upset among the Re-Amp participants, that our first group meeting couldn't begin by putting, say, an environmentalist in the room with a utility executive. The emotional charge was simply too great. I couldn't construct a container, a process, that would productively channel their charge into a positive outcome.

So I turned to Yvonne's SCT functional subgrouping, knowing that within a group of similar interests—though there would be differences among the apparently similar—the differences wouldn't be so great as to blow the container.

TIMEOUT: Humanizing

As a part of humanizing this way of working, and in addition to Yvonne, I want to give thanks to my mentors in trauma psychotherapy, principally Dr. Peter Levine, and in Somatic Developmental Psychology, largely Marianne Bentzen of Denmark. They continually modeled the critical nature of deliberately constructing, maintaining, and adapting a container to ensure that a client's emotional energy didn't slip over the edge in chaos—i.e., did not allow the process to re-injure the client, abiding by that "do no harm" maxim from Hippocrates[90].

Fundamental to this was the practice of compartmentalizing the charge such that upset at one level couldn't suddenly cascade into other levels, triggering a string of ever-increasing levels of distress. A very crude (though visually illustrative) example would be that of a controlled demolition that safely removes an obsolete building without causing collateral damage. The detonation is compartmentalized in time and the charges contained, channeled in a direction that will accomplish the desired outcome in a healthy way.

Back to Re-Amp

Thanks in large part to my remarkably gifted partner in the project, LeeAnn Mallory, the results were nothing short of remarkable—for each of the groups. True to Yvonne's words, the first 5–10 minutes of, for example, the environmentalist's meeting, were filled with smiles, excitement, and pats on the back. They were delighted at having their own say without concern about the economic development folks or the utility execs or the regulators, etc.

But before too long, they were engaged in some very feisty, spirited debates about what their goal should be. Should it emphasize policy or activism or green consumerism or…? As the day and the

---

[90] Despite popular opinion, this is actually from his work *Of the Epidemics*, not the *Hippocratic Oath*.

design unfolded, they moved steadily from positions of difference to increasing awareness of their similarities, emerging at the end of the day aligned on a shared goal and aware of the forces at play over time in the larger ecosystem that determined the fate of their shared goal.

What's more, the level of information exchanged and the relationships forged, from both the evolution of their goal and the behavior over time (BOT) graph explorations (more on those in the "Team Clarity" section below), were equally remarkable.

We were then ready to come back together as a whole group for the first time since redesigning the project—able to see and appreciate the similarities among the apparently different. And to grasp that. Based on their BOTs, each had admirable, mutually-beneficial goals and each were struggling to do the right thing in a complex environment.

In the end, Re-Amp was positioned to be surprisingly successful— growing from 24 organizations to 170. It was ultimately endorsed by 8 Midwestern governors—passing significantly impactful energy efficiency, clean energy, decoupling and other policies, rules, and regulations across those 8 Midwestern states.

Fundamentally, it was our ability to tap into and champion the passions of each individual in the heretofore unaffiliated groups that enabled success. Then, once they were activated, to consistently maintain our integrity by continually assessing—whether live in front of the room, in individual conversations, in subgroup meetings or in whole group meetings—whether or not we are on the path to addressing those concerns—on the road to achieving our needed, reality-based (and because of that, heartfelt) outcomes.

Okay. That should give us a decent grasp of functional subgroups for the moment. Next...

Conversant's Cycle of Value: Mining the Value in Difference

As you'll recall, we are specifically using functional subgrouping at this level to discover the differences among the apparently similar. We're doing so because it's been well-proven, time and again, that there's value in diversity—as evidenced, for instance, by the richness in the diversity/differences in Nature, in a healthy Society, or in a thriving Business.[91] And it's critical to survival— specifically as called out by "Ashby's Law of Requisite Variety". As Don Lockton puts it, Ashby's Law goes like this: "Informally, practically, [Ashby's Law] says that in order to deal properly with the diversity of problems the world throws at you, you need to have a repertoire of responses which is (at least) as nuanced as the problems you face."[92]

There's a proven, though insufficiently known, methodology to ensure that we can distill value from our differences. Mickey Connolly and my brilliant friends at Conversant have developed (and continue to evolve) a truly seminal body of work that, too, is rooted in what it means to be fully human—though you're much better off reading Mickey's book about it, *The Communication Catalyst*. Until then, let me give you a brief run-through based on one of their most compelling graphics.

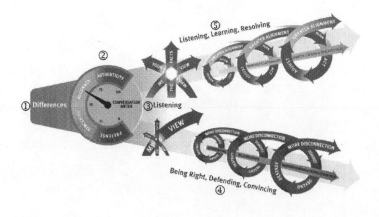

---

[91] https://blog.capterra.com/7-studies-that-prove-the-value-of-diversity-in-the-workplace/
[92] http://requisitevariety.co.uk/what-is-requisite-variety/

Our ability to realize the value inherent in "Differences" ① is a function of the quality of our conversations, as indicated by the "Conversation Meter" ②. We can converse at one of four levels:

Pretense—e.g., I'm nodding silently, even smiling, as you speak although I have absolutely no intention of following through on your idea—a form of dishonesty

Sincerity—e.g., "I'm going to tell you the absolute truth—you're a jerk!" Truthful (my truth, anyway), but not at all helpful—and would actually be harmful

Accuracy—i.e., I'm citing valid facts and figures as evidence of my perspective and beginning to inform our decision-making—relevant truth

Authenticity—i.e., I can be trusted to speak with the intention of benefiting the whole, looking for an intersection of our interests, our mutual benefit—displaying true leadership.

That fork in the road at "Listening" ③ between the upper fork and the lower is easiest to demonstrate from the lower (literally) end first—the Cycle of Waste ④. When we operate from Pretense and/or Sincerity:

- I express my view (that one thick arrow dominating those two thin ones), giving (at best) token recognition to your view and to the facts
- You naturally *disagree*
- I naturally *defend*
- The resulting *disconnect* in our relationship *destroys* value
- Again and again and again—accelerating our descent into waste.

By contrast, in the "Cycle of Value" ⑤, when we operate from Accuracy and/or Authenticity:

- I give equal recognition to your view, the facts, and my view (that intersection of three equally sized arrows)
- Enabling us to *align* with Reality and one another

- Which gives us the ability to *act* together
- From which we can learn and *adjust*
- Realigning and repeating—accelerating ever-increasing cycles of value.

With a Team or Subgroup, we'll typically put this up early on in the day—both as a way to frame our conversations throughout our time together and to remind ourselves when we stray. It also serves as a meta-concept for the process as a whole over time. That is, we'll continue to use these cycles of Align, Act, and Adjust from here on—at this level and beyond—because the frame generates ever-increasing value as we move into execution, scalability, and sustainability—the latter 3 abilities that arise from our 6 levels.

Now onto the third of our five Level 3 essentials:

A Shared Goal

Once who's in which Team or Subgroup is clear, we can begin to think about the third of our five tools—each subgroup's goal.

As I shared earlier, the relationship & clarity strands of our work will continue to blend/blur a bit as they transition from individual strands (initially) to a weave (eventually) in the later phases. It's through the emergence of a clear, reality-based goal that relationship truly deepens.

As I spoke to in the Individual level—and as you'll see in the next section on the Organizational Level—the single most important starting point is for the team to create a *shared positive goal*—a team goal that eventually sits within and supports the overall organizational goal (more on this later). But it is ideally a goal they elicit, or at least believe in, for themselves. Without that, we have a group, but we don't have a team. Even the Nobel-nominated philosopher Martin Buber speaks to this in his book *Ich Und Du* (*I and Thou*),1923, demonstrating that, without clear purpose (in our context, without a clear goal), a community/group cannot sustain itself.

Once the individual subgroups are determined (using the learnings from our individual interviews), each subgroup convenes and first determines what their goal is. What's critical at this point is ensuring that we're weaving each individual's goal into a higher order group goal that includes and then transcends the individual goals.

To ensure this, the first act in our day is to introduce ourselves by taking 5-10 minutes to orient ourselves individually to what we each believe our goal for this domain of the ecosystem should be. We then share that as the basis for birthing our shared goal. And, though we don't ever use the word consensus,[93] shared alignment inevitably shows up.

By the time we get to the whole group/organizational level (coming next), their individual and subgroup goals have been integrated into their larger, overall system's goal—developed by simultaneously holding in mind/in their awareness both their individual and subgroup perspectives as well as the needs of the whole.

The Real World: Map OneSonoma (M1S)—Responding to Sonoma County's devastating fires of 2017:

Beginning during the night of October 8, 2017, California's deadliest and most destructive firestorms up to that moment in time[94] literally swept through Northern California—taking, in Sonoma County alone, the lives of 25 people, destroying 7,023 homes and buildings and leaving 112,380 acres of charred landscape in its wake.[95]

A crisis of this magnitude catalyzed the recognition on the part of Sonoma County's community leaders that the recovery process represented an opportunity to rebuild in a way that redesigned and reset the well-being for all Sonomans—including those without sufficient

---

[93] This work doesn't advocate consensus as a decision-making principle since such a requirement enables a single individual to effectively veto forward progress. Still, it consistently emerges.
[94] At that moment in time, we had no idea the magnitude of firestorms yet to come.
[95] For more on these fires, see this link https://en.wikipedia.org/wiki/ October_2017_Northern_California_wildfires.

resources to weather such events. Further, it represented an opportunity to create an inclusive, resilient, and thriving future for all Sonomans.

As a part of this journey, the individual interviews and individual maps made explicit 7 thematic domains of critical interest—7 subgroups, including: housing and transportation, workforce and education, equity and inclusion, labor, economic development, overall community health and, finally, governance.

We, as a design team, offered these up as 1-day subgroup meetings that any leader could attend and allowed them to attend as many subgroups as they wished—requiring only that they be genuinely interested in the subgroup topic. This insistence on genuine interest— vs. being assigned to a group or attending because it was in their job description or their boss directed it or they "should" attend—ensured that every participant would be fully engaged—fully contributing to the work of the group from a place of personal interest, expertise, and/ or passion (that word again).

And because everyone was fully engaged, we were able to quickly get to a shared positive goal and *engage in the reality of that goal* via a fact-filled/reality-based conversation—vs. opinion-driven or ideological exchanges[96] —about the pattern of that goal's BOT (via a "Behavior Over Time Graph", the next of our five tools).

But before we jump into that part of our day, before the BOT, a bit of context via one of the subgroups. The Economic Development subgroup was composed of representatives from both the business community (e.g., the Chamber of Commerce and the Economic Development Board) as well as those concerned about overall community economic well-being (e.g. the United Way of the Wine Country and other local NGOs). And, though they each came from different points on the economic compass, they quickly aligned on an extraordinary goal. Don't worry, I'll share that in moment. But first…

---

[96] It still amazes me that, when we shift a conversation from opinion-based/ideological to a sufficiently fact/reality-based (when properly structured), most of the conflict simply "dissolves."

In keeping with the principle of emergence, we had each individual leader take a few minutes in silence to write down what they believed the goal for this subgroup—this dimension of the ecosystem—should be. Again, we do this within businesses with equal, if not even better, success—as few have seriously thought about their true goal/purpose beyond throwaways like "shareholder value"[97].

As we went around the room, each reading out their individual goal, something deeply meaningful and valuable became readily apparent—as it does each time we do this. Though they were gathered around a shared passion, there were clearly differences in each of their goals. Yet their differences were not insurmountable. Each was deeply concerned, at their core, about the distribution of both income and, as importantly, wealth. This extended to a concern about the follow-on impact that the lack of sufficient economic opportunity had on housing, health, education, and beyond.

What emerged was a goal driven by a *standard*—an agreed-upon, well-defined metric by which our progress could be measured. They settled on the *Social Progress Index* + Resiliency (in response to anticipated fire, flood, and drought) as their target/goal. Specifically, they landed on "Score 90 on the Social Progress Index while assuring resiliency (environmental, social, and economic) by 2028"—SPI+R for short.

You'll recall that the first essential to gaining team clarity is discovering a *positive* goal. We, like Robert Fritz[98] (more on his contributions in a moment) insist on a positive goal. In this instance, we have an example of a reality-based, positive, measurable, time-specific goal via the M1S Economic Development subgroup. But we don't have an example of a negative goal, a useful counterexample. So to offer you a study in contrast...

---

[97] See "The World's Dumbest Idea," *Forbes*, Jun 26, 2013

[98] Robert Fritz (co-founder, along with Peter Senge, of Innovation Associates) has written and taught extensively on the creative process—especially in organizations. For more on his work, see www.robertfritz.com or *The Path of Least Resistance*.

The Real World: CARE Guatemala's "Negative" Goal:

When Jim and I first began to work with the CARE Guatemala team, they had a negative goal[99]—i.e., the elimination of poverty and social injustice—a much-needed condition, to be sure. Yet when we think about it for a moment, negative goals are usually an attempt to remove obstacles to a much more motivating, desirable, and collectively sharable positive goal.

In the case of Guatemala, as we delved into that goal with the team from CARE Guatemala, it soon became clear that they couldn't even align on the *definition* of poverty. Some K'iche and Mam peoples, living in the traditional ways, would have been classified, based on the global income standard, as living in poverty. But if allowed to live in and evolve their traditional ways, they were happy.[100] Others living and working in, say, Guatemala City—and not defined as poor—were deeply unhappy. So if you consistently ask the question "When you eliminate poverty, what will that get you?", you eventually come up with (and they did) a very different goal—in this case, economic self-determination.

This is a goal that includes (and has the potential to significantly transcend) both poverty elimination and social injustice. Additionally, when we began the larger conversation with the rest of Guatemalan Society, CARE's goal of eliminating poverty had historically garnered insufficiently powerful and/or committed advocates at a national level. There just wasn't much enthusiasm on the part of those in a position to affect change for eliminating poverty and social injustice—a decades-old conversation that seemed intractable.

---

[99] Neuro-Linguistic Programming (NLP) has something to say about "positive/negative" goal orientations. They offer (and, based on experience, we tend to agree) that individuals are of two primary types: fundamentally orienting *toward* something (i.e., positive goals) or *away from* something (i.e., negative goals). And, while we do seem to see this in our work with teams and organizations, we're not convinced that such an orientation is a permanent condition, believing that every individual does, at some level, have something they are "for" to orient toward, something waiting to be discovered and declared.

[100] BTW, I'm not referring to the term "happy" here casually. Instead, to more rigorous standards like Gross National Happiness that measure overall well-being vs. unidimensional economics.

But the goal of economic self-determination garnered serious, enthusiastic, and broad support from the rural communities, the education sector, the business sector, policy sectors—even military leadership. And quite quickly, the larger group of 30 stakeholders from across Guatemalan Society came into shared alignment that this was, indeed, their goal, too. As a result, CARE became an actively sought out participant in a variety of national-level conversations about the future of Guatemalan Society—something previously unheard of in their 47-year history of work in Guatemala. And we consistently evoke similar shifts/step-changes in attention (and intention) each time we reveal such a positive (vs. negative) goal.

TIMEOUT: The Reinforcing Nature of Relationship & Clarity

Here I'd be remiss if I failed to bring attention to the iterative, reinforcing nature of this way of working. By iterative, I mean that we're repeatedly deepening and expanding both Relationship & Clarity at each level, bit by bit—growing these assets that are essential to scalability and sustainability as our enterprise matures/evolves over time. By reinforcing relationship (much more my point at this juncture), I mean that deepening Relationship surfaces more Clarity just as seeking Clarity drives/deepens Relationship. You could imagine it like the twin strands of a double helix with each strand—one Relationship, one Clarity—both impacting and supporting the other. Hence, the notion of the blur between Relationship & Clarity.

Practically speaking, as the rest of this way of working unfolds, I suggest you gauge for yourself just how what we reveal going forward about how Clarity positively impacts Relationship—and vice versa—something you'll see play out even more in the next chapter.

Okay, now the goal has emerged from the Subgroup/team. It's time for our 4th of 5 tools: The BOT.

Team Clarity (and Relationship) via graphing Behavior Over Time (BOT)

At the highest level, team clarity is generated by *discovering and assessing the team's goal, understanding its behavior over time, and,* from that standpoint, *mapping the system as a whole.*

Exploring behavior over time is an ideal foundation for establishing three vital resources: 1) a well-grounded subgroup/team goal, one clearly situated in physical reality by 2) exposing the team to the shared learnings, knowledge, experience, and passions of the Team/Subgroup members (things that typically never happen when we ask folks to "read these articles" or "watch these videos" or "do this to prepare"—they're simply too busy), and 3) using both of these clarifying elements to deepen that crucial third—their Relationship—to self, one another, and Reality (again, blending Relationship & Clarity).

Behavior over time (BOT) graph[101]

What needs to be said about the BOT's invaluable role here won't make much sense in the abstract. We need a framework within which to anchor the really important characteristics of the BOT that make it an indispensable, even pivotal, moment in the project. So with that in mind, let's pick up the thread we began with the Map OneSonoma Economic Development subgroup…

The Real World: back to Map OneSonoma

Building off of their goal as a starting point—Score 90 on the Social Progress Index, while assuring resiliency (Environmental, Social and Economic) by 2028—we then shifted into exploring the behavior of that goal over time. Here's the collective discovery and alignment that emerged from their structured BOT conversation:[102]

---

[101] For more on behavior over time graphs, just search the term or see my instructional video at scottspann.com/impossible.

[102] For a video walk-through of this BOT, see scottspann.com/impossible.

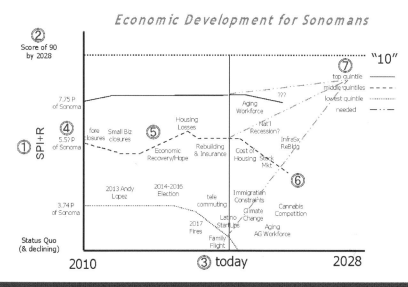

Economic Development for Sonomans

A bit about interpreting their BOT graph along two dimensions—structure and content.

You may ask, "Why the 3 sets of lines"—something we don't usually do in a BOT? In addition to aligning on a standard (the SPI+R), they then went a step further. The Team realized that current inequities in income and wealth meant that we needed to acknowledge the initial conditions of differing socio-economic groups if we were to achieve equity of opportunity (not, btw, equality—a very different path). This would enable understanding of historical imbalances that negatively impacted all of Sonoma County. So they chose to explore it in quintiles—roughly the top fifth, middle fifth, and lowest fifth. Back to their BOT…

First, the structure, the container that ensures a constructive (vs. conflicted) conversation at a high level. We laid out the structure in 7 steps:

1. Place their goal on the vertical axis (in this case, abbreviated as SPI+R)

2. Further define the goal by identifying the endpoints, clearly specifying success (10) and failure (0) on a scale of 1-10

3. Determine the timeframe needed to understand the systemic impacts on the goal over time (from 2010-2028)

4. Propose where we were at the beginning of the timeframe—i.e., in 2010, supporting the level(s) with data vs. opinions. In this case we needed to track levels for 3 different quintiles of the population

5. Extend and explore the graph from there, offering supporting facts at each inflection point for each of the 3 lines

6. Given the trajectory and anticipated future events, predict the unchecked future path for all 3

7. Project the needed future path if their goal is to succeed, again for all 3.

Second, the content. Once they were unanimously aligned on their goal, our job was to agree about the path that goal had taken over the last 10 years. What unfolded during our conversation was a rich exchange of information and data supporting the different perspectives on the fate of their new goal over time. Before any single point of view could be charted, however, the group had to do two things: 1) come to alignment, i.e., true consensus (not just compromise) about the state of the goal at that first point in time ④ and 2) the cause for any changes to that state at each inflection point in the graph ⑤. By the end of that conversation, the group had a felt-sense experience of exploring, validating and/or modifying their opinions by aggregating and integrating their previously fragmented perspectives about the state of their goal in Sonoma County. Once they'd worked up to "today", we offered an observation—and asked a tough question.

The observation: "The behavior of the system over time includes the fact that you've been raising more and more money, hiring smarter and smarter people, doing better and better projects, getting better and better results—and yet the state of your goal is getting worse and worse."

The question: "Given that this is a system—an amoral beast with significant momentum—momentum and inertia that will cause it to seek to continue to respond as it has historically, how is this system likely to behave going forward?" With just a bit of discussion, they all agreed that, without some significant change, the system would continue to perform as it had—i.e., the downward trend would likely continue ⑥. This realization was a somber moment for the group—the realization that without significant intervention the desired—actually, the needed—goal would fail. The fact that it was a shared realization made it even more sobering—made the need to respond even more real.

So we now had to ask, "Given what the system naturally seeks to do, *what* must happen by *when* if you are to prevent this negative impact? What then emerged was another spirited, though brief, conversation in which they all agreed that there must be an immediate positive shift in their system—that it must improve sharply to a significantly higher level for the lower two quintiles (only somewhat higher for the upper quintile) over the next 10 years ⑦. After that, the rate of improvement could begin to level off, while still progressing toward the ideal.

Now we had a complete and reality-based image of the state of that 3rd thing—their goal—to which they were all committed. It was a challenging realization—one that captured the paradox of what would naturally happen if the system was left unchecked and what *must* happen (even though the "how"[103] was not yet, by design, identified) if this worthy goal was to survive. We then pointed out that their task as leaders was to internalize this paradox, these two poles.

Fixating on one line (the lower) had previously been the role of cynics. Fixating on the other pole (that upper line) had been the role of idealists. Neither of these attitudes would successfully solve for this.

---

[103] Recalling Peter Block's "The Answer to `How' is `Yes!`"

The level of true innovation needed to alter the path of this system would only arise from the dynamic structural tension (to borrow from Robert Fritz) that exists when one successfully internalizes this polarity—when one simultaneously holds both in their nervous system, literally. So now a bit about innovation…

Innovation 101

When the team as a whole can clearly see the typically stark distinction between the behavior likely to be produced by the system and the behavior they, as leaders, want to—even must—elicit from the system, they experience a state of what Fritz calls "structural tension"[104]—an internalized tension, reflective of external reality—tension that naturally seeks resolution. Usually, the startling, shared clarity of the magnitude of this gap renders the typical means of solving the problem moot. Typical organizational fixes are simply inadequate. It is out of the convergence of three things—1) this gap, 2) the collective recognition that there is such a gap, and 3) the emotional, physical (literally) and mental energy generated by this gap—that the requisite level of creativity emerges. It is from this internalized state of being/becoming—this recognition of what is (i.e., a catastrophic trajectory) and yet, what must be (i.e., the reality-based necessity)—that the team as a whole commits to using truly innovative principles, practices, and processes to solve their problem.

What 1 Word? Capturing the Team's Energy Assets

Over the course of our conversation, we've built up a distinctively different, more potent emotional, physical, and even intellectual energy in the room at this point—an asset we want to be sure and inventory—one we mustn't lose track of.

By way of stark contrast, usually when the subgroup meeting opens, I make it a point to ask the group how we "need to be" in order

---

[104] For a more elegant understanding of this, see Robert's blog post about his insight here https://thefloweringbrain.wordpress.com/2013/12/01/the-power-of-structural-creative-tension/.

to solve this problem or to avail ourselves of this opportunity or… (whatever their stated outcome). Invariably, they'll say that it requires that we be "open-minded, focused, respectful, realistic, opportunistic, visionary…" the stock, muted list one gets as a leader or facilitator in most business-as-usual processes.

Yet, at the conclusion of this BOT exercise for the Map OneSonoma Economic Development subgroup—from this entirely new, collectively shared, aligned perspective of the glaring gap between what will happen without a radical intervention in both the "what" and "how", and what must happen if their goal is to survive—there was a palpable shift in the emotional and physical energy in the room. So we deliberately made note of this shift by asking, "What '1' word captures how we[105] need to be if we're to close this gap?

They identified, among an impassioned (as evidenced by their voice tonality, facial expressions, and body language) list of behaviors—the need to be "radically innovative", "radically compassionate", "brave/courageous", to "accept responsibility", "listen deeply", "align with reality", and so on. These words allowed us to remind ourselves of the commitment, enthusiasm, and determination of the group—as individuals and as a whole—a shift that they sustained throughout the remainder of our work and beyond—a shift essential to being able to innovate in truly unique, ingenious ways.

Our Innate Response to Relationship and to Reality

Having done this with literally hundreds of leaders, I'm convinced that the palpable shift in energy is the result of being in clearer, deeper relationship with: 1) ourself(s) about what's happening to what we care deeply about (our goal), 2) with others who share a similar degree of

---

[105] We deliberately use the pronoun "we" as a way of enabling individuals to bridge from the general (we) to the specific (I) as a means of deepening our individual and collective "contract" with ourselves, one another, and the project/goal. Said another way, it's much less threatening for one to speak (initially) to the "we" than the "I".

caring, and 3) with Reality itself—based on our fact-based exploration of Reality. Humans are uniquely equipped to respond innovatively to reality if they/we are sufficiently (and accurately) aware of it. But to be truly innovative, we still need a critical element—shared alignment about *how* the system that drives/determines this goal actually works—in the form of the map of their ecosystem.

BOT as the initial condition for evoking Collaboration

Over the course of working in this way—and throughout my practice as a psychotherapist—I've come to realize that humans are innately designed to collaborate and succeed—hence, the name of my company—Innate Strategies. We've simply, through our culture and many of our social institutions, been taught not to. Yet if I choose to believe in—and design for—that innate ability, we consistently produce surprisingly fruitful outcomes.[106]

While you've just seen an example of what a BOT process looks like, it's such a pivotal and catalytic event that you deserve a bit more about how it generates this shift toward collaboration.

Coming to shared alignment about how your goal has been behaving over time is pivotal to changing the condition of a system— especially as a team—and eventually as an organization or network. Is it trending up or down? Up or down from a high point or a low point? Is it stable or erratic? And what other systemic forces are determining its fate?

Since the system's goal—which, in fact, defines the boundaries of the system—is often new to the team, they generally have no explicit alignment (yet) about how it's been doing. The BOT process equips the team to come into alignment about: 1) the ideal state of their goal, 2) its current state, and 3) its likely future state—over a time period that has relevance to both the team and the system. The BOT also serves to scrutinize—even test—the goal as the team delves deeper

---

[106] For more of what I choose to believe—and the benefits, see Chapter 6.

by establishing the high and low endpoints of their goal's possible behavior—the ideal and worst-case outcomes.

The rigorous structure of the Behavior Over Time process—and the corresponding structure of the work—channels previously siloed individuals into group collaboration, even consensus, without ever requiring it of them—without ever mentioning those words. Collaboration emerges organically as a natural by-product of the work (back to that "structure determines behavior" maxim). By the time their journey through the BOT is complete, they've experienced coming to shared alignment and understanding, not only about the behavior of the system over time, but also about the magnitude and direction of the change they must, as a team, evoke if they are to achieve their systemic goal.

TIMEOUT: In the context of real work (vs. a training)

The felt sense of this experience is critical to the eventual and continuing success of the Whole group down the line. I've seen too many times when trainings or presentations or lectures about the value of collaboration or communication have been conducted in the absence of real work. This creates at least three problems.

First, it often takes leaders and staff out of production—something that we typically can't afford in a right-sized, just-in-time, lean world—dwarfing the cost of the stand-alone training because of the lost-opportunity cost of their day job.

Second, unless it's tightly coupled to real work, any learnings remain largely cognitive and/or superficial—not benefitting from the internalization typically required to effect positive, lasting behavioral change.

Third, by giving individuals the real-world experience of the change first, then examining, cognitively (in real time), the principles and practices that evoked the change/experience, we give them three frameworks/senses from which to apply the process going forward: physical, emotional, and cognitive.

Moreover, we've/they've now lived Yvonne's/SCT's promise. That is, individuals have now, as a subgroup/team, weathered the "differences among the apparently similar" and come out stronger for it. Even at the level of their nervous systems, they are now aware that they can confront conflict, resolve it, and, as a result, create greater value than they started with—by orders of magnitude. Yes, nervous systems do learn, as my psychotherapy clients (and I) experienced when working through trauma. This experience then ports to the whole-group level when/where they'll need to appreciate and integrate the similarities among the apparently different (again, true to Yvonne's words).

The Integrated Map: mapping the system as a whole

We've arrived at the last—but definitely not least (quite the contrary)—of our tools/processes at the level of the subgroup/team. It's last because we needed the prior work to create: 1) the motivation that would compel leaders to *reach* for the map (vs. imposing it on them) and 2) the energy needed to interrogate and improve the integrated map—all of which was generated via the goalsetting and BOT experiences with one another.

In preparation for the subgroup meetings, we create a draft ecosystem map that represents their "world"—i.e., the system that determines the fate of their goal. When we say "map", we're referring again (as we were at the individual level) to a causal diagram—a word and arrow expression of their system—one that represents their system's goal, how that goal is achieved, all of its bits and pieces, the interactions among all of those parts, and the effect of those interactions on each part and on the system (and on the actors/stakeholders) as a whole.

So how do we develop an integrated map in a way that represents Reality—at least the shared reality of those involved in the process—the participants and key actors/stakeholders? We do so in part through those individual interviews—and their accompanying individual maps—that we described earlier. In any systemic engagement, we interview a 360° set of key stakeholders in the system—those individuals who have credibility in and knowledge of the system in the eyes of the other actors/stakeholders in that system—whether those stakeholders who will eventually be engaged at this level of the process or those stakeholders we'll need to reach out to as we progress.

TIMEOUT: Credibility, Knowledge, and Influence

Now is a good time to speak about those eventual stakeholders.

In every project to date, once a critical mass of leaders has achieved a level of relationship & clarity sufficient to tackle their "impossible" issue/opportunity, they need to engage a next level of actors—that is if they're to systemically execute on their strategy and achieve their goal. So as we design the project, we need to ensure that those we interview have three characteristics: credibility, knowledge, and influence.

While knowledge and credibility are self-explanatory, by influence we mean that—once these leaders are ready to act—they, as a group as a whole, also have the ability to influence the next level of others to act—whether via their leadership role, their organization, their network, or their celebrity. What's critical here is that, from the beginning and at each subsequent level, we're assessing credibility, knowledge, and influence with the end user in mind—whether that's a CEO, a legislative body, a market segment, a venture capitalist, a voting population, etc.

We need this because, eventually, we'll be asked, "Where did this come from?" or "Who determined this?" When that moment arrives, we need to be able to call out the list of those who, not only contributed to—but even more importantly—aligned *on* this process from beginning to end.

For example, in the case of Minnesota's Education Transformation Initiative (ETI), we were able to (from among nearly 200 total participants) build on the credibility, knowledge, and influence of Minneapolis Mayor RT Rybak, School Superintendent Bernadeia Johnson, State Senator Brandon Petersen, US Bank CEO Richard Davis, and far too many more to list here. The point is, as we moved steadily forward, we were able to clearly demonstrate that we'd made a good faith effort (within the constraints of available time and money) to integrate and optimize the views of a 360° array of stakeholders/leaders across economic, social, political, ethnic, geographic, professional, and other dimensions. This, along with the solid execution of the resultant leadership team, helped to ensure the continued success of the venture, long after the mapping and strategy phases were completed.

One last important bit here. The strength of our relationship with each of these credible, knowledgeable, influential leaders was birthed in that first interview and individual map. Keeping in mind the long-term value of each of those we engage serves to highlight the importance of adding value with each touch—in every interaction.

So back to how the map evolves. In the individual interviews, you'll recall that we ask each leader about what they're trying to cause in their current context. We ask it in this way for two reasons. First, they can only authentically go into depth about what they themselves are seeking. Said another way, they can't typically go in depth on behalf of others—e.g., other leaders, members of the organization, the organization itself (as it's an abstract entity), etc. To do so, except in extraordinary cases, would be to speculate beyond their own personally verifiable awareness.

Secondly, and most importantly, we really need to know, as precisely as we can, what they need the system to provide for them—how the system needs to function if they are to willingly—even enthusiastically—make a good faith contribution, especially if they are to engage over time.

It's only by engaging them in this way that we can be confident that our eventual system map will be inclusive of the elements essential to their success. And why is this critical? To borrow from the influence example above, if Mayor Rybak's needs—and his aspirations—didn't show up in the eventual map, why would he "play" with us? Why would he contribute his time, energy, intelligence, and social capital to this effort?

BTW, as part of humanizing this work, this test acknowledges and activates the human/mammalian expectation of—even drive for—reciprocity, one of the handful of qualities that fuel the scalability and sustainability we'll dig into in those later chapters at the levels of the market and the larger ecosystem, respectively.

The Real World: Minneapolis Mayor RT Rybak

As evidence of this need to add value, here's a quick, illustrative story about RT's level of engagement. We had a hell of time getting on RT's calendar for the interview. He's a busy guy with a pre-existing pile of very hot topics to deal with, even before we[107] came along. But we persisted and eventually got the interview. Whew!

Still, he was a busy guy and getting his attention for anything beyond the 1-hour interview was a long shot. But when I shared his individual map back with him—in a way that added significant value to his educational and even economic and social policy platforms—he was convinced that this approach went well beyond business-as-usual

---

[107] The "we" here included the clear–headed and incredibly capable Design Team of Amy Hertel, Becky Erdahl, Al Fan, Chris Smith, and Phil Soran whose leadership was key to success.

and was worth the time and energy he had invested. So we at least had his attention.

But still, he was a busy guy. So the idea that he would now invest a day of his time to attend a subgroup meeting was a fantasy. But we persisted—and, much to our surprise, he came. And our ability to share the fact that he was to attend added to our own credibility—his leadership and celebrity influence prompted others (who were on the fence) to also attend.

Still, he was a busy guy. So entertaining the notion that he would ever consider attending a 2-day strategy offsite—a meeting of all of the subgroup attendees—seemed clearly beyond reach. But we persisted and he again agreed to come—again, to our surprise—and again boosting overall attendance to 40+ key leaders—significantly beyond our expectations.

Then something tragic for RT and his family happened. Less than a week before our strategy summit, while cross country skiing, the incredibly lean, fit, athletic RT had a heart attack—had to be hospitalized and underwent angioplasty surgery, including the insertion of two stints. Whoa!

So understandably, we made plans to proceed without him. Yet…

He came to the 2-day event—*less than a week after his surgery.* Astonishing!

So we need to deliberately ask ourselves why and how this happened. What so compelled RT to invest that kind of time and energy, especially in light of what he and his family had just endured?

Well, first of all, this is clearly a testament to RT's fortitude, commitment, and leadership. That cannot be overstated. It was/he is remarkable! At the same time, I offer this story to also make explicit the power of working in this way, as we are consistently surprised when our expectations are consistently exceeded.

Done well, you/we have the potential to so engage others—even already overcommitted others—at a level that they find incredibly compelling. So compelling, in fact, that they'll overcome seemingly "impossible" odds to engage. It presents us with both a priceless opportunity and the humbling (and somewhat daunting) responsibility to make sure their investment of themselves is worth it.

Back to our Integrated Map

Returning to how our map emerges, when we're at the individual level, we ask leaders what they're seeking to cause within the emerging system and what's required to cause that. We're basically asking them about their mental model of Reality.[108] We all have and operate out of our mental models—our unavoidably incomplete representations of reality. We just rarely make them explicit, much less rigorous.

Some of the most interesting (and least successful) decisions we make are the result of incomplete, untested, incongruent—even inaccurate[109]—mental models.[110] By making these mental models explicit, we can test them, validate them, make them more complete and more congruent—and more valuable—to ourselves, to others, and to the Whole.

An explicitly mapped mental model enables our thinking to be: 1) communicated as clearly and simply as possible; 2) shared with others to be enriched by the questions, insights, even criticisms they offer; and 3) utilized to make better, more congruent, and more successful decisions. Once these individual stakeholder maps/perspectives have been validated, we can use them as the palette from which to design a single, integrated systems map.

Invariably, when we do this, all of the stakeholders are able—for the first time (as with the GNSC's Supply Chain)—to see their whole world—all of its parts and pieces, the interactions of those parts and

---

[108] For more about mental models see the NLP (Neuro-Linguistic Programming) literature, in particular, Steve Andrea's book *The New Technology of Achievement*, 1996 and any of Robert Dilts' work (www.nlpu.com). Or the early works of Bandler and Grinder.

[109] As is often attributed to Mark Twain, "It ain't what you don't know that gets you into trouble. It's what you know for sure that just ain't so."

[110] For some fascinating examples of incomplete mental models, see John Sterman's book, *Business Dynamics*, 2000.

pieces, and the impact of those interactions on the other aspects and stakeholders that make up our system. These systems maps—these complete, congruent, and validated shared representations of reality— form the basis for determining where, when, and how we will intervene in the system to achieve our shared goal. But before we can make those determinations, we have to validate the map.

TIMEOUT: It's not about the Map!

Right now seems like a good time to call out two critical things.

First, we need to remind ourselves that all models are wrong—but some models are useful.[111] I'm frequently asked, "But what if our model is wrong or incomplete or...?" Well in fairness, the integrated map is a hypothesis. But done well, it's a damn good hypothesis— and, invariably, the best available one out there—especially given the way it emerged from a diverse, 360° set of leaders with the credibility, knowledge, and influence needed to help catalyze the resultant relationships and clarity into action—at scale—built (as it should be) by an experienced, systems thinker/modeler and usually validated by 4-7 subgroups totaling typically 60+ people.

Additionally, it's deliberately NOT cast in stone. Out of necessity it's in a state of continual, though ever-stabilizing, emergence. As we scale and as others are attracted to—and included in working on this issue/ opportunity in this way, they need to know that the effort is open to— actually authentically curious about—whether or not their perspectives are included in and/or explained by the Map. In this way, the map serves as an ongoing storyboard—ensuring that we continually learn about the complex-adaptive system, even once we've integrated it. That said, we've consistently found that the maps presented to the subgroups are roughly 95% accurate, needing only slight—though

[111] Box, G. E. P. (1979), "Robustness in the strategy of scientific model building", in Launer, R. L.; Wilkinson, G. N. (eds.), *Robustness in Statistics, Academic Press*, pp. 201–236, doi:10.1016/ B978-0-12-438150-6.50018-2, ISBN 9781483263366.

significantly valuable—refinements. Once validated, they remain surprisingly stable—even over time. And there's a reason for that.

It may help if we think about a system via an analogy. Take our physical human bodies. For example, I can train my body to lay on the couch or I can train it to run a marathon. It's the same body—the same system. It's simply a matter of how I'm weighting/training/investing in the various resources in the system: VO2 max, body fat percentage, heart rate variability, etc.

So back to our map. Once we've created a validated view of a system, it's typically fairly durable—unless something radical shifts in the larger ecosystem.

Secondly, though it may seem like heresy here (so I offer this cautiously): It's not all about the Map. _Please, please don't get me wrong—hear me out._ The map is an incredibly valuable artifact—an important and essential artifact and an indispensably useful one—especially once we've analyzed it. (see "Analysis" in Chapter 4, below).

Still, what's most critical if we're to emerge ready to make a difference in physical Reality, is the _conversation_ and resultant _relationship-building_ that the map enables. This _must_ be in the forefront of our awareness as we design our strategic conversations—to stimulate our relationship with self, with one another, and with Reality itself. You'll recall that it was the overemphasis on the map (a really good map, btw) coupled with the failure to sufficiently design for the vital relationship component that jeopardized the success of the Re-Amp project cited above.

BOT/Map Mashup

The capability and eagerness/energy of the group to validate the map arises out of their BOT work based on: 1) the power of their shared goal, 2) their internalization of the systemic forces impacting their goal, and 3) internalizing the direction and magnitude of the shift required to accomplish what they most care about.

This experience ideally positions them to interrogate—even attack—the integrated map. I don't use the term attack as a pejorative. The group needs to fiercely engage with the map because we need to now internalize a felt sense of the structure of the system that determines the fate of our goal. The best way to do that, within the limited timeframe of our group meeting, is to challenge the map at every juncture.

The Real World: Consilient, a startup

So to better understand what that looks like, literally, let's take a brief look at one such integrated map just to give you a sense of what we're talking about.

Let's take Consilient, a 120-person startup in Silicon Valley, seeking to integrate and automate typical real-world transactions like, say, a fender bender with your car. It's one that requires coordination between the insurance company(s), rental car company, towing company, the body shop, the owner, and others. Consilient was committed to doing so in a way that captures all communication in one app—vs. the usual hodgepodge of phone calls, emails, faxes, letters, forms, sticky notes, conversations, etc.

Before you look at it—lest you freak out at the complexity of this beast—know this: Once this is validated and we perform the analysis, it resolves into a much simpler strategy map that serves as the basis for strategic communication and execution, one usually representing roughly 10-15% of the original map—something I'll share when we speak about Analysis a bit later in Chapter 4.[112]

(Note: The format of this book simply won't accommodate any of these larger, integrated maps. So please go to scottspann.com/impossible for a bigger, color view of this one and reference this page number.)

---

[112] For a walk through of this (& in color), visit scottspann.com/impossible.

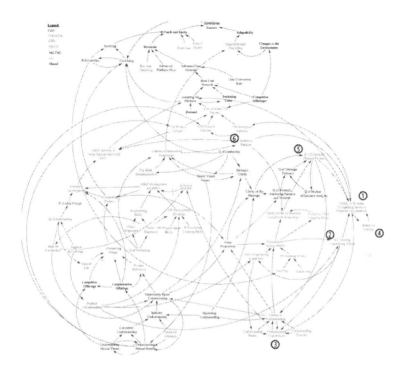

Wow! Looks complicated, eh? While it's all too easy to let this larger version of a causal diagram overwhelm you, there are two things to keep in mind.[113]

First, if you spend a bit of time with just a bit of it, you'll see that it follows the same rules, logic, and flow as the individual causal maps we looked at earlier in that it follows the kind of math required to cause any outcome. For example (as an act of compassion, I will NOT walk you through this whole thing), if you take the Ability to Develop Compelling Services, Products and Opportunities ① at the far right hand edge of the map (at 3 o'clock) as but one requisite outcome, this company came to shared understanding and alignment that this was a function of (see each of the six arrows feeding into this variable/resource): ② the company's KT (Knowledge Transfer) Training Consulting Ability;

---

[113] Again, if you need more on reading causal diagrams, simply search "causal loop diagrams" or "reading causal loop diagrams". Or go to www.pegasus.com and search there.

③ their Understanding (of Customer) Expectations; ④ the quality of their modular Solutions Library; ⑤ the Q(quality) of (their) Enterprise and Channel Partners working with Consilient on those solution sets, and finally, ⑥ their own Ability to Execute.

Secondly, in the event that a map like this is a bit puzzling in places, please know that that's not unusual—as they are rarely designed as standalone items. Maps like these are often shorthand for a conversation that has emerged between the participants in the project—intended more to guide causal storytelling than to serve as the full and final freestanding explanation of their Reality. When needed, we append a glossary—or better yet, make a video—to smooth the transition between the shorthand and the fuller comprehension sought by those not directly involved in the original conversations.

TIMEOUT: Literally "holding" the Conversation

A word here about clarity and systems maps.

Getting to this level of shared understanding and clarity represents a significant accomplishment for the team members involved in creating it—whether the map is at the level of the organization, the market, or the ecosystem.

In Consilient's case, they'd listened to each other's stories about their part of the system in the form of their individual systems maps—inquired about and even modified those individual maps—in some cases modifying the underlying assumptions about their goals. All the while they were engaging in a rigorous conversation about the validity of one another's perspectives of their world and how each/all of those work in reality. This created a constructively structured (vs. the typical unstructured) conversation. It is one where a team can actually arrive at shared understanding and alignment about a complex system—its goal, how it achieves that goal, all of its parts and pieces, the interactions among all of those parts, and the effect of those interactions on their system as a whole. This is a very rare thing. In almost every case, each team member sees things about their organization that they haven't seen despite 5 or 10 or 20 years of working in the industry. This happens time and again in organization after organization.

It happened for the participants in the Guatemalan project—for doctors, lawyers, economists, political leaders, educators and others. Across the board they understood—for the first time—how the different interests in Guatemalan Society impacted, for better and/or worse, one another and the system as a whole. And they got to that understanding through a series of fairly straightforward 1-on-1 conversations—as each stakeholder's world was presented to the participants in small group conversations. There, the initial understandings (or misunderstandings) about a segment of their world were explored, discussed, debated, modified, and validated by a small group of 3-4 people. And this was repeated until the systemic understanding stabilized—until we all agreed that we were collectively accurately representing Guatemala. Most satisfying about the outcome of those conversations was their realization that most of the conflict in the system wasn't personal—it was *structural*.

For example, those in the President's section of the map/system didn't realize that, when they created a policy that favored the wealthy segment of the economy—say a tax break or a subsidy—three years later, the road that would have enabled a remote village to get their corn to market didn't get built. As a result, the village's economy was jeopardized. This led to the realization that it wasn't a deliberate ideological attempt to "destroy our local culture" or an intentionally personalized issue of classism or racism (something much harder to solve for). It was a function of how their system was designed/structured[114]—and something within their power to solve for.

---

[114] This is in no way meant to minimize the real-world existence of rampant structural racism—which did/does exist. However, this realization enabled the group to "solve" for this specifically vs. trying to tackle "structural racism" in a vacuum.

So it's in this sense that, on the one hand, it's not about the map—that the map simply, literally holds the conversation. On the other hand, it *is* about the map—as the group is pointing at (or fussing at or, in some cases, yelling at) the wall—at the map or at me calling out that "The map's wrong" or "Scott's wrong." The important point here—the absolutely critical point here—is that they're not pointing, fussing, yelling, etc., at each other! To do so would damage trust in and relationship with one another—damage the fabric of relationship quintessential to their combined future success.

Mapping: A Vehicle for Containing and Resolving Conflict

There's another deep learning here—one that came from my time as a trauma psychotherapist. It's the critical concept of titration[115]—a concept borrowed from chemistry and one of the critical adavantages of working through the map bit-by-bit.

In chemistry, titration enables the mixing of strong acids with strong bases to neutralize them. For example, HCl and NaOH are each dangerous chemicals—ones not to be exposed to. However, if you titrate the mixture—slowly release a drop of one into the other—you get a series, drop by drop, of minor perturbations—but no strong reaction. Rather, you're left with two elements crucial to life—salt (NaCl) and water (H2O).

We applied this concept in trauma psychotherapy to make absolutely sure we didn't reactivate a traumatic event as a whole—didn't bring too many charged elements together at once, as that would literally retraumatize the individual—actually deepening the traumatic neural pathway—making things worse, not better. Instead, we'd isolate a minor reaction (via titration) from the traumatic event—e.g., the tightening of the client's right shoulder or the shifting of their breath

---

[115] A concept from "Somatic Experiencing," the work developed by trauma therapist Dr. Peter Levine, with whom I trained—a revolutionarily effective approach to deep-seated trauma.

from their belly to their upper chest or micro-movements in their neck or hand. We'd consciously isolate this from the traumatic experience as a whole—allowing it to play out on in isolation—without reference to the larger story of the trauma until it resolved—the psychotherapeutic equivalent of chemical neutralization.

While there's obviously much more to this, proceeding in this way—titrating via a series of smaller reactions—allowed us to eventually resolve the traumatic experience as a whole, often enabling the individual to emerge stronger post-trauma than they were even pre-trauma.

So how does that apply here? The map, by its very nature/structure, isolates the myriad resources and relationships into micro-reactions—allowing us to ask, "Is it true that when this one thing happens, this one (and, for the moment, only one) other thing happens?" Full stop!

Now, admittedly, those in the room are tempted to say "Yes, but then this, then this, then…"—triggering a chain reaction of overreaction—much like exciting the whole traumatic chain/episode would be for a trauma client. However, through the map, we're able to suspend that temptation by promising those individuals (as we did with the GNSC) that we'll get to that part of the map in just a bit. But for now, we're working this bit, then the next bit and the next and the next.

This titration ensures that the leaders in the room stay focused on the here and now in this present moment and don't let their minds and emotions activate a charge bigger than the conversation can handle. It basically compartmentalizes potentially explosive aspects of the relationship into sub-conversations that can contain, channel, and resolve the charge inherent in the larger, more complex, troublesome issues/opportunities.

Innovation 201: On the other side of conflict

The insights gained by the group from the systems mapping process come in two forms: 1) the *conversations* that create, validate, and evolve the map, and 2) *the map itself*. Probably the most beneficial and transformational are the conversations, although the value of the map itself can't be overstated. The sharing with one another that takes place in the validation conversations of stories, examples, and data ensures that: 1) their perspectives are accurately represented in the map, 2) they truly appreciate each other's perspectives of and contributions to the system, and 3) inevitably come to *comprehend* (intellectually) then *apprehend* (actionably) how various aspects of the system affect each/all of them and their goals. This ability to see, converse about, and contain the system—this ability of the map to literally hold the conversation—enables (often for the first time) sane, well-structured, and productive conversations about a complex, usually mutually confused, and conflicted issue.

These insights (even internalizations)—coupled with the sense of urgency and vitality[116] that emerges from the realizations in the BOT graph—combine to form a robust platform for a mindset shift. They're insights that compel, that fuel, that together drive and guide, at the next level, innovation—innovation that resolves problems at their root cause—as opposed to the periphery of symptomatic solutions. For one client, the planning department in a world class resort community, their systems map alone was enough to enable them to disentangle and then heal a serious internal conflict—one that had grown to the point that staff was coming into the office on different shifts simply to avoid interacting with one another.

Moving beyond conflict sets up the possibility for...

Flow: Innovation, energy, and insight

Have you ever had a time when you were totally "on!"? A time when you were "in the zone"? When you were fully immersed in what you were doing? When nothing else existed outside of you and the object of your attention?

---

[116] For more about the vitality available in the face of (and even because of) impending mortality, see Peter Koestenbaum's and Peter Block's *Freedom and Accountability at Work*.

Psychologist Mihály Csíkszentmihályi named this highly focused, unusually productive state "Flow".

Csíkszentmihályi describes 6 factors and 3 components essential to experiencing a Flow state,[117] this state of optimal creativity, innovation, and potential action.

The 6 factors are:

- Intense and focused concentration on the present moment
- Merging of action and awareness
- A loss of reflective self-consciousness
- A sense of personal control or agency over the situation or activity
- A distortion of temporal experience, as one's subjective experience of time is altered
- Experience of the activity as intrinsically rewarding—also referred to as autotelic experience

…those six factors that combine with…

The 3 components:

- Immediate feedback
- Feeling the potential to succeed
- Feeling so engrossed in the experience, that other needs become negligible

…all 9 coming together to create the initial conditions for Flow.

In the years before this way of working revealed itself, I was fascinated by Flow and Csíkszentmihályi's work. I've experienced it

---

[117]https://en.wikipedia.org/wiki/Flow_(psychology). You might want to refer to a source other than Wikipedia: https://positivepsychology.com/mihaly-csikszentmihalyi-father-of-flow/

myself in national and international handball[118] tournaments—at times when the level of play and the needed reaction times exceeded anything I could consciously manage. This was most pronounced in doubles competition when my partner and I were both in the flow—seamlessly, spontaneously covering the court—responding at speed, unconsciously and reflexively, almost as if we were one organism. And I'm guessing that you, too, if you've ever engaged in a high-performance activity—be it dance or music or even writing or coding—have touched into this space.

What Mikhaly was up to was figuring out how to ensure the initial conditions to reliably, repeatedly, and even predictably invoke the state of Flow.

In that same vein, when we consciously invoke this way of working with the deliberate intention to evoke Flow, I'm continuously struck by the number of times we're able to enter into these states of awareness as a group. When intentional about it, we consistently achieve such frames of mind by attending to the principles and practices we've covered so far. When this happens, it's spontaneous—not the result of forcing it or announcing it. It simply arises.

And we can anchor these states—to borrow a term from NLP[119] (Neuro Linguistic Programming)—often by simply flashing their BOT graph back up on the screen along with their "1 word(s)" from the conclusion of the BOT workout.

The Real World: The IT Leadership Team of a Top-3 Bank

In the late '90s, as a byproduct of one of its larger mergers, the IT leadership team of one of the top three banks in the U.S. was confronting an overwhelming project load resulting in late and/or incomplete projects—and an accompanying loss of credibility.

---

[118] Michael Murphy also chronicles this across many different sports and athletes in his book *The Psychic Side of Sports* (1978)

[119] Steve Andreas, Op. cit.

Compounding that was an external report from a global consulting company recommending 100+ fixes. Not unlike with the GNSC and their 127 initiatives from the field, the cure was looking worse than the disease.

To make matters worse (oh yes, things can, it seems, always get worse), the impasse prompted by such an overwhelming situation provoked conflicting views among the IT leadership team about which recommendations were of highest priority. This was crippling their ability to respond so much so that we were lucky to get the 2 days of their time needed to sort this out. Eventually, though, they agreed that it was time to do something fundamentally/radically different and sequestered themselves with us in the Iroquois Hotel in New York City.

In the second half of our first day, after we'd exposed this embattled leadership team to some of the principles and practices described herein, something startling spontaneously shifted. We suddenly noticed a distinctly different feel to the room/to the group. What had been an awkwardness, a hesitancy, a bumpiness to the conversations and even the body language, was gone! And its place was an ease, an engagement—people building on one another's conversations, peppered with words like "yes and" (vs. "yeah, but").

The SAVI Grid

Yvonne Agazarian and her colleagues describe this with great precision in their SAVI Grid (System for Analyzing Verbal Interaction), a tool for analyzing and then improving group/team performance below.[120] The team had moved from the upper left-hand box (red in its intended form[121]) to the lower right-hand box (green), even occasionally dipping into laughter.

---

[120] Co-developed along with Claudia Byram, Frances Carter, and Anita Simon
[121] To see this in color, go to scottspann.com/impossible

SAVI® Grid
System for Analyzing Verbal Interaction
CLASSIC

	PERSON		TOPIC
	Personal	Factual	Orienting
Red AVOIDANCE	**1 FIGHTING** Attack/Blame Righteous Question Sarcasm Self Attack/Defend Complaint	**2 OBSCURING** Mind-Reading Negative or Positive Prediction Gossip Joking Around Thinking Out Loud Social Ritual	**3 COMPETING** Yes-But Discount Leading Question Oughtitude Interrupt
Yellow CONTINGENT	**4 INDIVIDUALIZING** Personal Information Current Personal Information Past Personal Opinion/Explanation Personal Question	**5 FINDING FACTS** Facts & Figures General Information Narrow Question Broad Question	**6 INFLUENCING** Opinion Proposal Command Social Reinforcement
Green APPROACH	**7 RESONATING** Inner Feeling Feeling Question Answer Feeling Question Mirror Inner Experience Affectionate Joke Self Assertion	**8 RESPONDING** Answer Question Clarify Own Answer (with data) Paraphrase Summarize Corrective Feedback	**9 INTEGRATING** Agreement Positives Build on Other's Ideas or Experience Work Joke

Silence, Laughter, Noise

Note: The Grid is intended to be used in conjuction with SAVI ® training.
Taken out of context, the content of the Grid may be ambiguous, confusing, or misleading.
SAVI® is a registered trademark of Yvonne Agazarian, Claudia Byram, Frances Carter, and Anita Simon. Copyright © 2011 Simon & Agazarian.

When I took a moment to bring this to our collective attention—to make it explicit—we were each/all similarly struck by the marked, palpable distinction between the mood of our morning session and how it/we had morphed by mid-afternoon.

So we consciously took note of the distinction—each in our own way—as a cue to aid us in recovering this sense of flow if/when we began to waiver. One cue was to explicitly name it as the "Flow" phenomenon. This ability to: 1) create the initial conditions to evoke Flow coupled with 2) our own, individualized anchors (back to NLP) ensured that we were able to maintain our own optimally motivated, creative, and productive state for the remainder of our time together.

Even more gratifying was the fact that the IT leadership team was able to successfully identify, from the dozens of possibilities, the 7 initiatives the team as a whole aligned on as the highest leverage projects to enable them to restore their value-adding contribution to the firm, as well as their collective credibility as an IT leadership team.

Internalization: Your BOT

Again, what value can you take away from this? What can you go do to begin to harness your "impossible" issue/opportunity—now!? Well, I certainly wouldn't recommend that you try to build your own large-scale, integrated map. That definitely falls into the "don't try this at home" bucket, at least not until you've had some significant practice at the smaller map level.

The single most powerful thing you can do from here is to gather your team together to create your own BOT (behavior over time) graph. And while you may be perfectly capable of doing so based on my descriptions above, if you like, feel free to reach out and (as a part of needing to scale this work) I'll link you to both the written instructions and the accompanying video to help ensure your success. As I hope I made clear above, the amount of shared understanding, alignment, and energy this exercise alone generates can catalyze a significant breakthrough for you, your team, and your organization.

Okay, we've progressed through 3 of our 6 organic levels. Time to take on the 4th ...

Chapter 4: At the Level of the Organization

Organizational Relationship x Organizational Clarity = Execution

> **TIMEOUT: This Relationship x Clarity = Execution is a "Moonshot"**
>
> About that RxC=E formula here, it is especially critical at this level that we absolutely ensure both relationship & clarity. This next level is our version of a moonshot. If we're off by even a few degrees, as we engage 30 or 60 or 80 people in a room (much less a whole organization), if we don't pay attention to both relationship & clarity, we risk amplifying any conflict or confusion beyond the group's ability to contain, direct, and produce value from their differences.[122] So the groundwork we've invested in with the prior levels really pays off here.

Organization

Almost by definition, the word "organization" denotes that a team alone—even a leadership team—can't pull off a systemic goal. It requires the combined capacity and cooperation of an integrated set of teams—an organization—often even a whole ecosystem. Generally the next step in that direction is to work with that aggregation of teams we'll call "an organization"— though it may take the form of a corporation, a government, an NGO, a network, etc. Just as the team

---

[122] Mickey Connolly, op cit.

must emerge from their own process with the ability to *innovate*, the organization must emerge with the ability to *execute*.

This level, much more so than the Team level, represents a convergence of all of the prior work—so much so that it would be easy to overwhelm ourselves. So let's simplify this a bit by limiting this level of our conversation to three critical, interwoven processes (leaving the rest for the practitioner's manual) as follows:

- the Whole group/System goal
- the Analysis
- the Strategy Summit.

And I'll forewarn you that even this limit of three topical areas can be a bit much. Still, I'm going to deliberately avoid that "how-to" level of detail— saving that for the practitioner's manual—staying focused here on the level of "how do" we harness complexity in the face of the "impossible".

Integrating Organizational Relationship & Clarity.

In order to demystify the mechanisms for creating each of these two, we've been deliberately (and artificially) discriminating between Relationship & Clarity all along—as if they aren't intimately related— as if one isn't intensifying the other. But we now need to acknowledge that each step activates both Relationship & Clarity in a way that creates a reinforcing loop—a virtuous cycle.

Though they've not yet gathered as a whole group, so far, the individuals and subgroups have typically/ideally engaged in individual interviews and individual maps; discovered team/subgroup goals; aligned around how their goals behave over time; and, finally, explored and validated the integrated, inclusive map of their system. As a result, they have both a cognitive sense (clarity) and a felt sense (relationship) with themselves, one another, and Reality. And they have a stark sense of what will likely happen if they don't intervene in a radically different way—and, usually, soon.

TIMEOUT: The Myth of Separateness

As I write this, COVID-19 is laying bare the myth that any of this (or any of us) is somehow separate—that the action of one of us doesn't impact the well-being of another. This is especially so in the context of this present moment—of our collective "Now".[123]

Now we need to take that deliberate buildup of energy and channel it into execution through:

- Deepening organizational relationship by:
  - Aligning around our global goal
  - Inventing and crosspollinating our strategies and
  - confronting our reality
- And expanding organizational clarity by:
  - Analyzing our map and discovering our levers
  - Designing and testing specific strategies and
  - Taking 1 next step.

So now we're going to weave relationship & clarity together, blending the twin strands of this work.

It all begins with aligning around our global goal…

A Positive, Reality-Based, Measurable, Time-specific Goal (+RBMTSG).

Though we've touched on the importance of the Goal along the way here, I want to emphasize that this is an absolutely crucial bridge between the work of the subgroups and that of the whole group. It's crucial at this moment in the flow of the work for two reasons: 1) for deepening/weaving both relationship & clarity, and 2) for anchoring

---

[123] When I make time to reflect, I find Eckhart Tolle's *The Power of Now* (1997) a great way to remember and inhabit this awareness— this state of being— this felt sense of relationship with Now.

the analysis. Overall, it's the critical bridge to economic, social, and/or environmental Reality.

Given that, I'm going to go deep on "goal" here—on each of the criteria indispensable to the goal, possibly repeating some of what I've already shared but, at the very worst, consolidating it all here—where it all absolutely MUST come together.

TIMEOUT: In defense of goals

I'm acutely aware of what some object to as the claimed fallibility of such a goal—or some even of goals in general. I'm also well aware that true emergence applies even (or especially) to the goal—that judging our performance based solely on a goal ignores the dynamic complexity of our World—that we alone don't cause our goal—the role of luck, or fate, etc. And each of these is a valid concern. But we miss two valuable considerations by not setting such a goal.

First, in so many cases we do need to know the magnitude of the challenge—we have to hit a number—be it a revenue number, or the replacement of GHG producing energy sources with renewable sources, or housing units, etc. And setting a goal forces our conversation about that need—it channels or constrains our thinking relative to that opportunity, enabling us to anchor our conversation in reality-based facts vs. ideology-rooted opinions divorced from reality.

Second, because we're aware from the outset about the complex-adaptive (i.e., unpredictable) nature of our world, we're careful to not be so focused on our goal as to ignore and/or jeopardize other critical needs in the ecosystem or enterprise. In fact, this whole body of work is deliberately designed to include and optimize for the whole of the critical issues, opportunities, and/or stakeholders. We're simply using our goal as an indicator as to whether or not we're on the right path—as a steppingstone toward the path we've consciously—individually and collectively—chosen of our own free will. Is our strategy and execution moving us generally in the right direction? Or are we wandering off into a ditch?

To both of these points, John Doerr's[124] excellent book *Measure What Matters* does a crystal-clear job of describing the use of goals. He calls them objectives and key results (OKRs), capturing both their subjective and objective aspects. And he relates their application to the successes of Intel, Google, YouTube, Bono's ONE Foundation and many others—in both the for-profit and non-profit realms.

The Real World: a global technology company

For example, our recent work with a $30B legacy hardware company and their need to pivot to an everything-as-a-service, edge-to-cloud company required, and they determined, a reality-based, positive, measurable, time-specific goal—one that immediately awakened everyone—both within and outside the company—to the scope and slope of change required—individually and organizationally.

Their goal was an order of magnitude multiple of their current performance in the marketplace and in the markets—one that clearly called for a r/evolution within the company—an internal one that could then be reflected externally—if they were to survive the dynamics of their increasingly competitive ecosystem. And yes, it seemed "impossible", unreasonable, impractical, unachievable. Yet it simply mirrored the Reality of their situation in the emerging, evolving industry.

Organizational relationship & clarity begins here...

So the criteria: a positive, reality-based, measurable, time-specific goal. Let's examine those criteria.

---

[124] John Doerr, *Measure What Matters: How Google, Bono, and the Gates Foundation Rock the World with OKRs*, (Portfolio, 2018).

Positive: There are, from my perspective, two key aspects to "positive": 1) how our human neurology responds to positive vs. negative stimuli and, therefore, mindset; and 2) the impact of positive (vs. negative) on our mood.

As for neurology, check this one out for yourself. We are literally wired for the positive/desired outcome. For example, when I'm mountain biking or snowboarding or (pick your favorite performance activity), if I relate to Reality in terms of "Don't hit the tree", or the rock, or the…, of course I invariably hit it.

But instead, when I simply focus on "Take the open path to the right (or wherever)", my body smoothly, effortlessly responds to my intention—and I successfully maneuver around any obstacles, able to prepare for the next one.[125] In my experience (particularly as an internationally competitive athlete[126]), this applies to other aspects of my physical world. And it's intimately related to my internal personal and external professional world as follows…

I've mentioned before my good (and brilliant) friend and colleague, Mickey Connolly of Conversant. He once shared with me (and I've passed along) something I've continued to find acutely insightful. Mickey put it something like this: "When I find myself tense, anxious, uptight, upset, or stuck, it's usually when I'm in the presence of something I'm *against*. If I can get myself in the presence of what I'm *for*, my body relaxes, my breath opens up, my mind clears, my spirits lift, and I find myself back in a creative mindset."

So by insisting on a positive goal, we generate a compelling end state as a part of the pathway to our solution—rather than simply voicing the complaint of a negative/against goal. And, as it happens (though I doubt it's an accident), we again find ourselves aligning with

---

[125] See, for example, Timothy Galloway's classic *The Inner Game of Tennis* (1972).
[126] For those who care to know, at the time of this writing, I've finished in the top 4 internationally in my chosen sport, 4-Wall Handball—an arcane, but delightfully demanding sport where I get to continually play (literally) with these principles.

the principles of David Cooperrider's "Appreciate Inquiry" and Jerry Sternin's "Positive Deviance".

Reality-based: We spoke in the beginning about the essential role of Reality. So rather than making you page back to it, I'm going to deliberately repeat what we shared early on about "So Why Reality?"

Yes, I'm deliberately using capital "R" Reality, as I'm speaking to THE reality, not "your" reality, as in "Well, that's *your* reality;" or "my" reality, as in "Well, that's not *my* reality." Once we open that can of worms, we're lost in opinions and ideologies—in our theories about what is or isn't—what works and what doesn't. (As Daniel Patrick Moynihan famously clarified, "Everyone is entitled to their own opinion, but not their own facts".)

I'm speaking about the Reality that we have created—that we have literally *caused.* The systems that produce Reality(s) like income inequity, out-of-control prison populations, climate change, political polarization, etc. I'm speaking of objectively verifiable Reality[127]— those things that confront us in our World today—issues that are seemingly impossible to resolve.

Continuing…

That reality is not only the measure, the standard to which we can hold society, our leaders, and even ourselves to account. Ultimately it's also the 'change agent' (and I think that Robert Fritz[128] would agree) that determines what our goals need to be vs. what seems comfortably achievable or practical or reasonable. It is Reality that determines what we simply *must* accomplish if so much of what we care about is to thrive—Reality, not ideology. And (luckily?) that Reality that we've by and large caused has a structure that determines its/our behavior— whether via our legal systems, our tax policies, our transportation systems, our educational systems, our economic systems, etc. And because we've caused these structures, we can 'uncause' what's harmful

---

[127] For example, as defined by Jordan Peterson and/or Sam Harris
[128] Robert Fritz, op cit.

and, instead, design for more of what's most mutually beneficial— for ourselves and for Life itself."

So any goal that doesn't put us clearly on the path to Reality— regardless of whether we, alone, can achieve it—is a form of denial— of self-deception that distracts from what's truly at stake.

Measurable: I've spoken to the necessity of this before. But to recap, enumerating/quantifying a goal tells us two things. One, it clarifies those ambiguous aspects of most goals. For instance, what do we mean by "all customers" (or "all people" or "all employees")? What's the magnitude of that? Two, it calls out specifically what target are we committing to—forcing us to get into sufficient relationship with one another and Reality to come into alignment around such metrics.

Time-specific: As with "measurable" above, we have to (as individuals and as a group), align our intention(s) with physical reality. Systems do break when allowed to go beyond certain thresholds at certain points in time. Just look at Jared Diamond's *Collapse*[129] for examples of whole societies that pushed their systems beyond their limits into states from which they've never recovered. So we need to have some sense of "by when" the measurable must happen.

Further, the timing determines the "slope" of the ramp rate for key resources. For example, with Map OneSonoma in 2018, understanding that we MUST have 26,074 additional housing units by 2020[130] (when their annual rate of production over the last 20 years came nowhere near meeting that level) gave us a pretty good indication of the slope of the production curve—and that it would require radically different approaches to housing. Even different approaches to how we imagine/ envision housing.

It may even require delving deeper into the true purpose of housing in order to satisfy the fundamental needs that housing is but one response to. Similarly, when the GNSC's leadership realized the measurable

---

[129] Jared Diamond, *Collapse: How Societies Choose to Fail or Succeed* (2005).
[130] See *County of Sonoma, Permit Sonoma, Need for New Housing* here; (2018).

need to triple the output of its supply chain, the specific timing had the impact of crystalizing and catalyzing their sense of urgency.

Goal: As a guiding principle, I'll remind us of Alan Watts[131] offering that we need a "3rd thing" (in our case, a goal) by which to assess our relative position in reality. And of Martin Buber's insight that a community—and, I'd offer, an organization, network, etc.—can't sustain itself without a goal/purpose[132]—its own "north star".

There's one more thing that we've observed about goals—in particular the goal at the whole group level, what we'll call a "global goal". In the absence of a good global goal, the intelligent thing to do is to default to "my own" local goal. By that I mean that, if my company (or my country) doesn't stand for something that's beneficial to me—and to the whole—then I'm in the position of needing to look out for myself and my own because, evidently, no one else is. This has the unintended consequence of placing us into competition with one another in what is perceived to be a zero-sum game—which all too often, becomes a self–fulfilling prophecy.

The Real World: an F100 merger:

Early in my return to the business world from my career as a psychotherapist, I was focusing on leadership development and cultural change—in particular, mergers and acquisitions. With one F100 client, I was asked to sit in on the integration team meetings where decisions were being made regarding which systems to adopt—e.g. which human resources system to go with; or which accounting system; or which finance team; or…. The problem here—for both the merging companies and the leaders at the table—was that there existed no good global goal—no real strategy guiding the merger other than the all-too-popular, vague, non–specific claims popular at the time.

---

[131] Alan Watts, op cit.
[132] Yes, there is a clear distinction between "goal" and "purpose"—and "mission" and "vision." In most cases, the "goal" is a step on the path to "purpose"—or, at least, it better be. ☺

This is not an uncommon malady, by the way. Too often, leaders appeal to Wall Street with palliatives of "creating synergies", "eliminating redundancies", "increasing market presence", "scaling purchasing power", etc.—rarely clarifying how such a move will generate/cause the net gains such a move entails.

In the case of my client, without a clear, well-articulated, and enumerated "3rd thing" with which to guide their decision making— without an external point of reference—the justifications for which systems to go with defaulted to "mine is better than yours" debates— debates that were destructive to the individuals, the organizations, and ultimately their employees, customers, and shareholders. It's useful to note here that upwards of 90% of all mergers and acquisitions fail.[133] And this lack of goal clarity—one of the critical initial conditions needed to help guide the operational and cultural evolution—prede- termines the resultant destruction of relationships—and value.

Said another way, a well-designed emergent goal is inclusive of and reflective of the needs of the system as a whole—in the context of reality—such that it optimizes the potential gains across the system. By so doing, it forms the basis for optimal decision making, even (or especially) about the toughest of issues.

At each of these five junctures in exploring the anatomy of our goal—positive, reality-based, measurable, time-specific—culminating in the goal itself, we deepen the weave of both our relationship and our clarity with self, another, and reality, reinforcing those fundamental building blocks requisite for our eventual success.

TIMEOUT: That promise to deal with bullies

Since this way of working self-selects those who primarily care about the whole, I only occasionally encounter bullies. Yet too many of those leaders with whom I work eventually do encounter them. I was surprised to discover, in support of that reality, that a study cited in

[133] https://hbr.org/2016/06/ma-the-one-thing-you-need-to-get-right

the *Washington Post* (2016) asserts that "21% of CEOs [in the United States] are psychopaths."[134] So they seem to be a fact of life.

Bullies tend to be able to operate through a strategy of "divide and conquer", especially in environments with low levels of transparency—something we'll see as essential to both scalability and sustainability in our chapters 5 and 6.

An appreciation of the mechanisms that enable bullying holds the key to containing it. The primary anti-bullying mechanism is (as you'll recognize) to focus on what we're "for" in this way of working—vs. focusing "against" the bully. And what we're striving for here is the continual deepening of both Relationship & Clarity such that the group becomes so clear and connected relative to what's most needed—the antidote to "divide and conquer"—that they step into their collective power and voluntarily begin to act relative to their goal and to Reality (given, of course, the right mechanisms[135]).

The Real World: a newly forming Network

Though I much prefer to offer the real-world credentials of those I've worked with—wanting you to be able to better tie what we're learning to our economic and social landscape—given that bullies are, by nature, vindictive, I'll especially avoid naming clients here to keep from introducing a possible irritant for those still involved in this ongoing project. Bearing that in mind, I'll keep this brief…

A newly forming network of systemic actors had historically operated in silos, having very little relationship with or even much specific knowledge about one another. And it was to the advantage of a major power broker in the ecosystem to keep it that way as a means

---

[134] https://www.washingtonpost.com/news/on-small-business/wp/2016/09/16/gene-marks-21-percent-of-ceos-are-psychopaths-only-21-percent/
[135] See also Jim Collins, *Turning Goals into Results: The Power of Catalytic Mechanisms*, Harvard Business Review (July-August, 1999).

for maintaining control. To that end, one leader (who was funded by the power broker) continually engaged in attempts to disrupt the project—increasingly so as we began to make significant progress. (BTW, this individual—having historically bullied key members of their own staff—had already been compelled by his Board to undergo psychotherapy—immediately following the "successful" completion of which, he fired the complainants "for cause".)

There had been 1-on-1 attempts to contain his interference. However, that simply fed into the divide and conquer tactics on the part of the bully. So his disruptions were successful in consistently intimidating individual members of the group, primarily because the group knew that the principal reason this individual was included in the project to begin with was because, if he hadn't been included, he would have sought to eventually harm both the venture and the individuals.

As the network moved sequentially through the levels (from Individual to Another to Team/Subgroup, now arriving at the level of the Organization/Whole Group) the groups' individual and collective levels of Relationship & Clarity continued to deepen and strengthen. They had become so demonstrably united that, when the bully now attempted to disrupt them, a strikingly new, spontaneous behavior emerged.

This time, when the outrageous attempt to derail the flow that was emerging occurred, the group turned in unison and simply looked at the bully. Then, again in unison and without uttering a word, turned back to their conversation and continued on their way as if nothing had happened. Basically, the group ignored him—now experiencing his distractions as irrelevant to their newfound purpose and process.

What was even more striking was the response of the bully. He immediately began to perform the kinds of appeasement behaviors Frans de Waal[136] describes in his book *Chimpanzee Politics*—behaviors that are hard-

---

[136] Frans de Waal, *Chimpanzee Politics: Power and Sex Among Apes* (2007). A great read—almost like reading about everyday scenes from the office.

wired into our brain's mammalian limbic systems and exhibited from marsupials to wolves to primates—even, apparently, to human bullies.

The bully began to ask if he could get people tea or pillows or offer them his chair. It radically changed both the bully's behavior and that of the group going forward.

For me, this clearly demonstrated the value of building the strength of the group via designing for Relationship & Clarity vs. attempting to counter the influence of the bully—yet another example of "For" (the group) vs. "Against" (the bully). And you can ponder for yourself whether individuals aligning to overcome bullies is borne out in other settings by checking out, among other sources, the smaller scale of group psychotherapy (see again Yvonne's SCT) and/or the larger scale of the 2011 Egyptian revolution (see Wael Ghonim's *Revolution 2.0* and his Facebook coordination of the protests that helped to oust Mubarak[137]).

It continues to be my experience that what keeps all of us in check, bullies included, is ultimately Reality itself. It's simply inarguable—even bullies can't successfully argue with it—not for long, anyway.

The good news is that we, as a species, are uniquely sensitive to Reality so long as we're not buffered from it by way of disinformation or isolation or too much privilege.[138] We instinctively seek to help others when we see them in need. We have an emotional reaction to injustice and seek to right wrongs. It's by creating the initial conditions that enable us to grasp Reality that we come into alignment as a group around a purpose for responding to Reality. And it's through that that we progress, even (or especially) in the presence of bullies.[139] And we have progressed—despite the complexities we've spawned along the way.

---

[137] Wael Ghonim's *Revolution 2.0: The Power of the People Is Greater Than the People in Power* (2012)

[138] One of my favorite authors (when I'm falling to sleep at night) is the creative comedic fantasy writer Terry Pratchett (knighted by the Queen for the genius of his political satire). It was from him that I learned (among other things) that the word "privilege" originally meant "private law", i.e., their own legal system.

[139] In Carlos Castenada's series, the Yaqui shaman don Juan Matus points out the essential value of a "petty tyrant" capable of causing harm in one's development. Though many see the series as fictional, the essential learning re: the value of a "bully" as "grist for one's mill" still holds.

Now that we've kept the promise to take stock of that troublesome topic of bullies, let's get back to what we're "For"…`

The Goal anchors the Analysis...

When it comes time to convert the rendering of our system (in the form of the integrated map) into something actionable (via our analysis), we'll need a standard by which to assess things such as: the relative (to our goal) readiness of key resources, or the expected and also needed trend of resource development (again, relative to our goal). Even the sequencing and pacing of key resource acquisition and/or development is a function of our +RBMTSG (our positive, reality-based, time-specific goal). Its magnitude and timeframe define the relative health or fitness of our system much like an upcoming athletic competition sets the specifications for body fat, VO2 max, endurance, strength, speed, etc.

Without knowing where we're headed, we can't make useful, reality-based decisions about where to focus—much less align on those decisions. By way of metaphor, how could we choose an airplane if we don't know where we're traveling, with how many people, and when we need to arrive? So why would we ignore such a vital way of orienting ourselves about these "impossible" enterprises, these (ad)ventures—in which we invest so much time, money, talent, and even stress?

Okay, enough about +RBMTS goals…let's assume we've got one. So now what…?

Analyzing your map and discovering your levers

Now we're jumping over to the clarity strand for a bit. We now have a really good map—one we've validated in subgroups, with our group as a whole and, in many cases, in extended individual conversations. And we're aligned on our goal. We're now at our own "necessary but not sufficient" moment.

I was once engaged to review the work of one of the premier systems thinking/modeling groups in the world. My client shared the model with me then asked what I thought of it. "I don't know," I mused. "I'd have to think about it." Then of course I had to think about *how* to think about it. And, in order to share my thoughts, how to think about it in a way that others could understand, assess for themselves, and act from, too.

Since then, we've had to design[140] a set of analysis principles and practices that would consistently and reliably work across scores of such maps—and in ways that enable the leaders themselves to make their needed decisions, vs. forcing them to blindly default to an "expert" to make decisions for them.

The former stays true to the emergent and self-organizing rules adapted from the Cynefin insights—the latter would drop us into the nebulous world of black boxes—where those tasked with execution have only a vague idea how decisions arose—more importantly, why they're doing what they're doing. Even more troubling, how to adapt when circumstances change. And as the COVID-19 pandemic; the riots following the killing of George Floyd (and too many others); and the unprecedented firestorms beginning in 2017 and continuing through 2021 in California, Colorado, and Oregon (and other states) made startlingly, painfully, and tragically clear, we are in a high change world, right?

Such a break in our chain of evidence—our deeper understanding of reality (via our analysis)—would disrupt the integrity of the whole process of emergent impact—leaving it/us vulnerable to the inevitable shifts we'll encounter as we move forward. An "expert-only" analysis (btw, we *do* need experts, just not *only* experts) risks negating the ability to internalize the full process as part of the path to leading with

---

[140] Again, I want/need to credit my good friend & colleague, Jim Ritchie-Dunham, who seeded my step onto this path and who describes his take on analysis in his book *Managing from Clarity* (2001).

authenticity— with congruence and credibility. It also thwarts the scalability and sustainability of levels 5 and 6.

So how to jump into this section on the Analysis? A systems map, alone, is not sufficient for intervening in a system. We must deepen our understanding about how the system behaves.

Systems have both momentum and inertia—they tend to keep on doing whatever they've been doing—and aren't easily diverted from their path. It's sometimes useful for me to think of a system as an amoral beast—doing what it does simply because it's driven by its goal and its structure. It's simply doing what it was built or has evolved (often by accident) to do. So we've found it more effective and efficient to apply a handful of system-thinking-based assessment tools to the map to more fully understand the system and how to influence it. Applying these different analytical tools is akin to viewing it from different perspectives—literally like picking it up and rotating it, allowing the "light" to strike it at different angles with each view offering some new insight into its behavior. In addition to the Behavior over Time tool, we may also look at the system through the 8 lenses of:

- *Cross Impact Matrix analysis*—a software program that mathematically identifies those levers with the greatest influence based on the structure of the map

- *Systems Archetypes*—those generically recurring loops/patterns in systems (whether ecological, biological, economic, or social) that cause a system's behavior—akin to getting caught in a riptide—if you know you're in one, you can work with it to safely recover—if not, you're likely to fight it, exhaust yourself, and drown

- *Leadership's own leverage identification, weighting, and scoring*— asking the leaders in the process to identify, for themselves, what they believe are the most impactful levers and weight and score them

- *Readiness rating*—assessing the strength of key organizational resources on, say, a scale of 1-10, relative to their goal

- *Trends analysis*—distinguishing between how the individual resources in the system have trended historically, are expected to trend in the future, and need to trend if the system is to achieve its goal

- *Places to Intervene in a System*[141]– Donella Meadows' brilliant insight about the relative impact of different categories of leverage points, for example, shifting a mindset is more potent than changing a goal is more powerful than changing information flows, etc.

- *Prior analyses, reports and recommendations*—using insights from prior work to both validate and/or strengthen the map while reinforcing our insight regarding other possible levers

- *Others*—which we'll not cover at this point but that include stakeholder assessments, social network analysis, systemic vs. dynamic leverage, performance indicators, loop dominance— each applied based upon what's most useful to the key decision makers.

Regardless of which combination of tools[142] we use, these analyses are populated, integrated, and distilled to clarify specifically where in the organization we can most efficiently and effectively intervene to move the system as a whole in the desired direction at the needed order of magnitude.

But before jumping into this, a warning…

TIMEOUT: Skip this part, please…seriously

I'm going to do something unusual here. I actually recommend that you skip this part, seriously. It's technical. I included it for those who care to wade in a bit deeper because the Analysis is, unequivocally, a pivotal part of working in this way—enabling us to translate the map from say, 120 possible intervention points (akin to GNSC's world) to a

---

[141] Donella H. Meadows, *Places to Intervene in a System*, Whole Earth Winter 1997.
[142] For more information on several of these tools, see *Managing from Clarity* by my friends/ colleagues Jim Ritchie-Dunham and Hal T. Rabbino (2001).

relative handful (like the GNSC's eventual 7)—making the map much easier to strategize with, to organize around, and to communicate. Over the past 20 years, I can only think of one client who was so familiar with their system that they could move to strategies based on the map alone. I've included a deep dive on Analysis here only because it plays such a crucial role that leaving it out would have given rise to a hole in our flow here—especially for those who want to more thoroughly understand how we distill the strategic value out of the map.

So now that you've been forewarned, I'll leave it to you to decide if you prefer to skip to the next section (the Strategy Summit) or stay the course. BTW, even if you do skip the nitty gritty, you may still find value in the real-world case examples. So with those caveats, here we go…

Cross-Impact Matrix Analysis:

(This tool is more commonly known by the French acronym MicMac.)[143]

Without getting deep into the math (it is deep), I'll simply say that this technique is used by, among others, our intelligence services to assess what we'll term "nodes of high opportunity within networks of great uncertainty".[144]

As it's applied here, it helps to think about it as the ability to identify a relative handful of elements on the map that are of high influence across the system—i.e., elements that drive more of the other system elements that are located downstream from its position—but are subject to low exposure to the rest of the system—i.e., they are not driven by more of the system from upstream. An even more simplistic explanation would be to say that it shows us, mathematically, which

---

[143] http://en.laprospective.fr/methods-of-prospective/softwares/59-micmac.html
[144] https://en.wikipedia.org/wiki/Cross_impact_analysis

variables have the greatest downstream impact while exposed to the least upstream constraints.

For example, in overly simplistic terms, if one variable influences, say, 20 things downstream but is exposed to just 3 things upstream, it's a relatively higher leverage opportunity. That is, as compared with one with similar downstream potential yet exposed to 10 upstream variables. It requires the use of the Cross-Impact Analysis and a computer because it's not possible for the human mind to trace the complications presented by the numerous feedback loops when the model runs through to say, the 32nd order of computation. Said another way, simply looking at the map in the 1st order—the map we see on the page representing just the first revolution of the system, the first turn of the crank—conceals the true behavior of the system as it iterates. The true behavior of the system is a function of the feedback loops over time.

This analysis typically distills down to roughly 15% of the total number of variables—those with both high influence and low exposure. This is extremely valuable as the intent of any analysis is to constrain the number of potential levers to the smallest, though still impactful, set possible. Said another way, it's precisely because we can't do everything that we need to (via analysis) reduce our universe of possibilities to the most essential—in this case, to the 15%.

I can't overstate the value of this analysis, as it often reveals insights that are only brilliant in retrospect—insights that make good, common sense, but only once they're revealed to us. For example …

The Real World: The Nature Conservancy and the Great Lakes Fisheries

Once a bountiful, seemingly inexhaustible source of low-cost protein, the Great Lakes—the largest collective body of fresh water on Earth—represents an opportunity to recover at least a meaningful portion of its once prolific capacity—its ability to sustainably, renewably provide a rich, diverse array of economic, environmental, and even social wealth.

The Nature Conservancy (TNC) was bold enough to conceive of and confront this challenge, this opportunity. Drawing on a diverse set of interviews from scientists, commercial fishers, indigenous peoples, government agencies, academics, and environmentalists (among others), we developed and validated a map of the ecosystem—subsequently convening to explore the analysis—one that included most of the 8 lenses described earlier. Thanks to the work of our whole team (including Anne Murray Allen, Bob Johnson and Kell Delaney of Conversant along with Scott Sowa and Michael Reuter of TNC), the outcome of this meeting was nothing less than remarkable.

By way of comparison, in our initial meeting in January—which, due to the constraints of the process, did not follow the structure of the subgroup and BOT work described herein—was a feisty one—with one key group consistently struggling to align—lacking a sufficient container or protocol to ensure that all voices were heard—much less "discriminated, understood, appreciated and included."[145] On the bright side, though, we did gain a solid understanding of the diversity of opinion regarding the task before us—diversity (yet) to be integrated into a cohesive, inclusive whole.

Our April meeting—just 3 months later and with very few intervening meetings—was, by stark contrast, a delightful one—a deep learning for them—even for us. When I initially ran the MicMac, I thought I'd gotten it wrong—that either the software was malfunctioning (I ran it on several different computers to double-check it) or the map itself was off. The reason for my skepticism was that one particular cluster of variables consistently showed up mathematically as high leverage—those in the realm of aquaculture.

Then I was gob-smacked by my own foolishness. I was biased! Early in my career, I had established the Texas offices of The Nature Conservancy and, during my time there (and, now obviously, beyond) was completely committed to the preservation of native species.

---

[145] Again, referring to Yvonne's insight.

As a part of the Great Lakes Fisheries process, we'd engaged in several conversations about proper goal setting—i.e., +RBMTS Goal. Following that protocol, they eventually determined that their goal was: "By 2030, Great Lakes Fisheries are more diverse, resilient, and abundant through restoration of self-sustainable native fish stocks and *an overall 15% increase in availability of harvestable species*" (emphasis mine).

It turns out that that last phrase—"overall 15% increase in harvestable species"—implicitly demanded that we include aquaculture in the equation—as it was the optimal path to that aspect of their goal—and that of the other stakeholders, if we were to fulfill their economic and social needs.

And that wasn't just a function of my opinion. It came primarily from the fact that roughly 25% of those selected to be interviewed were, in one way or another, supportive of the aquaculture sector. So the map naturally fully represented the role of aquaculture in the Great Lakes Fishery ecosystem—economically, socially, and environmentally.

Viewed from that perspective, the leverage accorded aquaculture by the mathematical analysis made perfect sense. It was only my bias toward "native" that caused me to doubt the emergence of aquaculture in the analysis—to doubt the map and, ultimately, to doubt myself. My bad! ☺

So to emphasize this learning about myself as a cautionary tale for the group, I shared this story about my own foolishness as a part of the analysis presentation the next day—not realizing that it was a bit of a bombshell. The room as a whole immediately erupted into a furor—decrying that aquaculture was not on their horizon and had no business being called out as part of their strategy.

Wow! I didn't see that coming.

But then a delightful, truly priceless (at least in my world) thing happened. Over the course of just the next 45 minutes, through an authentic conversation,[146] they collectively, collaboratively recognized

---

[146] Again, based on Conversant's Conversation Meter & Cycle of Value.

that, if they were to authentically show up as leaders for the system as a whole-and not just for TNC's hopes and/or biases for the system—they had to embrace, not just native species, but aquaculture, too. They truly took on responsibility for their goal—they arrived at "systems leadership".[147]

They chose to not just maximize their environmental portion of their equation, but also to optimize the system in a way that included the social (much needed low-cost protein) and economic (much needed jobs and accompanying local economic multiplier) represented by that "15% increase in harvestable species." Aquaculture was clearly an indispensable lever.

This is an excellent illustration of the value of ever-increasing specificity in the goal setting process and conversation. Without such precision we NEVER would have discovered this embedded confusion. Well, actually, we would have, but only late (months or years late—too late) into the execution phase—and at a time when it could have seriously harmed the project.

It's also a good illustration of the value of the structure of the map—its ability to literally hold their conversation. These two—the goal and the map, combined with the irrefutable illumination provided by the MicMac—triggered that conversation.

This triad, when paired with the skillsets of my colleagues at Conversant and TNC's leaders, created the requisite initial conditions. Further, it deepened both the relationship among those in the room—as they went beyond their opinion-based biases and deeper into the reality-based facts—and their shared clarity—as they quickly internalized the relative importance of an aspect they would have otherwise omitted.

I and my colleagues from Conversant were immediately struck by how far this diversified—even conflicted—group had come in just 3 short months—from feisty exchanges in late January to quick, clear

---

[147] In the spirit of *"The Dawn of System Leadership"*, Stanford Social Innovation Review, Winter 2015.

alignment in early April. And the boon of working in this way has been consistently, reliably, even predictably replicated both before and after this striking example.

Systems Archetypes:

Archetypes in systems are patterns that are commonly observed (and commonly at play) across all kinds of systems—economic, biological, social, political, business, and environmental. And there's a limited number of them, ranging from 8-12—depending on how you interpret them. As for their impact and importance, a metaphor may help…

I find it useful to think about Archetypes like riptides. When someone at the beach finds themselves caught in a riptide, the typical response is to fight against it. That natural but ineffective reaction to swim against it is likely to result in exhaustion and, well, you likely know what's next (drowning). Instead, the response to a riptide, once you understand its pattern, is to work with it until you can get to a point of safety and return to shore—then get on with your life.

The same is true in systems. The natural reaction is to fight against the archetype which often only serves to reinforce its destructive impact—continuing to drive the system down—continuing to exhaust time, money, and talent while driving up stress. But if you understand the archetype(s), you can work with it and get yourself, and your system, safely on its way.

So another caveat here—one in keeping with making the best use of your time.

First, there are several of these archetypes and describing them in actionable detail would move us in the direction of the practitioner's manual—not the job of this book.

Second, one could devote a whole book simply to this topic (and some have).[148] Again, not our job here.

---

[148] For more on these (and so much more), I'm long overdue in calling out Donella Meadows' great read *Thinking in Systems: A Primer* (2007) produced posthumously.

Third, there are several serviceable descriptions of archetypes easily available, for instance, via Wikipedia. With that in mind, I'm not going to try to offer full elaborations for each—or (my apologies here) even try to offer detailed, working examples of each.

Instead, we'll do three things: 1) list them, at least the ones I find most valuable along with a (too) quick, (too) short common example or two. 2) offer one real-world example that applies them in practice, and 3) make sure to cover them at the needed depth in the practitioner's manual.

That said, unless you *really* want to learn something about archetypes, you may want to finally take my advice and skip this bit—moving on to the next analysis section, Leadership's Leverage Identification...

TIMEOUT: Archetypes and Sensemaking...

Much of what we've explored here falls in the domain of sensemaking—our collective, collaborative efforts to frame our complex experiences as meaningful. Sensemaking is even (or especially) applied in the life and death reality of warfare as central to the conceptual framework for military network-centric operations (NCO) espoused by the United States Department of Defense (Garstka and Alberts, 2004[149]):

(Note: though this next passage, because it speaks to networking, is also relevant to our scalability level, I'll go ahead and share it here to keep it in context—simply reminding us of it when we get to levels 5 and 6. I'm doing so because what we've forged up to this point epitomizes, particularly in the last sentence, what the NCO deems most valuable.) Continuing...

"In a joint/coalition military environment [akin to many of the networked environments required to solve our 'impossible' problems], sensemaking is complicated by numerous technical, social, organizational, cultural, and operational factors. A central hypothesis of NCO is that the quality of shared sensemaking and collaboration will be better in a robustly networked force than in a

---

[149] https://en.wikipedia.org/wiki/Sensemaking#Reference-Garstka,_J._and_Alberts,_D._2004

platform-centric force, empowering people to make better decisions. According to NCO theory, there is a mutually reinforcing relationship among and between individual sensemaking, shared sensemaking, and collaboration."

While this whole process is specifically designed to enable sensemaking, System Archetypes are one atypically valuable tool for sensemaking. And, like much of sensemaking, they're an imprecise tool—much like Fuzzy Logic, based on degrees of truth instead of true or false Boolean logic.[150] So when applying the Archetypes, you make your best effort to conform the Archetypes to the systemic story and vice versa. My point here is to cut yourself some slack as you seek to make sense of your Integrated Map through the lens of the Archetypes (some slack, not a lot). ☺

So first, the list with a too-short example (knowing that you can simply go to this footnote[151] for more):

- **Reinforcing loop**—e.g., earning periodic interest on an investment over time
- **Balancing loop**—e.g., a thermostat
- **Limits to success**—e.g., (healthy) weight loss from fasting
- **Balancing loop with delay**—e.g., steering a sluggish boat
- **Success to the successful**—e.g., the wealthy gaining control of an economic or political system
- **Fixes that fail**—e.g., borrowing to pay interest on debt
- **Growth and underinvestment**—e.g., an undercapitalized startup
- **Shifting the burden**—increasing caffeine/stimulants when tired
- **Tragedy of the commons**—e.g., overgrazing a shared pasture

---

[150] https://searchenterpriseai.techtarget.com/definition/fuzzy-logic
[151] https://thesystemsthinker.com/wp-content/uploads/2016/03/Systems-Archetypes-I-TRSA01_pk.pdf

- **Escalation**—e.g., price wars at neighboring gas stations
- **Accidental adversaries**—e.g., good friends arguing about conflicting politics, opinions, or beliefs
- **Drifting goals**—e.g., settling for things in life or work.

The Real World: Minnesota's Education Transformation Initiative (ETI):

While we've performed similar analyses in the corporate sector, given our NDA's, we're not allowed to share those. So here's one we can…

We've touched on this one before—it's the project that included Mayor RT Rybak. So I won't repeat the context here. I will, however, cite the archetype portion of the analysis as it greatly clarified what had happened to Minnesota's educational system—giving us shared insight for getting back on track.

Before showing you that analysis, let's set just a bit of context—not about the client—rather about Systems Archetypes. When applying System Archetypes to any of the maps, I literally pull out the list of Archetypes—walking through them one by one and asking myself whether or not a particular archetype is in play in the system. Once I've identified which ones are active—say 3-5 or so—I then ask whether or not there's a particular sequence to these—i.e., how one Archetype leads to another then another and so on.

Once the list is clear, I then sequence them in a way that enables us to understand (and tell) the larger story of the system's evolution (or, too often, devolution) over time.

TIMEOUT: 1:1 Matching to the Map

Some apply the Archetypes generically, telling the story in general terms without tying it back verbatim to the integrated map. And there's still value in that. But there's greater value in linking the archetype analysis directly back up to the map—word for word—to reinforce our emerging common language, integrating the various analyses into a rigorous, common sensical whole—supporting our decision regarding where to act.

In the case of the ETI, the relevant archetypes were:

- Addiction
- Success to the Successful
- Shifting the Burden
- Tragedy of the Commons
- Accidental Adversaries.

BTW, we're going to walk through these one at a time showing first the graphic, then explaining it. Once I've walked through each individually, we'll link them up—giving us the view that tells the whole story.[152]

They played out beginning with "**Addiction**", which is a variant of Shifting the Burden:

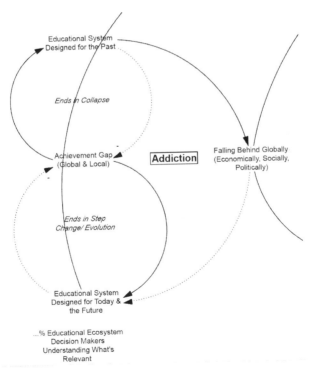

---

[152] Since this is black & white for publication, a solid line represents a reinforcing relationship; a dashed one an inverse relationship. To see this in color via video, go to scottspann.com/impossible.

"Addiction" to the past

Through our interviews and mapping with students, teachers, parents, business leaders, and others, we discovered that the existing education system was perfectly suited for educating our youth for the past.

Yet what we need is a system designed for today and the future. According to the Archetypes—and our interviews, maps and ensuing conversations—every time we in the system experienced an achievement gap, we increased our existing pattern of educating for the past—in other words, "doing more and more of the same and expecting a different result", which momentarily/symptomatically closed the achievement gap. However, doing so caused us to consistently fall behind globally, thereby damaging our economic, social, and political ability to re-design our educational system for the future (the root cause of our gap). The fix here is to evolve our educational systems for the future which would then enable us to close the achievement gap without falling behind globally. Since this wasn't happening systemically, it pushed us into **"Success to the Successful"**…

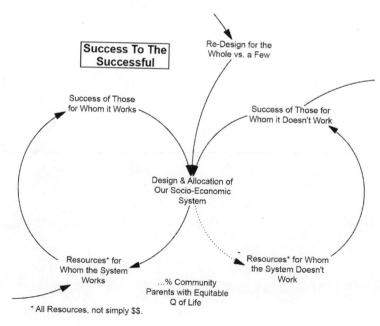

Given that the current educational system was not preparing our children (or our society) for a prosperous future, those parents with the means would move their children (and the accompanying per child resources) out of traditional public education and into other options that would meet the needs of the future. This resource reallocation results in fewer resources for those remaining in traditional public schools.

As these alternates became more successful, they were allocated more and more resources—further diminishing resources available for traditional schools. This resulted in greater success to those receiving more, while the performance of those receiving less fell. The fix here is to design a system that works for the whole vs. a few—to design that future-oriented system. Since that wasn't happening, this then drove us into *"Shifting the Burden...*

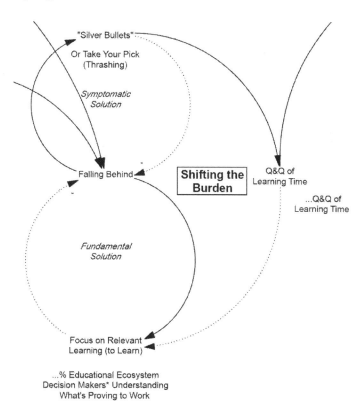

Students in traditional systems in Minnesota continued to fall behind. In response, we relied on "silver bullets"—trying a host of ideological fads to solve our educational woes, many—of which were just variants on "educating for the past". This, then, took away from a focus on what students, parents, and business leaders considered relevant—as well as distracting decision makers (and draining resources) from the fundamental solution: evidence–based approaches vs. fads. As this accelerated, it led to a *"Tragedy of the Commons"*…

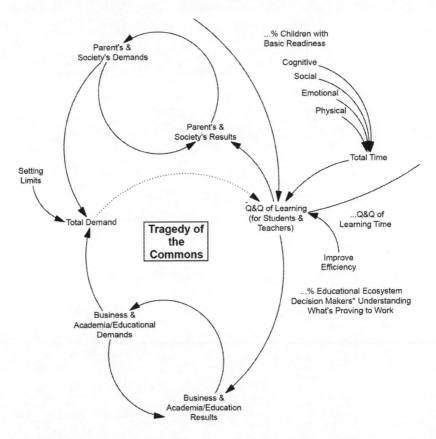

The common resource—i.e., the "commons"—shared by students and teachers is the quality and quantity of learning time, which is a function of total time available—time for cognitive, social, emotional, and physical needs. In response to the intermittent reinforcement of the partially successful system, demands from two sectors—parents and society, on the one hand and business and academics, on the other—increased. As a result, total demand began to overwhelm learning time. Since we can't increase total time, the fix here is to improve efficiency based on evidence-based approaches—those proven to work. However, we were still responding with silver bullets—which culminated in "*Accidental Adversaries*"...

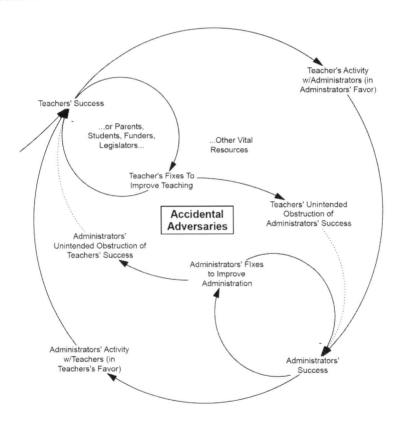

Once we've reached this point, we've lost track of a mutually beneficial global goal—our unifying factor, our "3rd thing"—one that appreciates, includes, and integrates our diverse perspectives and efforts. When that happens, we each silo, we each default to our local goals—those things that we know we must do to fulfil our individual immediate obligations/needs—especially in the absence of a worthy global goal.

Consequently, what would normally be mutually reinforcing actions—the outer ring with solid arrows—then flips to actions that move "me" forward but may impede "you"—the inner loop—especially those components feeding the dashed arrows. As a result, our world becomes parents vs. teachers vs. students vs. legislators vs. ... Those who should and could be allies now become adversaries—each fully believing, from a non–systemic point of view, that they're doing the right thing.

When we integrate these[153], we can see the progression (digression?) of the archetypes—how one presages the next and the next and...

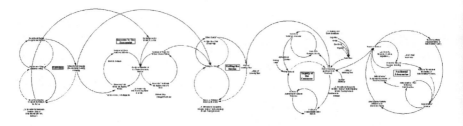

It's quite tragic how many of our systems seem to culminate in Accidental Adversaries—where those of us who would normally be working together to solve our mutual problems—political, economic, social, environmental, and so on—end up at odds with one another. This predominates when the actors are relying primarily on Ideologies (such as trickle-down economics) about how our World works rather than seeking to understand the Reality of how our World really works. Hence, the value of math and science. Now, however, Reality-based views are, more than ever, increasingly available to us.

Psychotherapists call such unrealistic responses "denial" and understand them as part of recognized pathologies. It is the specific

---

[153] Again, my apologies for the tiny image—you'll find a legible version at scottspann.com/impossible.

design intention of this work to bridge that gap by uncovering what each actor is fundamentally "for" vs. "against", enabling them to align on how to bring their reality-based goals about in physical reality.

Said another way, I've been continually encouraged by how many times—when we model the ultimate outcome of an opinion-based, ideological position using a rigorous inspection of the math of that position—the originator's own resultant realization converts to a fact-based understanding that reverses their previous opinion-based stance. When that happens, clarity arises from the prior confusion—and tensions in the relationship resolve.

And there are those times when a leader sees and understands the "math"—the harm/irrationality of their position—but because of concerns about power or compensation or image, chooses to act against the best interests of the Whole—be it the firm, organization, community, or the group. In one clear business case I can recall that an individual's destructive behavior became so obvious (via such leadership's mapping process) that they were "freed" to explore other opportunities elsewhere in their industry.

Now on to the 3rd of our 7 analyses…

Leadership Leverage Identification

Those first two analyses are vital because they—along with Donella Meadows' *Places to Intervene in a System*, coming up soon—are truly systemic analyses. That is, they have their origins in a deep understanding of how systems behave. Despite the vital value in those three, we can't allow the analysis to become a black box out of which magically appears whatever the systems "expert" deems to be valuable. Doing so would create: 1) a disconnect from your ability to internalize the system, along with 2) a dependency on an external party—one you would simply have to trust. It's not that they're not trustworthy. It's simply that, as leaders, we must ultimately internalize (vs. externalize) both the knowledge and the responsibility for making such decisions.

So we blend the approaches. We conduct those three above-mentioned systemic analyses. Meanwhile, we engage leaders individually, from their unique perspectives, in: 1) identifying the top 10 or 20 levers, 2) weighting them, 3) rating each lever's readiness, and 4) assessing how each lever is trending over time. We'll look at an example of this in a bit, but for now…

And we only engage those leaders who have been through the map validation process—needing to be sure that whoever engages in the analysis has a shared baseline of understanding about how their system works.

They engage in the Analysis by:

1. Identifying and weighting levers, circling their choices on the map (usually limited to ~15% of the total elements on the map), then

2. Assigning a limited number of points to each chosen lever

3. Rating each lever's readiness relative to their goal (on a scale of, say, 1-10)

4. Adding trend information—specifically historical, expected, and needed trends.

We then aggregate this information from each leader to generate a value sorted list of each parameter. These, then, are incorporated—along with the other analyses—into the overall analysis as we move into the next step of their collective strategic decision making.

Places to Intervene in a System:

Donella Meadows[154] was an extremely gifted Systems Thinker who tragically passed away suddenly and much too soon. One of the gifts she left us is her *Places to Intervene in a System*, originally published in Stewart Brand's *Whole Earth Magazine*, Winter 1997.

---

[154] Donella Meadows, Op. cit.

It came to her as a spontaneous epiphany. As she tells it, "So one day I was sitting in a meeting about how to make the world work better—actually it was a meeting about how the new global trade regime—NAFTA and GATT and the World Trade Organization—is likely to make the world work worse. The more I listened, the more I began to simmer inside."

"'This is a HUGE NEW SYSTEM people are inventing!' I said to myself. 'They haven't the SLIGHTEST IDEA how this complex structure will behave,' myself said back to me. 'It's almost certainly an example of cranking the system in the wrong direction. It's aimed at growth, growth at any price! And the control measures these nice, liberal folks are talking about to combat it—small parameter adjustments, weak negative feedback loops—are PUNY!!!'"

She goes on to explain,

"'Suddenly, without quite knowing what was happening, I got up, marched to the flip chart, tossed over to a clean page, and wrote:

PLACES TO INTERVENE IN A SYSTEM (in increasing order of effectiveness):

9. Constants, parameters, numbers (subsidies, taxes, standards)

8. Regulating negative feedback loops

7. Driving positive feedback loops

6. Material flows and nodes of material intersection

5. Information flows

4. The rules of the system (incentives, punishments, constraints)

3. The distribution of power over the rules of the system

2. The goals of the system

1. The mindset or paradigm out of which the system—its goals, power structure, rules, its culture—arises.'[155]

---

[155] http://donellameadows.org/archives/leverage-points-places-to-intervene-in-a-system/

Everyone in the meeting blinked in surprise, including me. 'That's brilliant!' someone breathed. 'Huh?' said someone else."

She later went on to expand this list of 9 to 12[156], but I've consistently found the original 9 best suited to working with leaders.

The way we apply them is to go through their Integrated map, variable–by–variable, and decide whether or not one of the 5 most effective (from "information flows" down/up to "mindset or paradigm") applies to each. In many cases, a single variable may represent more than 1 of the 5—making it an especially attractive lever—when viewed through this lens.

The results of this analysis, then, are tabulated as a part of the Analysis Summary sheet, an example of which I'll share at the end of this segment on analysis.

The Real World: A $30B Technology Company:

In a recent engagement, one of the variables in their Integrated Map (designed to enable them to pivot from a legacy company to a successful 21st century technology competitor) was, for the various historically separate business units, the Ability to Dynamically Align on Metrics. For them, this represented all 5 of the most effective levels, specifically:

1. *A mindset/paradigm shift*—from independent business units to an integrated portfolio—now targeted collectively on client acquisition, satisfaction, and/or renewal

2. *Their goals*—from individually determined goals to goals that add up to overall client acquisition, satisfaction, and/or renewal

3. *Self-organization*—Within this new mindset/paradigm and within the context of these goals, this alignment enables each business unit to now design their own (yet still collaborative) pathway to achieve these new metrics

---

[156] Ibid

4. ***The rules***—Since now the company's Executive Team would hold themselves and their business units—individually and collectively—accountable for the new metrics

5. ***Information flows***—in that the transparency afforded by these new metrics would serve to inform both leaders and staff regarding the relative success of each aspect of the business—relative to their overall goals—keeping them apprised of their success (or not) in using the rules to self-organize toward the goals that would enable their paradigm shift.

Okay, just one more bit of analysis technicality to get through…we're almost done! Whew!

Prior analyses, reports and recommendations:

In some cases, leaders have already engaged in other approaches in their attempt to solve their "impossible" issue/opportunity—in prior attempts to harness their complexity. These are valuable investments that need to be fully mined—whose value still needs to be harvested/safeguarded for two important reasons.

First, there's been significant investment— investments of people's time (usually leadership, staff and/or external experts); money (whether internally or externally sourced); and talent (from leaders, staff, and experts—either in the creation, review, and/or implementation of these other recommendations). So we need to make sure we build on that investment instead of discarding it. In many cases, ignoring them represents not simply a loss of prior investment—which should be enough motivation to incorporate them—but also risks negatively impacting the morale of those originally involved.

Secondly, such alternate perspectives offer yet one more way to validate the Integrated Map. By going item by item through the prior recommendations, we're able to determine whether or not our current Integrated Map includes those elements that are part of the recommendation.

In almost every case, because of the math inherent in the Integrated Map (in combination with the 360° perspectives used to construct it) the Map includes and transcends the prior reports. In those few cases where something's missing, the structure of the map's design typically enables a straightforward adjustment. So far, there has been one time when such an adjustment was required…

The Real World: diaTribe and the global diabetes epidemic

The diaTribe Foundation is committed to improving the lives of people with diabetes and prediabetes—and to advocating for action.[157] And for good (well, for not so good) reason: Diabetes quadrupled from 108 million in 1980 to 422 million in 2014 and continues to escalate globally at a truly tragic rate. Diabetes is estimated to have caused 106 million deaths in 2016 and is the 7th leading cause of death.[158]

In pursuit of their mission, their founder, Kelly Close, and her team annually host a gathering of diabetes experts—doctors, scientists, advocates, business leaders, policy makers, designers, drug makers, media professionals—in an event known as their dSeries.

In preparation for d19 (2019),[159] we drew on input from 30+ experts in the field. We used their perspectives of the diabetes ecosystem as the cornerstone for the d19 gathering at the St. Francis Hotel in the heart of downtown San Francisco across from Union Square.

Given that this is an annual series of events—and that many participants make recurring annual investments in this innovative event—we needed to be exceptionally thoughtful about how to include the value from prior events—their prior contributions. diaTribe's d18 event included a significant investment in scenario planning—one that yielded rich insight from the more than 50+ leaders who took part that year.

While our Ecosystem Map initially covered 97% of their scenario elements—we had missed one bit—a significant bit: burnout. It was

---

[157] https://diatribe.org/foundation/
[158] https://www.who.int/news-room/fact-sheets/detail/diabetes
[159] https://www.dropbox.com/s/48g5v1hx46i5yfm/d19%20Executive%20Summary.pdf?dl=0

something that, despite our careful expert input and review, eluded us. But it was one that, once called out, everyone recognized as a critical element.

First, let me share just that portion of the diabetes Ecosystem Map as its origin point in the overall map—then point out why it was so impactful throughout the map.

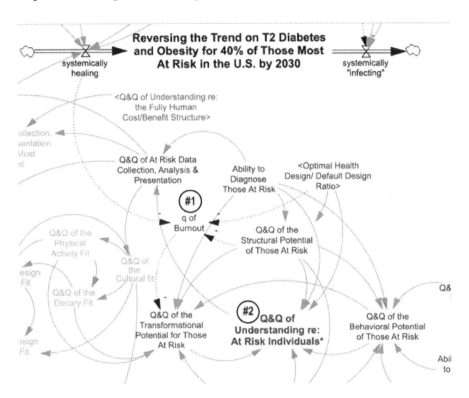

Burnout, near the center @ #1, first occurs in this portion of the map— the portion capturing the larger dynamic of At Risk Individuals (#2)— because those at risk are the ones first exposed to burnout. They continually struggle to overcome the structural design (called out in other sectors of our Integrated Map[160]) our Food Systems, our Mobility Systems, our Behavioral Systems, and even our Built Environment—each of which, in their own way, contribute to obesity and diabetes. (Another instance—as

[160] Yep! There is a video walkthrough (& color version) of this at scottspann.com/impossible. ☺

you'll recall from our 4 fundamental questions in the very beginning of our conversation—of structure determining behavior.)

However, though burdened with burnout, those At Risk are not the only ones who experience burnout in their struggle to stem the tide of diabetes. Others in the system, too, eventually succumb to burnout as the number and severity of those at risk increase and the success rate falls. It is an epidemic—one in slow motion—but an epidemic, nonetheless. These include, per their ecosystem map (relevant portions of which are unveiled below):

- Those seeking to encourage/influence those at risk (#3)

- The medical professionals optimizing health (OH) for those at risk (#4), as well as those using the "default" approach, and

- Those most impacted (TMI) key stakeholders who are supportive of those at risk, including families, employers, and cities (#5).

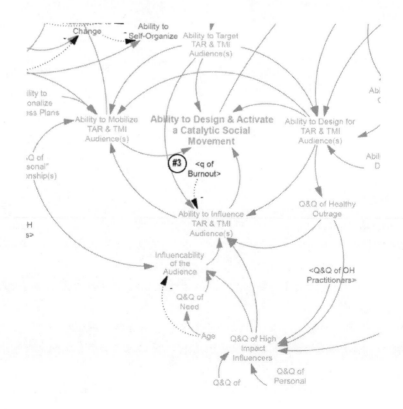

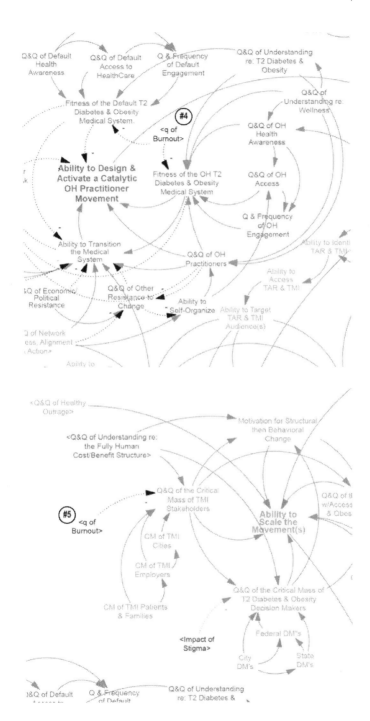

As this application of pre-existing work demonstrates, it can be strikingly valuable to expand the analysis—to the degree that our time and money constraints allow—by making a good faith effort to include broad, deep sources of input. And if we're not able to do so in the initial phase of the work, we can, given a well-designed map, adjust as we continue to learn—part of the emergent nature of working in this way—part of hosting a living, emerging map.

Wow! Congratulations! You made it! That's it, the last of the analyses.

And again, "So what? Now what?" How do we make sense of all this information? How do we convert it from potentially overwhelming information into actionable insight?

Well, in 3 ways:

- An Analysis Summary
- An Analysis Survey
- A Strategy Map

…as follows…

The Analysis Summary(s):

While some systems thinkers ascribe value to just one or another of a preferred analysis, let's not follow that path—for two reasons.

First, for exactly the same reason that some prefer one form of analysis over another, there's clearly value to be gained from each of the analyses. What I find most interesting and informative is contemplating which elements from the map show up over and over again, regardless of which view/analysis we take.

For instance, which show up in 7 out of 7 analyses? Or 6 out of 7? 5 out of 7? What's the finite set of variables that occur most frequently regardless of the specific analysis? Those are clearly elements that we would only ignore at our peril.

To make that as obvious as possible, we compile each of these analyses in a workbook—culminating in an Analysis Summary sheet. This Summary sheet is a 2x2 matrix (see below) whose: 1) vertical axis is an alpha description of the variables that comprise the systems map and 2) horizontal axis represent the various analyses conducted. The final column of the 2x2 is simply a count function. It denotes in how many of the analyses did an individual variable show up as significant— as potentially high leverage. This is then sorted by count (highest to lowest) to pull the strongest candidates to the top of the pile.

The Real World: diaTribe's d19 Analysis Summary

To make this as straightforward as possible, let's continue following diaTribe's process through their 2-day strategy event. Below you'll find their summary, sorted by count.

diaTribe Integrated Ecosystem Map Analysis
Analysis Summary

#	Variable	Leverage	Leverage TTI	Score	Readiness	Trend	Levels	Archetypes	d18 Scenarios	Count	Potentials	15%
9	Ability to Design Food Systems for Optimal Health		2	2	10		20	1	1	6		
10	Q&Q of the Critical Mass of T2 Diabetes & Obesity Decision Makers		3	3	14	8		2	1	6		
19	Ability to Personalize Wellness Plans		16	17	4	3	9		1	6		
25	City DM's	10	8	7		2	10		1	6		
26	Q&Q of Understanding re: At Risk Individuals*	5	12	13	1	1			1	6	5	
3	Ability to Access TAR & TMI		6	8	13	14			1	5		
5	Ability to Design & Activate a Catalytic Social Movement		7	6	18	21	18			5		
12	Ability to Design Political/ Economic Systems for Optimal Health		4	4			4	1	1	5		
17	Ability to Influence TAR & TMI Audience(s)		5	5		25	14		1	5		
18	Q&Q of the Transformational Potential for Those At Risk	14	14	17	9				1	5	5	
11	Ability to Design Mobility/Activty/Exercise Systems for Optimal Health	10	12		12	21				4		
15	Ability to Diagnose Those At Risk	3	15	11	11					4		
16	Q&Q of Emotional, National Security, Environmental & Other Benefits		9	9	9	15				4		
17	Q&Q of RePurposed Funds	13	11	10		27				4	4	
18	Reversing the Trend on T2 Diabetes and Obesity for 40% ...				2	5			1	3		
13	Ability to Design Urban & Rural Built Environment(s) for Optimal Health				5	13	13			3		
14	Q&Q of Existing Costs				8	24			1	3	3	17
15	Q&Q of Personal Influencers (e.g., kids)				4	16			1	3		
16	Q&Q of Default Health Awareness		1	1	10					3		
17	Q&Q of Health Care Costs	7			22				1	3		
6	Ability to Design Behavioral Systems for Optimal Health		15	7	6					3		
7	Q&Q of Network Awareness, Alignment & Action	4			3				1	3		
35	Fitness of the Default T2 Diabetes & Obesity Medical System.		13	16	12					3		
4	Ability to Design & Activate a Catalytic OH Practitioner Movement				20	17				2		

In this case, we conducted 8 analyses, the 8th being integrating their prior d18 scenario planning work. We then sorted them by count. This yielded the following leverage opportunities as follows:

- 5 variables showed up in 6 out of 8 analyses
- 5 showed up in 5 out of 8 analyses
- 4 in 4 out of 8 analyses
- 3 in 3 out of 8 analyses.

And while there were more variables in the 3 out of 8 categories, we purposefully cut off the number considered high leverage at ~15% of the total so that we're in line with the output of the MicMac—wanting to be able to make "apples to apples" comparisons across the analyses.

In total, we've carefully, thoughtfully, rigorously distilled 17 elements out of a total of 113 on the diaTribe ecosystem map. But, as cited early on in this section, the analysis cannot, must not be a "black box"—must not be some "magical" process, opaque to the decision makers or to those ultimately acting on what will eventually become strategic probes. That's been the fate of too many "expert" analyses to date—a major reason so many reports/recommendations end up sitting on shelves gathering dust—eventually either tossed in the recycling bin or relegated to a never to be seen again backup drive.

As a part of the emergent aspect of working in this way, this Summary of feedback from the individuals involved—these 17 elements—become, not the solution, but the basis for a conversation among leaders about what they now, in light of this individual view, believe the true levers to be. This prompts—as you might expect—a lot of curiosity and inquiry about why some elements made it—and some didn't.

It's always vitally important at this point that we remind ourselves that everything in the map is essential—no element would have survived this long if not. Further, if we try to remove any single element at this point in the process, we'll cause quite a ruckus. In response to wondering about which ones made it, I typically return to a metaphor of the human body.

Everything in the body is essential to our well-being. So please don't cut off a big toe as we'll have to learn how to walk and run all over again. However, if you must choose only a handful of elements to absolutely ensure health, please prioritize the brain and the heart.

We bring this stratified count into the Strategy Summit (we'll speak to that near the end of this chapter) to guide our shared discovery and decision-making at this level—to fully understand what rose to the top—and why; to adjust either the map and/or the analysis—consciously—careful to do so in keeping with the principles of systems thinking and system dynamics (never in response to political or ideological or popular pressure).

As an example, let's recall for a moment TNC's Great Lakes Fisheries project cited earlier. Their analysis initially prompted a commotion due to ideological concerns regarding the inclusion of aquaculture as high leverage. Yet to their credit, as we re-examined the map and re-explored the analyses, it became clear that aquaculture was essential to the well-being of the system as a whole—socially, economically, and environmentally. Continuing...

When the time comes to shift from the analysis conversation to decision making, we move to...

An Analysis Survey: continuing with diaTribe's d19

To build off of the Analysis Summary above, let's pick up again with the d19 offsite of 60+ leaders. We'd already aligned: 1) on the integrity of their map, 2) on the validity of their reality-based goal and, following conversation similar to the one described above for TNC, 3) on their Analysis. Still, we needed a way to finalize and align our decision making across all 60+ experts/ leaders in a minimal timeframe. We simply had to move into strategic action planning, especially given our tight, 2-day timeframe.

In the face of such constraints, what has evolved over the years is our ability to resolve this last leg of the analysis trek via a survey that gauges just two things, yielding a third: 1) the number of leaders who select a given lever; 2) the total weight assigned to that lever and, by multiplying these two to simultaneously account for both frequency and potency, 3) a final score for each lever.

To get there, immediately following our Analysis conversation we distribute a color copy of the map and have each leader: 1) circle their (now post-conversation) high leverage variables of choice, 2) record those in the survey, and then 3) have them allocate their finite number of points across their selected variables.

We do so at this point because, if we're to move forward as an aligned effort, we need to ensure that everyone in the room has a chance to weigh in based on the intersection of the systemic and the leadership analyses—and their now collective (via conversation) considerations. Said another way, not creating the forum for both individual analyses (their first one) and collective exploration (this second one) would weaken the chain of our relationship & clarity-building process—we'd have been inclusive and emergent all the way up to this stage then suddenly, at a critical juncture, violated that. But by including this step, our chain is still intact.

Once the survey's complete, we share the compiled results like this (again, borrowing from d19):

d19 Strategic Ecosystem Map Survey Monkey by Score

Element	Total	Points	Score	Combining	Total	Ranking
Ability to Design Food Systems for Optimal Health	34	460	15640	360	16000	1
Ability to Design Political/ Economic Systems for Optimal Health	28	310	8680	1100	9780	2
Ability to Design Urban & Rural Built Environment(s) for Optimal Health	25	240	6000		6000	3
Ability to Design & Activate a Catalytic Social Movement	23	280	6440		6440	4
Q&Q of the Critical Mass of T2 Diabetes & Obesity Decision Makers	23	240	5520		5520	5
Ability to Influence TAR & TMI Audience(s)	21	205	4305		4305	6
Ability to Diagnose Those At Risk	20	190	3800		3800	7
Ability to Design Behavioral Systems for Optimal Health	19	220	4180	675	4855	8
Q&Q of Healthy Outrage	19	185	3515		3515	9
Q&Q of OH Food System Access	18	170	3060	855	3915	10
Impact of Stigma	17	220	3740		3740	11
Ability to Scale the Movement(s)	17	165	2805		2805	12
Ability to Mobilize TAR & TMI Audience(s)	16	195	3120		3120	13
Q&Q of the Critical Mass w/Access to T2 Diabetes & Obesity HealthCar	16	190	3040		3040	14
Ability to Design Mobility/Activty/Exercise Systems for Optimal Health	16	125	2000		2000	15
Q&Q of High Impact Influencers	16	125	2000		2000	16
Q&Q of OH Food System Infrastructure	15	150	2250	225	2475	17
Ability to Design/Structure* Systems for Optimal Health.	14	190	2660	360	3020	18
Ability to Transition the Medical System	14	170	2380		2380	19
Q&Q of OH Food System Profitability	8	90	720	225	945	20

It's rewarding (for me and for the group) to experience just how much this calms the waters of previous conversations about the analysis—just how much convergence emerges via this process, as indicated by the significant breakpoints in the scorring—from 16,000 to 9780 to 6000 and 6440. I think it does so for two reasons.

First, and perhaps most importantly, people really have to think through the map in order to come up with both their first (individual) set of levers—and then, going even deeper, this final set. It's one thing to follow, challenge, modify, and validate the map along the way—a critically important thing, to be sure. But being able to traverse the map on one's own is quite another.

These phases of review demand that one start to internalize the map—at least sufficiently to do this selection process. And this next, deeper, more rigorous step of discovery and scrutiny builds a hardy, more durable resource at the level of each individual leader—a resource they'll need if they're to continue to extract value from their map going forward—as they come to practice what since has come to be called "systems leadership".[161]

The second thing that seems to calm the waters is that, by and large, the groups do align—they do filter a formerly complicated map/list of 100+ variables down to a relative handful of elements to focus on. And the survey illuminates that.

There are typically clear breaks in the data. In this example, an overwhelming 34 leaders selected the top variable—20% more than selected the next highest scoring variable. And as we move down the list, we see a clear shift—a clear break in the list when we drop from 14 to 8, marking diminishing returns on going any deeper.

The reason for this represents a critical understanding about systems and Reality...

...one that's, time and again, overlooked. We're able to align at this level because there is a structure that determines the behavior of our system(s)—a structure we've taken great care to design and build from a 360° set of perspectives—maybe not perfect, but in good faith and to the best of our ability—a structure we've studiously validated with dozens of experts in the field—a structure we've now cross-examined, through a diverse variety of lenses, with a diverse variety of experienced leaders.

---

[161] For more on the intention underpinning "systems leadership," see: https://ssir.org/articles/entry/the_dawn_of_system_leadership

And such structures/systems operate throughout Reality—be they weather systems or hydrological systems or geological systems or…. Our understanding of them may be relatively imprecise, but it's getting/we're getting better—simply because there is a causal structure to Reality. So is it any surprise that we emerge aligned on Reality? (Well, frankly, we usually are surprised—delightfully so, since, when we set out, we were taking on what many believed was an "impossible" problem. ☺)

The Strategy Map: integrating the d19 diabetes Innovation Lab

So we've got a list! Now what?

I don't like lists, especially since Nature is not composed of lists. Life itself is not a list. Everything exists in relation to the whole of Reality.

The final analysis question then is "How are each of these elements, these levers, related to one another?" Well, it turns out that in every case they are. And in the case of d19, that looks like this:

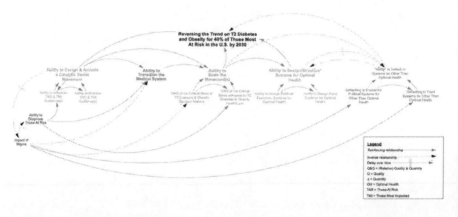

NOW we've got something. Now we can begin to act. This, when combined with the background information in the Map and the Analysis, tells us several things—it answers several questions, including:

- What drives what in our Strategy?
- What do we do first?

- Is there one element that impacts/enables everything else?
- Is one element (relatively speaking) strategically weaker?
- How do we sequence our diverse but interdependent activities?
- What are the criteria for satisfaction for "my" part of the work?
  - i.e., as defined by my downstream "customer's" need relative to our goal
- What impact will my actions (or inactions) have
  - On the organization or the network or the...?

...and so on. From here, it becomes so much clearer how we need to work together as a team, an organization, or an ecosystem to achieve what we've all declared as essential to the well-being of those we're concerned about—whether they be customers or stakeholders or shareholders or....

In this case, it illuminated the relevance of a crucial conversation that surfaced early during the first of our two days as the 60+ leaders exploring the analysis gained deeper clarity. It became clear that the "Impact of Stigma"[162] on the ecosystem was a critical element that impacts us all.

Via the Strategy Map, the strategic pathway also became clear—graspable by us all, as progressing from:

1. Stigma to
2. Social Movement to
3. The Medical System to
4. Scaling the movements to
5. Optimal Health systems to...
6. Then and only then beginning to address those systems that were designed for anything other than optimal health
7. All of which ultimately enables us to achieve our goal—further influencing Those at Risk (TAR) and Those Most Impacted (TMI).

---

[162] Something that originally surfaced in their d16 series

With this as a guiding framework, in addition to the strategy formulation framework we'll explore in a moment, the 60+ leaders at d19 were able to step into our design session the next day with Dennis Boyle (IDEO Co–Founder and Partner) at IDEO'S Pier 28 location on San Francisco's Embarcadero—a session Dennis had carefully crafted to take our strategies to the next level.

The Real World v1.0: Re–Amp's Strategy Map:

I find it encouraging that the Strategy Map is an innovation whose value has only increased over time. It first arose in that early project whose initial struggles prompted Rick Reed of Re–Amp to invite me in. That challenging dynamic forced the reinvention of how this was traditionally done—a simple list of possible intervention points. However, the need to render something much more actionable to the team of 24 that LeeAnn and I had worked with for the past 9 months resulting in the creation of the Strategy Map concept. In their case, after embarking on a process of rigorous mapping, exploration and analysis, their much smaller Strategy Map materialized as…[163]

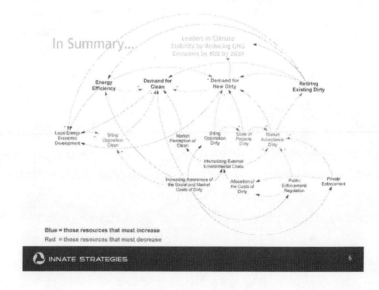

---

[163] Since this is black &white, the "red" arrows are those with a "–" at the arrowhead, blue are those without. Again, see scottspann.com/impossible for a much more legible color version—and the video. ☺

What was extraordinary about this Strategy Map was that it completely reframed and redesigned their strategies of the last 20 years, explaining so much of why they weren't succeeding. Here's part of the story this Strategy Map reveals…

Re-Amp's ability to achieve their goal (at the top of the map) is determined by the four "stocks" just below the goal, a pretty simple math, though only after you've analyzed it. It's the sum of:

- Energy Efficiency
- Demand for Clean (energy)
- Demand for New Dirty (energy)
- Retiring Existing Dirty (energy)

…all elements drawn directly from their map. The other elements below those 4 were the levers that emerged from the Analysis—the 11 actionable items that impacted the 4 stocks—the 11 as the means for activating the 4.

This illustrates how unintended consequences easily, innocently arise. That is, if we're not thinking systemically, the most straightforward way to begin to achieve that goal is (duh!) shut down an existing dirty plant. Doing so would immediately cut GHG output. BUT at the time, the electric utility system was predisposed to building Dirty Energy plants. The policies, incentives, etc., were not yet in place to channel demand toward Energy Efficiency and Clean Energy.

I often use the metaphor of a wild bear when speaking about systems. Both are amoral beasts,[164] doing what they do as a function of their design, their structure—not because of any deliberately malicious intent or evil nature. Bears are not inherently evil. That doesn't mean they can't do significant harm. So if one hits a bear with a stick, we'd

---

[164] I've since begun to seriously question whether or not wild bears and other animals are "amoral". See, for example, the film *Why Dogs Smile & Chimpanzees Cry* (1999) /or Frans de Waal's *Chimpanzee Politics* (2007)—and, especially, Jordan Peterson's work.

better not be surprised about how it reacts. And the same is true with Systems. In our case…

If we *did* somehow manage to shut down a dirty plant, we would have inadvertently caused something much, much worse—that "unintended consequence" thing you hear about. Our beast was preconditioned to build dirty plants because:

- Electric utility operators knew how to run and maintain them
- Manufacturing companies knew how to build their components
- Construction companies knew how to assemble them
- Coal companies knew how to supply the fuel they needed and
- Railroad companies knew how to deliver that coal.

So shutting one down would literally *cause* the building of a New Dirty plant. Then, instead of an old Existing Dirty plant—one with, say, a 5-year remaining useful life—you'd trigger the building of a New Dirty plant with a remaining useful life of 40 years. You'd have made your problem worse by a factor of 8!

And that's assuming you could even shut it down—as doing so would have killed jobs in the local community, something the community's immune system would reject outright.

Instead, the Strategy Map made it clear that:

- You had to first build up:
    - Energy Efficiency and
    - Demand for Clean
- While simultaneously blocking any New Dirty.

Then and only then could you:

- Shut down an Existing Dirty plant
- Now shunting demand
    - Away from New Dirty and on to

- Energy Efficiency and
- Clean Energy…

…as a way of both meeting growing energy demand and replacing lost Dirty jobs with jobs from Energy Efficiency and Clean Energy.

And they did just that. Over the next 5 years, in their 8 Midwestern States, they:

- Stopped any new coal plants in all 8 states
- Passed clean energy legislation in 7
- Catalyzed energy efficiency legislation in 6
- Triggered regulatory decoupling in 4

…and they continue their work today.

By clearly summarizing the analysis via our Strategy Map, we illuminated a crippling dynamic that would have resulted had we failed to formally collaborate across the system. Such a failure to "do the math" only becomes apparent when one maps the system—thereby avoiding "shooting ourselves in the foot".

Reflecting on the above Strategy Map suddenly crystallized one reason so little progress was being made, and it had to do with market forces, i.e., …

Imagine we have a 1000-megawatt system. If we, as an energy efficiency organization, succeed in passing a 10% reduction in energy usage, we now have 900MW of demand in a 1000MW system. So where's the demand for Clean Energy? (Answer: there is none.)

Flip it around. As a Clean Energy organization, we succeed in building a 100MW clean energy plant. We now have 1100MW of capacity in a system with 1000MW's of demand. So where's the demand for Energy Efficiency? (Answer: none.)

So every time our good friend in the Energy Efficiency space succeeded, we (in, say, the Clean Energy space) were inadvertently foiled. Similarly, every time we succeeded, they were thwarted. Go figure! This "duh!" moment only served to reinforce the need to collaborate across organizations and across the system to optimize our outcomes.

Once our Strategy Map is in place, we can now step into the last of the Organizational Level work—the execution level—now designing for strategic action.

The Strategy Summit:

Good news! We're not going to go too deep here, for three reasons.

First, I don't think going beyond the intrinsic framework here will do much good since each engagement at this stage deviates into its own unique language, culture, history, etc. What's much more useful is to understand the purpose and principles that must be achieved if we're to: 1) integrate the work up to this point in a way that continues to build emergent relationship & clarity and 2)come out of this ready to step into action.

Secondly, doing so would immerse you in a level of detail that would actually violate most of my NDAs.

Third, even those that don't violate an NDA, you'd likely find boring—unless you want to practice this yourself. And if that's the case, you'll want the next book, anyway. ☺

That said, I don't want to minimize the significance of this pivotal juncture because this is where we have the opportunity to experience an essential mindset shift. Rather than defaulting to the all-too-common conventional hierarchical governance systems (our habituated pattern), we are now in a realm that is best optimized by way of an emergent, self-organizing network—referring back to the Cynefin framework and Simple, Complicated, and Complex systems.

So in keeping with my promise to make valuable use of your time, let's go ahead and sketch this out…but we won't descend into a real-world case—since it seems that would simply bog us down, and we have quite a way yet to go.

The Purpose of the Strategy Summit:

In so many of these projects, we're asking leaders (or staff or partners or stakeholders or…) to collaborate across a system in ways they've not experienced before, i.e., systemically. When I worked at ARC International (home at various times to Robert Gass, Gary Koyen, Stan Aldrich, Leslie Jaffe, Cliff Mattson, Dennis Stratton, Caroline Fisher, and so many other talented colleagues), a key component in fostering organizational change at that point in our evolving (though not yet emergent) understanding about organizational development was ARC's "5-Box Model".

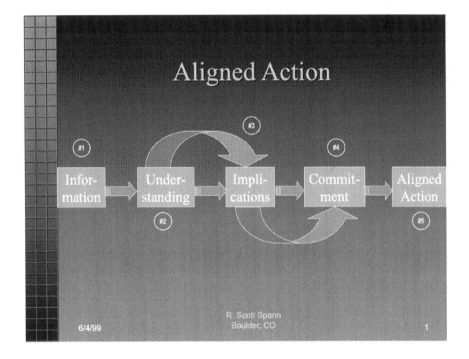

These 5 boxes tell this story…

We too often assume that if we give people information (#1), they'll immediately move into aligned action (#5)—something we still attempt today—something based on typical hierarchy and positional power—assuming that we can simply externally (vs. internally) motivate people. We all know how that goes—not! When that fails…

Oh! "Well," we seem to believe, "they just didn't understand." (#2) So we'll explain it to them and then they'll commit (#4). Nope! While it is a move in the direction of internal motivation, it's a necessary but not sufficient one.

It's not until they've had/we've had a chance to explore the personal and professional implications (#3) of what's being proposed that we can authentically commit—not until we have developed our own sense of informed consent—that the impulse to act moves from outside the individual to inside—that locus of control that endures when external motivation fades.

So while we've evoked many of these implications via the emergent mapping and the map validation process, the purpose of the Strategy Summit is to enable our group of leaders to have an *experience* of those implications that enables them to fully inform their decision based on their own interactions. Therefore, we must enable them to explore four crucial questions:

- What will I be working on?
- Toward what end?
- With whom?
- How?

…all in a way that builds *from* the work we've already done and *toward* the future we're choosing.

TIMEOUT: A temptation…

If we're working with an existing organization—either business or non-profit—I've seen too many organizations step back into their habitual way of getting things done—enlisting only those elements of our practice to date that they perceive as most needed to land a set of systemic strategies with the pre-existing team or teams. In all but rare cases, these "impossible" solutions span the whole eco-system—crossing intra- (even inter-) organizational boundaries—requiring many who've never worked together before (or even met) to collaborate—usually in the form of a network—regardless of their formal, legal structure. Not only that, the Complex-adaptive context/System they're engaging with requires that they operate in radically different ways than ever before— ways that, like any performance sport or activity, require whole new levels of understanding, learning, and most importantly, formal practice. This mindset and behavioral shift requires us to work through the full strategic flow (see below) since omitting any of the key elements results in a disconnect in the experiential weave of Relationship & Clarity critical to success. Said another way, there's a step-by-step logical and felt-sense flow to this paradigm shift that has been distilled and optimized dozens of times down to these essential, critical few. As a result, at this point in the development of the work, we're largely down to that finite set of steps required to pull this off. Given that, I'd encourage you to thoughtfully evaluate each step in the context of both your goal and your team/organization before dismissing any.

Despite that counsel regarding the pivotal, essential nature of this phase, rather than belabor this (given what you already know by now) let's simply lay out the rough framework, enumerating it for clarity's sake—annotating where needed (below)—while leaving aside the usual (though necessary) aspects of session opening, context setting, closing, etc.

The high-level flow goes like this:

1. Final explorations and alignment re our:
   a. Goal
   b. Analysis
   c. Strategy Map

        i. Based on the Analysis Survey selection

    d. Our mindset shift vs. our default behavior/assumptions

2. Moving to Strategizing by:

    a. Assigning ourselves to Teams Based on the Strategy Map & Levers

    b. Developing +RBMTS Goals for each Lever

    c. Developing 3–5 strategies for achieving those Goals

        i. Building on the need for Probes in complexity

3. Shifting toward Systemic Collaboration through:

    a. Cross-pollinating our Strategies

    b. Critiquing our Strategies with Ritual Dissent[165]

    c. Previewing our Refined Team Strategies with one another

4. Committing to our Future via

    a. Rating our Strategies

        i. At the level of the Whole

        ii. At the level of our own Team

    b. Tactical DARCI Charting (see below)

    c. Conducting an overall Reality Check

    d. Choosing to take "1 Next Step"

This caution is largely a repeat of my caveat from the Analysis section about diving too deep into the weeds, as this is a bit technical. Like the Analysis section, I included it because, as I shared above, this is a pivotal part of working in this way—enabling us to translate our accumulated assets of Relationship & Clarity at the various levels (and their

---

[165] This is a specific process that I learned from Dave Snowden's work—one that, when properly constructed, deepens, hones, and integrates strategies both within a Team and across the system/organization/network.

resultant Abilities) into strategic action—to actually cause something to be different in physical Reality. While there may well be clients who can move directly from the Levers into Action, they have been exceptionally rare—too often believing they could make the shift—all too often reverting back to something akin to silos, then falling short. So with that in mind, I've included it here only because it plays such a crucial role that leaving it out would have given rise to another hole in our flow here—especially for those who want to more thoroughly understand how we initiate the needed mindset shift from Strategy into Action. So feel free to head over to Chapter 5, the Level of the Market and scalability…

Okay, since you're still here…

In the spirit of being deliberately sparse, I'm going to assume that the first few elements (1a–c) are clear by now. So let's jump to…

Mindset shift vs. Behavior (1d):

Something really interesting begins to show up at 1d—our mindset shift vs. our default behavior/assumptions. Once we've all re-examined and reinforced our alignment with our Goal, with our Analysis and with our Strategy Map, we now need to re-anchor ourselves in and re-inhabit the emotional/energetic state prompted by the mindset shift that occurred in our BOT (behavior over time) session. If we're to be truly innovative over the next (typically) two days, we need to reinhabit our "1 word" for the state of being we need to inhabit to close that BOT gap we discovered—that gap between what was likely to happen (if nothing fundamentally changed) and what MUST happen if our goal is to survive—much less, thrive.

So we do two things: 1) declare an intention about the step-change in the state of being that we need to inhabit beginning NOW and 2) test our intentions/shift via a brief, usually playful exercise, known as Red/Black. Bottom line, over two decades—in all but two episodes of this exercise—though leaders have clearly declared how they'll behave from now on, they immediately DON'T do any of those much-needed behavioral shifts. For example, over the brief course of the exercise, they don't keep an open mind, don't listen, don't take risks, be strategic, practice inclusion, innovate, etc. We suddenly discover that the #1 obstacle to our own success is, well, I think Pogo says it best…

Though we authentically *want* to behave in a new way, our habituated (too-often implicit, unconscious, and automatic) assumptions (and corresponding behaviors) about how our world works box us in— causing us to revert to our default settings— the very settings that got us here in the first place. Confronting this when we debrief the exercise—and our individual and collective performance—then sets the tone for catching and correcting ourselves as we go forward. For many, this realization persists, not just over the next two days, but beyond—even for Life as they are startled into a new level of awareness.

Moving into Strategizing (2):

As for #2, in the spirit of self-organizing and in order to scale (coming up next in Chapter 5), we'll need to begin to make our own decisions and take our own actions. While this began with the choices we made in the Analysis Survey, we continue to develop self-organization here by (in those cases where that makes sense) self-assigning to teams. There are many cases in which pre-assignments ensure that critically needed expertise shows up in the right place. And in others, our organizations have already assigned us based on our expertise and interest—via our jobs. Regardless, we absolutely *must* ensure that each team has at least one subject matter expert to safeguard the team from getting too far off track—too far out of alignment with Reality.

Once participants are in their teams, we use a tightly scripted and timed agenda along with behavioral rulesets to guide them in developing their own positive, measurable, and time-specific goals as the basis for formulating strategies for each goal. They generate several potential strategies/probes (in line with the Cynefin understandings) from which to eventually select one— while retaining the rest to later consider as potential future probes. These rulesets have the added advantage of helping teams begin to transition their regular interactions to greater levels of creativity and efficiency and, therefore, satisfaction—qualities essential to moving with speed relative to both the magnitude and sense of urgency of their goal.

Injecting Networked Collaboration: Cross–pollinating (3a)

Once we have several potential strategies available, we introduce the 30 to 40 to 60 or more leaders in the room to one of several cross-pollination/network optimization processes. Given that the room/group as a whole is attempting to simultaneously affect a whole system, we need to function much more like a network than we typically do in the kinds of conventional siloed hierarchies most of us have grown up in. The first process is one introduced to me by Matt and Gail Taylor[166] —

---

[166] I first read about Matt & Gail Taylor here (https://www.fastcompany.com/32920/group-genius). Little did I know that, years later, I'd have the opportunity to actually lead a project with them at the Noetics Institute.

one they modeled on Stuart Kauffman's understanding about optimizing information flow in a network. Kauffman[167] was able to demonstrate mathematically that, in order to ensure the optimal, just-in-time flow of information throughout a network, you're much better off randomly distributing that information in small bursts across the system (vs. the all-too-common all-hands-meeting delivery of a mass of information at once). This process also aligns with the optimal behavior in complex systems—where low amplitude, high frequency interactions (see below) function much better in environments with high rates of change—where high-amplitude, low-frequency interactions often fail.

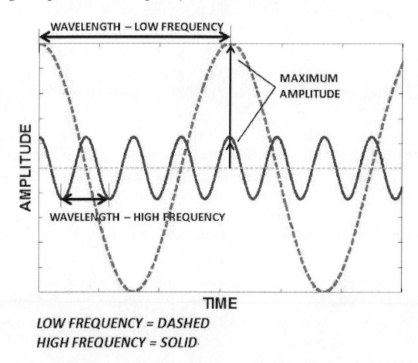

LOW FREQUENCY = DASHED
HIGH FREQUENCY = SOLID

Interestingly, interactions that follow the low amplitude, high frequency patterns (the solid wave) operate much more in line with the way that Nature or the human body behaves. The dashed wave is reminiscent of

---

[167] Kauffman, Stuart, *At Home in the Universe*, 1995.

the old Soviet planning days (Gosplan), with the first pattern ensuring a much tighter fit with Reality—the second inevitably leaving us vulnerable to drifting quickly out of touch with a dynamic Reality.

In keeping with these insights, we randomly assign each of the members in the room to brief, 5-minute exchanges with each other, during which time they swap information about what most "excites" and most "scares" them (feel free to choose your own prompts) about what's arising in our work together. After two or three rounds of this—with randomly different individuals—they return to their teams with a much better understanding of what's emerging across the system as a whole.

TIMEOUT: Imagine momentum...

So now imagine this: In this 2-day deep dive, you have a lever-age point, one you know will make a significant impact on shifting your system in the direction you need it to go. You have a team. You and your team have a positive, measurable, time-specific goal. You have several potential strategies for achieving your goal. And you and your team members have now had an aggregate of some-where between 15–20 random conversations with members from other teams across the system—enriching your awareness about what's becoming visible to the rest of the system/network/organi-zation. And to take it several steps further, each of the other teams is experiencing the same thing. As a result, if we're thoughtfully tending to this building momentum, we're doing so in a way that moves us ever closer to Csíkszentmihályi's Flow state.

Equipped with this, back in our teams, we choose a single strategy to focus on—retaining the rest for possible future reference—and/or for additional probes. We then flesh out that one strategy to include: specific phases of work, interdependencies, stakeholders, and timing—making sure that we have a clear enough description that we can readily communicate our strategy with our partners in the other teams via our next cross-pollination process…

Critiquing our Strategies with Ritual Dissent (3b):

Ritual dissent is a process developed by Dave Snowden—one of several things I learned from Dave for which I am continually grateful. Basically, every team sends each of their representatives to every other team. For example, at Team 1's table (the host) are reps (the guests) from, Teams 2, 3, 4, and 5. At Team 2's table, reps from 1, 3, 4, and 5. And so on. This fully cross-pollinates strategic representation from across the system.

The guests then first listen, uninterrupted, for 5 minutes to the host team's strategy. Then without comment from the presenter/host—in a conversation among just the "listeners"/guests—they critique that team's strategy via a rigorous, no-holds-barred exchange of ideas about the pluses, minuses, omissions, and additions that would ensure each strategy's fitness with the system as a whole. And they do so from the perspectives of their own strategies—the ones emerging from each of their own teams— implicitly weaving each of their own strategies into their feedback to the host. While I'm tempted to share more details here, that's dipping a bit too deep into the "how to".[168] Bottom line, the ROI on this process is remarkable—often cited as one of the group's highest value, most generative activities.

Previewing our Team Strategies with one another (3c):

We're now ready to preview our strategies with all of the other teams. What's critically important at this juncture is that we are listening to each strategy as we simultaneously hold in our mind's eye the global goal for our system as a whole. Fundamentally, we're doing conceptual, strategic math in our heads—i.e., we're listening to each strategy asking ourselves whether or not the integration of our strategies will,

---

[168] If you'd like to know how I use Ritual Dissent, feel free to reach out and I'll share the video and instruction set.

in sum and as a whole, enable us to get onto the path toward the accomplishment of our goal—or not. We stress "onto the path" here as we don't expect, in a 2-day offsite, to come up with the final, fleshed-out, step-by-step strategy—just enough to know that we're on the right track at the right order of magnitude. Fleshing it out will happen next in our "1 next step" (below).

Rating our Strategies (4a):

To test the soundness of our strategies, when all presentations are complete, I'll ask the room as a whole, "On a scale of 1–10, how confident are you that, if we successfully engage in these strategies, we will place ourselves firmly on the path toward accomplishing our goal?" We then take the information inherent in that rating back to our teams, ask ourselves that same question at our own team level, adjusting our own team's strategies accordingly. I deliberately don't ask the team-level question in front of the room as a whole because the last thing we want to do is shame individual teams, something that would be completely counterproductive and in violation of the spirit of the Appreciative Inquiry/Positive Deviance patterns we've been establishing from the beginning, and the essential efforts to continually build relationship.

DARCI Charting (4b):

The final step in this experience of exploring "what would it be like" together is to reduce our strategies down to the level of a DARCI[169] (or, if you prefer, RACI) chart. For those of you not yet familiar with it, DARCI stands for who is to be:

- **The Decider**—with whom does the ultimate authority lie
- **Accountable**—the one who tracks/counts actions being taken
- **Responsible**—those who will primarily cause/take action

---

[169] Again, I'm indebted to my longtime friend (one time colleague) Robert Gass for his evolution of the RACI chart; search "DARCI chart" and his name for more.

- **Consulted**—those whose feedback we seek prior to taking action
- **Informed**—those with whom we share information after action.

It takes this level of granularity—of getting right down on the ground into the experience of who specifically is doing what in the context of our lever, our lever's goal, and our strategy—in order for each of us to: 1) be in relationship with both our overall process and our teammates and 2) craft the needed clarity about what our relationship & clarity can produce, and, role by role, how.

Our Reality Check (4c):

It's only at this point, when we've actually written down (in the DARCI chart) what the work will look like, that we're able to switch modalities and ask ourselves how we really *feel* about what we've created—about our potential. This inquiry into our felt sense is an attempt to bring in anything that we might have missed—creating space for us to tap into our intuition. Why intuition? Throughout this process, we've been excruciatingly logical and rational—citing the "math" when building maps, asking for facts versus opinions, being very explicit about what causes what. Now it's time to step back and go a bit deeper on by inquiring about our confidence, i.e.,: "On a scale of 1 to 10, how confident am I that, if we successfully execute on what we've laid out here, that it will put us on the path to achieving our goal?" And we permission much-needed dissention by adding *"Or is something missing?"*

It's absolutely vital that we create this opening for whatever we may have missed. I've lost count of the number of times that people weren't "in" on our process/product until we did this. Though they often weren't consciously aware of it, there was some part of them that was holding back—that couldn't commit fully—because something unspoken was distracting them, diverting their complete intention and energy. This prompt awakens that "something" and brings it to the surface.

Briefly (again, no "how to" here), for anyone whose number is below an 8, we ask, "What would it take to move your number from (say) a 3 toward an 8, 9 or 10?" And we keep asking until we've exhausted their list—gotten to at least an 8. Often they call out something that takes them (and others in the group) all the way to 10. And we treat each of their issues/items as just as legitimate as any task—as anything else we're tracking—maintaining and managing this list just as we manage the strategies and DARCI charts.

By the time we're done, we have everyone up to an 8, 9 or 10. And again, speaking to the critical nature of this step, I've lost track of the number of times that people have said they weren't committed to this project/process until we did this exercise—only because they knew there was something missing, something they simply couldn't put their finger on—until now.

Choosing "1 Next Step" (4d):

In the spirit of emergence—and Conversant's Cycle of Value (Align, Act, Adjust)—it's at this moment in time (and it is a critical moment) that we ask, "Are you willing to take 1 next step?"

TIMEOUT: What's with just "1 next step"

This is another aspect of that mindset shift we're going for here—one grounded in the Reality (yes, that again) of: 1) working in complex-adaptive systems with 2) what it means to fully human. Regarding the former, we know from the Cynefin perspective that each of our actions (as in the trauma world) is a probe. Further, that when we probe, we need to *sense* the impact of that probe before we form a *response*.

This also corresponds with Conversant's Cycle of Value—the Align, Act, Adjust mantra—noting that the Adjust cycle is the one most often ignored—except in the life-and-death world of the military with their after-action reviews. So thinking in one-step-at-a-time terms encourages us to tend to this critical Adjust element—one that acknowledges the dynamic complexity of our world—that when we act, our world reacts.

As for the latter—what it means to be fully human—I'm appreciative of David Allen's[170] contribution here in his GTD process that optimizes getting things done (GTD) by having clients call out just the 1 next step for moving a project forward—an implicit acknowledgement of both the complexity of our world and the tendency for overwhelm when confronting it.

The first time in my career that I asked this 1-10 confidence question, I was admittedly, and understandably, a bit tense. We (my partner, clients, and I) had no idea what the answer would be. Though we had designed a process that would position each leader in the room to make an informed decision (back to that informed consent of the 5-Box model), we were handing the fate of this venture over to this diverse assemblage of organizations who may or may not choose to move ahead (we were, hopefully, building a network in this case—not working within an existing organization).

Now, while some may feel that this doesn't apply to a business, I'd ask you to re-think/re-feel that assumption. If we truly want/need our people to be internally motivated—to align, act, and adjust as part of a systemically informed and integrated venture, we need to know if they feel personally, individually ready, or not.

Continuing…

So this feels like quite a risk. But it is an unavoidable, even essential, risk. If we're to have a truly emergent, self-organizing response to our "impossible", complex issue/opportunity, we have to create the initial conditions that empower people to make good decisions and, well, let *them* decide!

In that first example cited above, I thought (and felt) that we'd given every leader in the room both the information (the cognitive)

---

[170] Allen, David, *Getting Things Done*, Penguin Books, 2001.

and experiences (the felt sense) they needed to achieve the levels of relationship & clarity required to make their informed decision. Still…?

When we do this, it's important to specifically remind ourselves—and, especially, the group—that we've:

- Interviewed a 360°set of credible, knowledgeable, and influential leaders
- Modeled each of their worldviews as small systems
- Combined those into an integrated map of our system as a whole
- Crafted a reality-based, positive, measurable, time-specific goal
- Analyzed our map, extracting the relative handful of key levers
- Integrated those into our Strategy Map
- Emerged from our Strategy Summit as working teams possessing the alignment we need to work our Levers, including:
  - Positive, reality-based, measurable, time-specific goal(s) both overall and for each Lever/Team
  - Strategies well-vetted and cross-pollinated
  - Reality checks of our strategies closing any gaps
  - DARCI charts…

…at which time we can ask,

"Show of hands, how many of us are ready to take just 1 next step?" …and then just wait.

Invariably—always surprisingly—the room is ready, and the hands shoot up. Over the years, we've had less than a handful of people who weren't yet ready to move forward, folks we don't press in this moment as we don't want to bring too much group pressure to bear on an individual (there's enough of that already). Though we do follow up afterward, offline—continuing to more deeply understand what we're not seeing/hearing—continuing to deepen Relationship & Clarity. We truly need to know what's missing for them if we're to continue to evolve our 360° view of Reality.

And that one next step is to engage in a 1–day meeting to explore what it would be like to begin to scale—to ramp up to be able to meet the needs of the market or constituency or beneficiaries or whatever your chosen audience/cause is.

TIMEOUT: A well-designed, emergent "Accident"

To be clear, we don't enter into the Strategy Summit with the intention that what emerge will be THE strategies to put immediately into practice. This is designed simply to give people the experience of working in this way—with others, with a shared purpose, from a shared view of Reality. However, once people allow themselves to relax into experimenting with this way of working, they inevitably emerge with plans that they later choose to execute. (More on that in the next chapter.)

So even though Reality needs us to align and agree to take at least one next step, we can't/don't force it. We let it arise of its own accord, and we're never quite sure where it will end up. So though I call "where" we end up almost accidental—"almost" as most leaders are quite uncomfortable with the loss of control that accompanies emergence. That aside, *that* we wind up here isn't. As we'll discover in the chapter on Possible, we, as humans, are specifically designed—developmentally and "divinely" by 3.5 billion years of evolution[171]—to end up here.

Internalization: 2 Takeaways

Given the depth we, as a group, have gone to to get here, it's likely clear that much of this—unless you really want to make a practice of this—falls into that well-worn warning "trained professionals, don't try

---

[171] I'm indebted here to Jordan Peterson's work and that of Iain McGilchrist.

this at home" realm. Still, you may need to move forward immediately on your own. In that case, there are two things from this level that I'd recommend—one from the Analysis, the other from the Strategy Summit.

While most of the Analysis requires study, practice, and experience (this is as much art as science/math), if you can only do one thing to continue to develop your needed Relationship & Clarity, I would suggest the Leadership Leverage Identification dimension as the means for at least initially selecting your Levers. It will establish a basis for your own rich exploratory conversation. I offer this one because, eventually, you and your team will need to individually and collectively Align (ala Conversant's Cycle of Value) on how to solve your complex issue/opportunity. Rallying around the Levers that arise from there, you can get into Action—probing your complex-adaptive system, converting that learning into Adjusting as the basis for re–Aligning and repeating. After all, we only truly learn when we Act—more precisely, when we interact with Reality. That has been the basis of the evolution of our scientific and technical development: hypothesize, test, learn, repeat.

Speaking of the importance of getting into Action, the one takeaway from the Strategy Summit that you may not already be practicing is that of +RBMTS Goals for each Lever at the Team level—goals whose collective, integrated math at least approximates your overall +RBMTSGoal. So once you've Aligned on your Levers as an Organization—rigorously designing each Team's goals for each lever—you need to test your math. That is, ask yourself, "If each Team were to achieve their goal, would that add up to our overall goal?" Doing so aligns with John Doerr's aforementioned *Measure What Matters* (2018) and the stratagem implicit in his OKRs (objectives and key results), reflecting both the qualitative and quantitative aspects comprising any truly powerful goal.

These two practices—and the principles they embody—though not perfect, will put you in a far better position systemically to harness your own complex, wicked problem than will most of the contemporary approaches. Done rigorously, they will position that shift in mindset so essential to your, your team's, and your enterprise's success.

Regardless of how you arrive at this point—whether with the full portfolio of principles, practices, and processes or simply those most ready to hand—you'll now need to scale.

Chapter 5: At the Level of the Market

Market Relationship x Market Clarity = Scalability

Okay. Remember that mindset shift we talked about in our first 20 pages or so? Well, we're here—or, rather, it's here.

Actively Weaving Relationship & Clarity...

Now we're in/you're in new territory. Here's where we'll be riding the leading edge of working in this way—surfing an emerging wave—one that requires present-moment awareness, alignment, and action (and conscious, rigorous adjustment)—at the levels of the organization, the team, and the individual—simultaneously weaving Relationship & Clarity together (in recognition of their real-world interdependence) in service to the market. Holding that metaphor in mind—much like a surfer, their board, and the wave merge—so, too, do Relationship & Clarity at the level of the Market need to merge—need to be recognized as the two sides of the same coin that they are. It's here that the aspiration for the Flow we're capable of (like any high–performance athlete) needs to take hold.

And *if there's a place that this way of working can break, it's here*. So, we need to get this right.

Market and Scalability

So two bits here: market and scalability.

First, I use the term "market" as a useful way to think about "for the sake of whom" (or what) do we do what we do—whether you're leading a corporation, a non-profit, a government agency—whatever. I find it useful because the marketing world, especially the sophisticated marketers of today, are well-grounded in the science of what it means to be human—what motivates us, what we find meaningful and/or compelling, and what we don't—responses hardwired into our nervous systems based on 3.5 billion years of evolution[172]. So if we want to scale—if we want to serve a broad audience of beneficiaries for whatever we're about—a product, a service, a cause—we need to understand how people operate at scale. Which leads us to…

Second, scalability. For each of the literally hundreds of leaders I've worked with, their Reality has been that they simply MUST harness their complex issue or opportunity *at scale*, whether that's the scale of the organization or the community or the ecosystem or even society.

And that's one hell of a challenge for us—principally because the majority of us have grown up in and been acculturated to conventional hierarchical systems (whether in our families, our schools, our workplaces, our governments…)—hierarchies that don't scale well in complex-adaptive environments, for reasons we explored in Dave's Cynefin model. And if we recall the contexts we explored early on, i.e.

- The state of Reality—current vs. needed
- The exponential rate of emergence of complex issues/opportunities—relative to our ability to solve them
- The increasing divergence of destruction (or loss or need or demand)—relative to regeneration (or gain or satisfaction or supply)

---

[172] See the work of both Jordan Peterson and Robert Cialdini (below) for more here.

- The nature of complex systems—vs. simple or even complicated
- The need to evolve—our mindset/paradigm shift…

…each/all of these speak to the need to be able to scale: ***what*** we do at an individual project level—but given the challenges we face—***how*** we do work at all.

This is the leading edge of working in this way—the leading edge of how we will move beyond the limitations we've imposed on ourselves—having been schooled primarily in Simple and Complicated systems (borrowing from the Cynefin model as a way to frame this part of our conversation). These are limitations we must move beyond if we're to solve the "impossible" issues/opportunities confronting us today.

Our need to operate at scale simply mirrors the fact that these issues themselves operate at scale. They include issues like climate change and scaling renewables & energy efficiency; structural income and wealth inequity; scaling future-relevant education and thriving-wage jobs; homelessness and scaling affordable housing; racism and scaling inclusion (i.e., as a part of economic growth); xenophobia and scaling mutually beneficial immigration: to say nothing of the need to innovatively respond, again, at scale, to human trafficking, political oppression and so many—too many—others. And they also include the social, environmental, and economic opportunities that arise for us as a society and as a species as we resolve them—vs. allowing them to persist. Can any of us realistically imagine a conventional hierarchy—a corporation, a government, a religious movement, a non-profit organization—capable of dealing with these issues? I think the telling question for us is, "How's that working for you?" to which the answer is inevitably "It's not!"

Yes, those institutions must be involved—must be aligned, too. But as we can see through the lens of Complexity—that lens of an ever-increasing pace and scale of change—we must, ourselves, learn to self-organize and self-manage.

TIMEOUT: In Defense of Hierarchy

I do not mean to say that hierarchies do not, nor should not, exist, btw. They very much do—and they are, in fact, essential to Life—as Jordan Peterson makes clear in *12 Rules for Life*.[173] Hierarchies have been around in animal nervous systems for at least 300 million years and account, at least in part, for the continued evolution of life itself. They exist—and must exist, socially, too—simply in their healthy form.

What I'm seeking to call out and address is the operational framework represented by conventional hierarchy and its tendency to become dominated by power or ego vs. the Reality of, well, Reality—be that the Reality of the challenge before us—or the Reality of meritocracy, of those most capable of doing the properly skilled work—the work that needs doing if we are to engage in healthy social, environmental, and economic development.

Said another way, hierarchies based on personalities and/or simple positional power (vs. Reality and/or meritocracy) are too easily corrupted by individuals overly concerned with self (yes, little "s" self)—vs. focusing on Self and Its continued development in the presence of what Reality confronts us with. Or, perhaps better said, the Reality(s) we choose to confront. In a healthy hierarchy, we're aligning our organizations—and the actors therein—relative to the hierarchy of a systemically sound (or as sound as we can muster) response to Reality. And, from there, populating and organizing the structure and function of our response (be it a company or an NGO or a network or...) to better mirror—better fit—with Reality in both its structure and its level of expertise.

So the trick here is our ability to evolve out of personality/power hierarchies into Reality-responsive hierarchies—responsive to: 1) the Reality of what it means to be fully (i.e., healthy) Human 2) in the presence of the World we've caused/co–created—such that the two come into alignment so that our ways of organizing are a strategic and operational fit with those Realities. Continuing...

---

[173] See https://www.youtube.com/watch?v=ViGdjc08Vt4&ab_channel=Bite-sizedPhilosophy or simply search "Jordan Peterson hierarchy."

Because of the need to engage in hierarchies based on the Reality of the work or our purpose or Reality—vs. hierarchies based solely on favoritism or power—this step-change—this evolution to self-organization/management—represents the most significant mindset/paradigm shift we face in working this way. And though I said it at the start of this chapter, it bears repeating: _If there's a place where working in this way breaks, it's here._ This is where we simply must change our lifelong habit of asking "Who's in charge?", lose our permission-seeking assumptions about dysfunctional (vs. functional) rules—most of which really don't exist—the whole point of the Red/Black exercise in the Strategy Summit—i.e., to lift the veil on the dysfunctional. Even the Taoists see this as counterproductivity[174]—this conformity to overly restrictive social conventions about what normal is and/or arguing about who's the "decider" (it's Reality, btw). Continuing to do what's normal isn't going to cut it.

Normal is what we've been doing all along. In our context, normal is the lowermost of those two diverging lines from our context conversations early on—the one that gives us the false impression that we're making progress—when we're actually losing ground relative to increasing destruction, loss, and need.

That said, we can't simply (remember, oversimplifying complexity drives us into Chaos) abandon what we've created to date. Nor can we oversimplify and risk a descent into chaos. We must transcend while including the most valuable aspects of where we've been. There is no "off" switch for today's world and an "on" switch for tomorrow's. We must transition from where we are to where we need to be—that is if we're to avoid massive disruption, destruction, and pain. In fact, it's our responsibility to ensure, to the degree possible, such a transition.

---

[174] Eva Wong, _Taoism: An Essential Guide_, Shambala, 2011.

Luckily, there are places to look to help us figure that out, figure out how to adapt, even how we must evolve as social beings—how we must learn to self-organize/manage. While I'll give some specific examples in a bit, they include paradigms from Nature,[175] the Military,[176] Architecture,[177] Science,[178] Ethology,[179] Business,[180] Complexity Theory[181] emerging management operating systems (in the text below), the Internet, network theory,[182] and more.

Again, wanting to safeguard your time here—and since each of these represents whole books and/or bodies of knowledge in and of themselves—I'll refer you to the footnotes so we can focus on how this applies to you and your "impossible" challenge in this/our context here.

Because it can break here, this is where we want to be particularly thoughtful—and particularly clear. We need to explore this together in the spirit that I suggested way back at the beginning of this book in the section entitled "Our Conversation". There I suggested that we each "need to gauge this for ourselves—to decide whether or not one should adopt, even embody, this work." That particularly holds true if one is to realize—even internalize—this aspect of mindset shift for themselves.

---

[175] Two sample sources here: Janine Benyus' Biomimicry is one—based on a practice that learns from and mimics the strategies found in nature to solve human design challenges; another is Elisabet Sarhouris—an evolutionary biologist who applies the lessons of Life's evolution to provide social, political, and economic solutions to our current challenges.

[176] General Stanley McChrystal's *Team of Teams: New Rules of Engagement for a Complex World* (2015) is an excellent real–world study on how the Special Forces had to abandon conventional tactics to create a scalable network capable of responding to Al Qaeda in Iraq—even touching on how NASA used such practices to put a man on the Moon.

[177] Christopher Alexander's *A Pattern Language*—we'll touch on later.

[178] Similarly, we'll touch on Stephen Wolfram's controversial *A New Kind of Science* later.

[179] See, in particular, Frans de Waal's *Chimpanzee Politics: Power and Sex Among Apes* (2000)— stunningly cautionary tale about everyday behaviors we see in many Human workplaces.

[180] See, for example, Collins & Porras' *Built to Last* (1994) and John Doerr's *Measure What Matters* (2018).

[181] Axelrod, Robert, *The Complexity of Cooperation: Agent-Based Models of Competition and Collaboration*, Princeton University Press (August 18, 1997).

[182] See Stuart Kauffman's *At Home in the Universe: The Search for the Laws of Self-Organization and Complexity* (1996).

To make the landscape of this shared exploration as distinct as possible, we'll examine it through the lenses of:

- Why this shift?
- What shift?
- How this shift?

So why this shift?

There are two dimensions to the "why" of this shift. One is reflective of *what it means to align with Reality*—the other reflective of *what it means to align with being fully Human.*

Reality & the Shift

We don't need to spend much time here, as we largely covered this early on when we contemplated both initial conditions and contexts. Drawing on that bit of our conversation, I'll quickly visually remind us of:

Our gap...

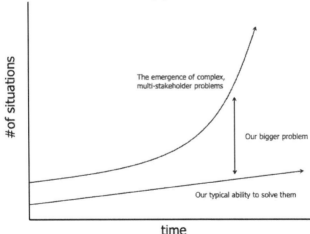

A fundamental hypothesis

…i.e., our emergence of issues/opportunities is exponentially outstripping our conventional ability to solve them. This is bad enough when a single dimension of our experience (as if anything exists in isolation) is impacted, e.g., the economy. It becomes abruptly and often catastrophically apparent when two or more dimensions of our experience collide, as with our COVID-19 pandemic impacting our healthcare systems and our economies—and inflaming our political systems, as but one example.

Something's fundamentally broken…

Something's fundamentally broken…

destruction, loss, demand, need…

regeneration, gain, supply, fulfillment…

…both
our What & our How

…i.e., our partial progress (that bottom line) misleads us to perceive/believe that we're becoming more successful (given that we *are* progressing in absolute terms) when, in relative terms (relative to our need—that top line), we're continuing to fall behind—self-generating a greater and greater gap.

The obvious legitimacy of these dynamics calls into sharp relief just how badly out of alignment with Reality we are with our current approaches to solving wicked problems in our increasingly complex world. Not only does "what" we're seeking need to shift radically (i.e., our +RBMTSGoals), but our radical shift must include our "how"—how we do what we do.

The adaptive Cynefin Framework

We dove deep on this early on. Its relevance here—as we've modified it—is the distinction it calls out between hierarchies and self-organizing/managing organizations. So let's refresh our memory with that quick visual.

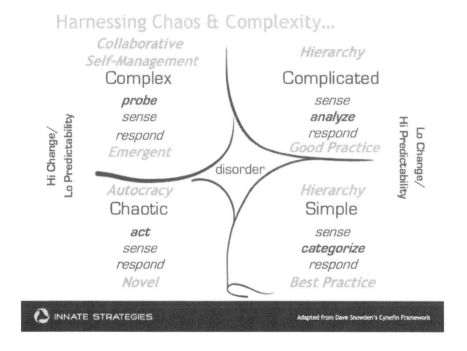

...i.e., as our World's rates of change continue to increase—while corresponding predictability continues to decrease, our complex systems call for emergent solutions and self-organizing/managing governance models with near real-time response times—vs. the delays inherent in most human hierarchies.

There's something here you may have noted (or questioned) up front when we first introduced the insights from the Cynefin framework.

When I first encountered Dave Snowden and trained with him, I was deeply concerned that—by employing cause-and-effect systems thinking/dynamics models (which reside in that Complicated quadrant),I had somehow unknowingly done harm to my clients—given that the solutions are emergent—lying in that Complex quadrant. Yet at the same time, I was struggling to understand how, despite such reliance on the Complicated maps, this way of working had done so much good—had enabled diverse, conflicted groups to solve their most intractable problems—even had a stickiness such that many of these groups are still engaged and operating today based on the source product, even years later.

Then it struck me! And in a way that's consistent with our "Fundamental hypothesis" and our "Something's Fundamentally Broken" learnings.

We're actually using all 4 quadrants, as follows:

Every situation I've been brought into is actually in Chaos. It's just that the time span over which we're experiencing the Chaos is long enough that we don't sense it in the same way that we do a hurricane or forest fire or COVID-19. So we don't register it as Chaos. Still, when viewed from the perspective of those two diverging lines, we're clearly in slow-motion Chaos, that of destruction, loss, etc.

So our actual progression through the Cynefin landscape moves from:

1. The Chaos of our presenting circumstance
2. to Complicated (the map *is* a complicated rendering of the chaos)
3. to Simple (via the Levers unveiled with our Analysis)
4. as a way of re-enlivening the Complex ecosystem as we launch our Probes and begin the process of reestablishing its Adaptive capability, illustrated as...

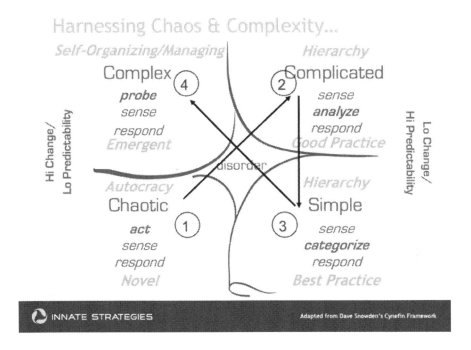

This is also completely aligned with how somatically oriented trauma resolution occurs—grossly oversimplifying here to make the point:

1. The client's presenting condition is experienced as Chaos in their life

2. We go through the Complicated phase of doing a trauma intake/inventory of all the possible traumatic events in their life to date

3. The Simple stage involves choosing the most likely event as an entry point (a Lever)

4. as the means for Probing the Complex-ity of their nervous system and consciousness in order to re-establish their ability to Adapt—both to the source trauma(s) and to the challenges of their world going forward.

Holding these three perspectives in mind (our Fundamental Hypothesis, Something's Fundamentally Broken, and the Cynefin progression) and viewing this from a meta-perspective, Reality is our ultimate change agent—regardless of our ideologies about how we wish the World should or would behave.

Just reflect for a moment on climate change, immigration, pandemics, fisheries collapse, population growth, deforestation, etc. If our responses do not in some way mirror our Reality—are not reflective of and responsive to it—we will fail. This again brings into play Ashby's Law of Requisite Variety: "In order to deal properly with the diversity of problems the world throws at [us], [we] need to have a repertoire of responses which is (at least) as nuanced as the problems [we] face."[183]

This problem statement is incredibly illuminating in that it forces us to look (again) at the "math" of the "what" and "how" of our situation. That is, if we're engaged with a reality that exhibits relatively low rates of change and high levels of predictability, then the math of the fit between reality and conventional hierarchy can be sufficiently "tight"—perhaps not optimal (see "Humanity & the Shift" next), but relatively tight.

If, on the other hand, the reverse is true—if reality is expressing relatively high rates of change and low levels of predictability, then the better fit is via a self-organizing/managing system—assuming comparable levels of competency—where more of humanity's innate traits (see the next section) can be activated and brought to bear.

Being fully Human and the Shift

One of the things we've not seriously delved into here is one of the (if not THE) primary reasons that this approach has been so consistently successful. This work expressly (though often implicitly vs. explicitly) relies on understanding what it means to be Human, how we're designed to function—e.g., our innate developmental pathways—those

---

[183] http://requisitevariety.co.uk/what-is-requisite-variety/

hardwired into us over 3.5 billion years of evolution. Hence, the significance of the word "Evolutionary" in the title.

Though I'm most often referred to as the "mapping" guy, I didn't start out that way—nor is it why I do what I do. I came back into the business/organizational world from the "human" angle—drawing on my skills/experience in trauma, developmental, and group psychotherapy—intrigued by what's possible when we recover our innately human instincts and abilities—when we're functioning more in alignment with our design intent.

Because of that aspect of my background, I initially focused on leadership development and cultural change—especially in the world of F100 mergers and acquisitions. I turned to systems thinking/dynamics when it became apparent that the complexity of today's enterprises had simply exceeded our capacity to "get our head around" them—clearly collectively and (for most) even individually.

What's evolved since then is something seminally different about this human-centric approach to applying system thinking/dynamics. And there's an analogy in today's increasingly cloud-based world that helps illuminate why this way of working has been so consistently successful.

Digital natives

The fitness of a particular approach to its ecosystem is often baked in from the beginning—part of its "genetic code". Google and AWS (Amazon Web Services), for example, are created and populated by what have been described as "digital natives". They entered our World having grown up in a digital world—experiencing it through a digital lens. Our increasingly digital world is second (well, actually, maybe even first) nature to them.

Their enterprises, therefore, have been designed from their first breath with an integrated view of their data. For Amazon (as a grossly oversimplified example), it's the integrated customer view—inclusive of the product view and/or service view. They know more about my buying habits—perhaps my health and even my moods—than I do!

By contrast (for example), legacy technology companies were often designed around their product lines—computers, servers, storage, etc.—with siloed data sets that allow them only partial views of their customers'/markets' activities. As a result, now that the Cloud is emerging as a dominant platform, legacy technology companies must scramble to convert their fractured data sets into federated database systems if they're to: 1) understand their customers/markets so as to 2) better—than the competition—serve their customers.

Analogously, the way of working we're exploring here arose from the beginning by trying to understand what human beings were designed to accomplish first: their innate, latent capabilities that—if awakened and supported/encouraged—would enable them to become more fully human. This was the point of origin around which the rich, invaluable toolset that is systems thinking/dynamics was repurposed, reassembled, sequenced, and applied—to reawaken and enable people to take advantage of their own healthy, fully human abilities—those skillful actions that naturally flow from their healthy needs/impulses.

Fully Human: A fully integrative approach

So what in the heck do I mean by "fully Human"? And why is it important?

When I trained in and practiced Somatic Developmental Psycho-therapy with the Bodynamic Institute of Denmark (primarily through the genius of my dear friend Marianne Bentzen), I became intimately aware of how we're innately designed to unfold from conception through adolescence—and beyond.

Because this body of knowledge is an integration of cognitive development (Jean Piaget), emotional development (Margaret Mahler), psychological development (Sigmund Freud and Erik Erikson), motoric development (Britte Holle[184]), energetic development (Wilhelm Reich[185]), and spiritual development (Buddhism[186]), it afforded a very complete, integrated understanding of how we're wired to develop both physically and psychologically.

While this is obviously a much deeper conversation/body of knowledge, I bring it up here because our current management systems—and even too many of our economic and social systems—work in ways that typically thwart our natural developmental pathways— thwarting even our neurology. We are *innately* designed to be:

- Secure in our sense of self and our right to exist (vs. anxious)
- Able to satisfy our own needs (vs. needy)
- Physically and emotionally autonomous (vs. co-dependent)
- Assertive (neither passive nor aggressive)
- Both visionary and pragmatic (vs. stuck in one pole or the other)
- Able to embody our opinions based on factual Reality (vs. untethered ideology/fantasy)
- Able to both excel individually while functioning as a healthy part of a Team and Community (vs. overly obsessed by either individual or collective rights)

When these innate stages of character development—of physical, emotional, intellectual, and even spiritual development—are allowed to unfold as designed, we are gifted with those among us capable of the kinds of remarkable accomplishments that truly contribute to Society and to Life itself.

---

[184] Britta Holle, *Motor Development in Children: Normal and Retarded*, Blackwell Science Ltd (December 31, 1977)
[185] https://en.wikipedia.org/wiki/Wilhelm_Reich
[186] https://hellomalavika.com/2012/09/22/chakras-7-year-development-life-cycles/

If a leader is to be able to solve "impossible" problems at scale – inspiring and supporting others living into these abilities – our innate abilities – is a prerequisite.

It has been the ability to reawaken what it means to be more fully human by embedding opportunities for the presence of these innate qualities in this way of working. Specifically, the repurposing and re-application of the tools afforded by systems thinking/dynamics is what accounts for the reliable, replicable success of this way of working across organizations, across industries, across issues, and even (or especially) across cultures.

Moreover, much like the solutions that emerge from this way of working, this work, itself, is continuing to adapt and evolve as we more fully integrate and apply what it means to be fully human to such an increasingly complex, fast-changing Reality.

What must Shift?

The most straightforward way to explore this aspect is to parse it into two dimensions: internal and external—i.e., mindset and mechanism.

Our internal shift: my/your/our paradigm and mindset

I said at the beginning of this chapter that, if this way of working breaks, it breaks here. And if it breaks, it breaks because we now need to operate out of a new paradigm—one that requires a foundational shift in mindset. And like any shift, it's a shift "from/to".

About the "from". As our early exploration of our context(s) at the beginning of this book makes clear, so much of the way we organize our work and world today is not optimal. Quite the contrary, as it does not align with Reality. Said another way, we simply have to figure out how to liberate our untapped human capability when confronted with today's (and tomorrow's) increasingly dynamic Reality.

As a result of the paradigm we've chosen to currently believe in, institutionalize, and operate out of, we only get glimpses of what it means to be fully human. Since the majority of us have grown up in, been educated in, work in, and are governed by suboptimal hierarchies, this from/to is a profound, fundamental, even seismic shift for us Individually, as a Society—and, in our now globalizing configuration—even as a Species.

That said, I *choose* to believe that this is doable. Actually, like so many of the challenges confronting us today, this simply MUST be doable—harkening back to Peter Block's "The answer to how is Yes!"—if we're to have a world worth living in. That is, this cannot be and, therefore (I feel compelled to believe), is not "impossible." This simply can't be, or else we won't be able to weather this age of wicked problems we've created for ourselves—to say nothing of what's awaiting our children and grandchildren.

But mindset and paradigm shifts are, if you recall Dana Meadows' *Places to Intervene in a System*, both extremely powerful and extremely difficult. Yet, as she puts it, "…there's nothing necessarily physical or expensive or even slow in the process of paradigm change. In a single individual it can happen in a millisecond. All it takes is a click in the mind, a falling away of scales from eyes, a new way of seeing."[187]

However, she goes on to say that individuals are one thing, but "Whole Societies are another matter. They resist changes to their paradigm harder than they resist anything else."[188] Luckily for us, we're operating in the middle, between individuals and whole societies—at the level of organizations and/or networks. And, as Yvonne and SCT would remind us, the most powerful layer for systemic intervention is the middle layer—that layer that has access to and is in communication with both the upper and lower (or inner and outer) layers.[189]

We're speaking here about scalability along two dimensions. First is the scalability of the work itself, meaning the ability to engage the

---

[187] Donella Meadows, op cit.

[188] Donella Meadows, op cit.

[189] Something learned all too painfully in the "organizational change" world when middle management was too often ignored or, worse, "ordered" to change.

larger set of actors required to hone and implement those strategies designed at the Organizational level.

The second dimension is the ability of that implementation to reach the larger population—i.e., the market, whatever that market may be—those who are the intended beneficiaries of our meta-goal, be it via a product, a service, a policy, an investment, etc. These two dimensions of scalability are reflective of one another. Typically, scaling to a larger market requires greater scalability in execution, whether that's by way of people or process, or both.

But causing a mindset shift requires—just as with any of the maps/systems we've examined so far—bringing a specific set of resources to bear in a specific sequence if we're to effect positive change. It's a fundamental tenet of systems thinking/dynamics that structure determines behavior—just as it's a fundamental tenet of the various healing systems I trained in and practiced—Rolfing® for instance.

In Rolfing® our structural alignment with the field of gravity determines how we move; in the models/practices of trauma, developmental, and group psychotherapy, the structure of our nervous systems and brain development determine our behavior relative to self, others, and reality. In each of these, there were—to borrow from Jim Collins' work[190]—catalytic mechanisms essential to establishing the initial conditions capable of sparking such shifts in mindset and, correspondingly, behavior. These mechanisms are an integral element of the subject of this work and in greater, more applicable detail, the next—the practitioners' manual. The most significant among these, though is…

Our external shift: our management mechanisms

In imprecise terms—we'll get more precise in a moment, but let's roughly frame this first—it's a shift *from* a personality/power-based hierarchical organizational/management structure *to* a reality-based,

---

[190] Jim Collins, "Turning Goals into Results: The Power of Catalytic Mechanisms", *Harvard Business Review* (July/August 1999).

self-organizing/managing network structure arising from a Reality-based meritocracy—the matching of skills with the Reality-based hierarchy of work. This harkens back to the Complexity quadrant of our adapted Cynefin framework. It's a shift that's emerging in response to what's arising in Reality.

And when I say "self-organizing/managing", I mean that in a very specific sense. There are healthy hierarchies in Reality–and those are essential! But, in keeping with the +RBMTS Goals we've been describing from the beginning of our conversation here, such hierarchies operate optimally because they are aligned with Reality. For example (now harkening back to our work with the GNSC—the Global Notebook Supply Chain), there was a "math" to achieving the reality of their goal, one that existed outside of any organizational structure. That math went like this...

Our ability to Scale to 30MM (a tripling of production) profitable, on-time deliveries in 3 years, with increasing quality and sustainably is a function of our:[191]

- Ability to make timely determination of present & future regional demand
- Ability to secure quality supply in alignment with demand on time & below mkt cost, sustainably
- Ability to produce high volume, low cost, on-time quality product at peak efficiency, scalably
- Ability to deliver 30MM units on time and at low cost through year 3 and beyond
- Ability to achieve and extend notebook market leadership
- Ability to influence the future structure and function of the GNSC ecosystem.

---

[191] Again, nothing unique here (that emerged in the leverage identification process). So no worries about confidentiality and NDA's.

This was their natural, reality-based hierarchy—irrespective of their hierarchy of positions or personalities. And if we refer back to their map, even those 6 elements comprised a next layer of elements that, themselves, formed a next level, and so on. That was the hierarchy of work needed to accomplish their goal.

As Rod Collins of Optimity Advisors put it in his *Huffpost* blog, "Thus, in nature, hierarchies are not a given, but rather are products of a bottom-up emergent process. This is an important distinction between nature's hierarchies and the social constructions we employ to organize human efforts."[192] This is quintessential reality-based hierarchy referring us back to the Cynefin notion of "Emergent." And, as such, this emergence needs to be rooted in meritocracy—a hierarchy of skills coupled with the work.

Such approaches have been successfully employed across a variety of organizations and efforts, including Wikipedia, W.L. Gore & Associates, Morning Star, Buurtzorg, Valve, Zappos, Linux, Whole Foods, Craigslist, LEGO, Threadless, and the Agile software development community.

In the presence of such reality-based hierarchies, what's now essential here is our ability to maintain:

- Awareness, Alignment and Action

…at the level of:

- The Organization, the Team and the Individual

More explicitly, we need to ensure that, at all three levels, all of us who are engaged in the effort are maintaining an awareness of why we're doing this (our global goal), specifically what we're seeking to accomplish (in measurable, time-specific terms for each Lever), and how we're going about that—from our strategies right down to our specific

---

[192] https://www.huffpost.com/entry/is-hierarchy-really-neces_b_9850168

Roles and Tasks—our DARCI chart. And this needs to be transparent to us as an Organization (or network), as Teams, and as Individuals. Our Awareness is a prerequisite to ensuring our ongoing Alignment—and our Alignment it essential to coordinated Action across our ecosystem.

And if we've been paying attention, it turns out that most of the mechanisms for accomplishing this are things we've already developed and experienced in our process so far—or that can be easily brought online. Though the detail will be covered in the Practitioner's Manual, I've at least summarized these mechanisms in a matrix I've termed (for reasons that will soon become apparent) a "Flight Manual" that, at a high level, looks like this:

Self-Organizing Networks
Strategy, Structure & Function in Action

	A "Flight Manual"								
	Self-Organizing Mechanisms & Protocols								
	Awareness			Alignment			Action		
Network	Ecosystem* Map	Strategy Map	Dashboard	Align, Act, Adjust	Global Goal	Team goal(s)	90 day cycle(s)	Common Circle	"Quick wins"
	X-pollination	Our Story	Surveys	Ritual Dissent	1-10 rating	Straw votes	"Default Setting"	a "Sherpa"	---
Team	CLEAR Team meetings	X-links	---	Conversation Meter	Team Strategy	DARCI +Chart	Team Lead	---	---
Individual	---	---	---	Purpose	Roles	---	Role Ownership	1 Next step	---

Of the 27 mechanisms listed here, 25 have either already been employed along our path from the initial Individual Level through to the Organizational Level or will be implemented in our 90-day Projects phase (see "How this Shift?" below).

TIMEOUT: Ripple effects

With the Flight Manual above, we're right on top of this issue of the inseparability of working in the midst of complexity—the wickedness of trying to artificially parse out individual threads from what is really, in these dynamic living systems, whole cloth. At the same time, the advantage of this is that a tool/mechanism developed in one phase of the work propagates value to other phases.

For example, while the Ecosystem Map (in the upper left-hand corner of the Flight Manual) initially provides Awareness at the level of the Network, it also does so at the Team and Individual levels along the vertical dimension. At the same time, horizontally, it increases Alignment and, in many cases, even points to strategic Action. The same can be said of the Strategy Map, the Dashboard, the narrative of our Story, and so on. Almost without exception, any tool employed up and to the left propagates down and across to the right—a further indication of the complexity of interdependencies between and among the resources and relationships that comprise our complex-adaptive ecosystem.

Illuminating this aspect of interdependence is crucial to, especially, the humanistic success of working in this way. It's as if, when we're engaging in each and every action (and, especially, interaction) along the way, we're aware of the interlocking weave of the whole we're seeking to create—that of deepening relationship & clarity at each of the 6 organic levels of our matrix. At each touch with the ecosystem—whether with the people or the process—we need to be adding a felt sense of value.

This appreciation for the need to exit each interaction having added value grew out of working as a Rolfer® and with trauma clients. As opposed to the fallacy that things have to get worse before they get better, we simply can't let someone with post-traumatic stress syndrome leave a session worse—we can't let someone with knee or shoulder or neck pain leave worse. If we've mastered our craft, we will only consciously stress the system in the presence of the resources needed to resolve that stress—whether we're talking human beings or human systems—our social, economic, or environmental systems.

How this Shift?

Okay, now that we've laid out the "why" and the "what" and some of the principles, let's get down on the ground with this by considering just "how" we need to interact to reliably and replicably apply the practice of scalability.

Just to remind us that scalability can and does happen, we should take note of a few real-world phenomena that speak to the possibility and power of scaling—specifically, critical mass, bell curves, and exponential inflection points (aka tipping points)—and their interrelatedness.

Critical mass

In physics critical mass is defined as "the minimum amount of a given fissile material necessary to achieve a self-sustaining fission chain reaction under stated conditions."[193] This property is the basis for our insistence from the beginning on assembling our 360° view of our ecosystem from the perspectives of a critical mass of credible, knowledgeable, and influential (CKI) leaders.

We choose critical mass here for reasons of efficiency and economy. We can't include everyone, not initially. That's left to scalability. So we'll need to evaluate each member of that critical mass relative to our three criteria—and even those criteria relative to our ultimate audience/market. That is, who will they/our market find credible, knowledgeable, and influential. In particular, however, it's the ability to influence that puts us on the path to scalability—with, at the same time, credibility and knowledge as a prerequisite.

The Real World: Scalability and Map OneSonoma

As you'll recall, in Sonoma we were seeking to impact a county of 494,336 individuals, each with differing needs, preferences, resources, metrics, etc. Doing so is quite complex—and initially does seem "impossible." But using the concept of critical mass, we scaled from an initial design team of four key leaders with the needed CKI (credibility, knowledge, and influence), getting us to the next level of 34 CKI leaders.

---

[193] https://www.britannica.com/science/critical-mass

Of that, a subset of 9 CKI leaders boosted our final Strategy Summit from an expected 30 leaders to an almost-overwhelming 85. Throughout our process, at every critical juncture, we consistently returned to this critical mass of 9 CKI leaders to ensure that we: 1) made the right, relevant decisions and 2) attracted the next level of critical mass.

(You've no doubt realized that these CKI criteria are closely related to Malcolm Gladwell's connector, maven, and salesperson roles, actors key to achieving a tipping point.[194])

A Bell Curve

When grappling with the sometimes-overwhelming notion of scaling, it can be useful to think of it like a bell curve—particularly Geoffrey Moore's insights in his book *Crossing the Chasm*.[195]

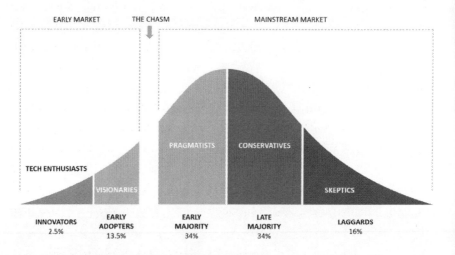

What's useful here is to think through, with your critical mass of initial leaders, each of these population subsets. In our experience, in every market we've encountered, there's been a leading edge of individuals

---

[194] Malcolm Gladwell, *The Tipping Point* (2000).
[195] Geoffrey Moore, *Crossing the Chasm: Marketing and Selling High-Tech Products to Mainstream Customers* (1991, 1999, 2014).

who are ready to make a shift in the right direction (i.e., a direction that's good for them and for the whole)—if they just knew what that shift was—just knew what to go do. When my friends/colleagues Matt and Gail Taylor and I were working with a group of 60+ global activists at the Noetics Institute (founded by former moon astronaut Edgar Mitchell), one of the leaders in a design conversation shared the pent-up demand for action. She said her constituency was beyond eager to act—demanding a path forward by asking, "Would someone who knows please have the decency to simply tell me what to go do?!" These types of individuals and leaders exist in the masses—in NGOs/NPOs, in corporations, and in Society, alike.

So it's up to us to think deeply about how each of these populations—in particular, the leading edge—make the shift—imagining, in practical terms, how to apply this way of working in a way that will catalyze that shift of mindset and opportunity essential to triggering scalability to the critical mass of the population required to accomplish our goal.

Inflection (Tipping) Points

So many of us are used to thinking linearly and can't fathom exponential growth. Yet reality is replete with exponential issues like human population growth, interest accrual on investment (or debt), rates of infectious diseases, etc. (Take the catastrophic case of COVID-19 and many of our decision-makers inability to grasp its exponential nature.) Any one of these can quickly outstrip our ability to mentally simulate future reality. For example, …

Try this: If you could fold a piece of notebook paper 42 times, how far would it reach? Seriously, if you don't already know the answer, stop for a moment and think about it. To support you here, I'll put the answer in the footnotes so I don't spoil the experiment for you.[196]

Didn't see that coming, eh? Nor do those who think about scalability in linear terms. And thinking in linear terms, they're right—we

---

[196] It reaches to the Moon—seriously—do a search! ☺

can't get there linearly. What tends to be forgotten is the power of exponential growth—growth we've experienced in the past—growth that we've been experiencing with ever-increasing speed. For example:

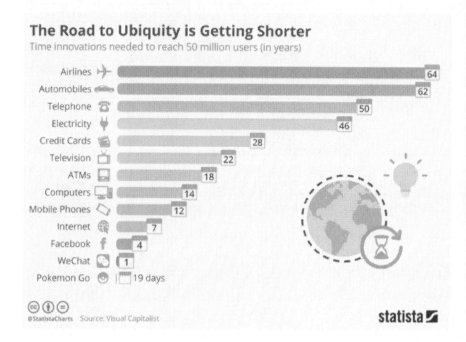

In combination, these understandings can be quite powerful, offering us light at the end of our tunnel should we begin to question our ability to do the "impossible". When we combine aligning a critical mass of leaders on the leading edge of the bell curve with our ability to get to an inflection point, we're well on the path to scalability.

Now that we've looked at the "how" from on high, let's drop down...

Deeper on the How

The "how" may seem daunting—in itself complex, even, per-haps, "impossible". And for some time, I pondered how we could possibly coordinate real-time, dynamic, emergent behavior in response to a complex, ever-changing environment. Then as I more deeply researched complexity theory, I ran across the Craig Reynolds video *Boids*,[197] something that, along with other complexity thinkers (including Robert Axelrod[198] and James Gleick[199]), actually goes to some of the nitty gritty of how such dynamics happen. Let's take *Boids* as but one example (btw, it'll really help if you can take a look at the Chris Reynolds' footnoted video on YouTube at some point—well, now, actually).

Boids: Coordinating Complexity

So imagine this: you're out in Nature, watching hundreds, possibly thousands of Starlings flock at dusk[200] (flocks can swell to as much as 100,000 in some places). Their murmuration appears incredibly complex as they turn, swoop, dive, and flow in unison—so much so that one has to ask, "How do they possibly manage such a coordinated feat?".

Well, Craig Reynolds set out to mimic that behavior and created an animated model[201] of coordinated animal motion—replicating that behavior (which is not to say that this is how Starlings actually do this). Long story short, he came up with 3 basic rules, plus 2, as follows:

- For the basic 3—using 3–dimensional computational geometry, he modeled these steering behaviors:
  - Separation: steer to avoid crowding local flockmates
  - Alignment: steer toward the average heading of local flockmates
  - Cohesion: steer to move toward the average position of local flockmates

[197] For a quick, updated version of his work, go here: https://youtu.be/GUkjC-69vaw
[198] See especially *The Complexity of Cooperation: Agent-Based Models of Competition and Collaboration* (1997) and *Harnessing Complexity* (2008).
[199] James Gleick, *Chaos: The Making of a New Science*; Viking Adult, 1987
[200] To see this, go here: https://youtu.be/eakKfY5aHmY
[201] For Craig's own story about this, go to: https://www.red3d.com/cwr/boids/

- Plus 2—elements he programmed in that are included here as they correspond to key principles for working in this way:
  - Goal Seeking: collectively pursue an agreed upon outcome—one we include here as it corresponds to our +RBMTS Goal
  - Avoidance: don't collide with an obstacle—one we always include as it corresponds in this work with the principle of "do no harm".

Patterns of Complex Coordination

What was so was thought-provoking about this is that this incredibly complex behavior (do take a look at the Starlings murmuration video in the link footnoted above) could be reduced to this handful of rules. And Reynolds is not alone in being able to distill complexity down to much simpler rulesets—for want of a better term. Others who see similar patterns and/or rulesets in complex domains include:

- Stephen Wolfram's controversial book, *A New Kind of Science*—postulating that Nature's laws can be described as simple programs;
- Christopher Alexander's[202] best-selling book on architecture, *A Pattern Language*—hypothesizing a set of timeless patterns that describe a problem and offer its solution, ranging from building materials to life experiences that ensure beauty and practicality in architecture—even reaching into the domains of human rights and freedom;
- John Doerr, formerly of Intel's rise and now with Kleiner Perkins—who calls out Andy Groves OKR's (objectives and key results) as a formula that, when scaled up, down, and across a venture, has significantly contributed to the success of organizations like Google, Spotify, Target, Bono's ONE Foundation, and TED[203]

---

[202] Co-authored with Sara Ishikawa and Murray Silverstein
[203] For more, see https://www.whatmatters.com/

- Elisabet Sahtouris, an evolution biologist, futurist, author, speaker, and consultant on Living Systems Design—who successfully applies the principles found in nature to topics as varied as organizational change, the corporate world, and global politics and economics…

…and we could go on. The nascent theme here, for those of us looking for it, is that there does exist significant evidence that complex behavior can be understood, distilled, and codified in such a way as to enable novel, fractal responses to complex situations in the real-world—ones that significantly surpass the performance of our typical personality/power-based hierarchal management models.

Coordinating Complexity at Scale

This deep knowing—that we simply must accomplish such fundamental shifts in both "what" and "how" we get work done on the path to evolving as a society and as a species—includes at least these 4 possibilities.

- **Holacracy**,[204] a rigorous way of running an organization that redistributes power throughout the organization to give individuals and teams the freedom they need while acting in alignment with an organization's purpose. Their interdependent principles include:
  - Purpose-driven—focusing on purpose at the level of the organization, the team, and the role/individual
  - Responsive—with each role/individual acting as a "sensor" for the organization using smaller, incremental decisions (vs. large, top–down decisions) to maintain agility

---

[204] https://www.holacracy.org/explore/why-practice-holacracy

- Explicit rules of the game—used to set clear expectations and transparent authority to reduce inefficiencies and hidden power/personality dynamics
- Transparent Roles & Responsibilities—to enable roles/individuals to evolve and organizations to scale…

…all of which is embodied in a formal constitution and continually guided by well–structured tactical (day-to-day operations) and governance (policy establishing/evolving) meetings.

- **Sociocracy[205] & Sociocracy 3.0**—a precursor to Holacracy, it is a dynamic governance model originating in the Netherlands, designed "…to achieve solutions that create harmonious social environments as well as productive organizations and businesses. It is distinguished by the use of consent [i.e., not "consensus"] rather than majority voting in decision-making…."[206] It employs the interdependent principles of:
  - Consent (vs. consensus) decision making
  - Organizing in Circles (akin to business units)
  - Double-linking individuals who serve as feedback loops and decision makers between higher and lower circles
  - Elections by consent to determine roles and responsibilities…

…all of which is underpinned by radical transparency (except for proprietary information or that which would threaten organizational or client security). BTW, Sociocracy 3.0 distinguishes itself from Sociocracy as a "free social technology for growing agile and resilient organizations" with roots in (and appreciation to) Sociocracy.

---

[205] The concept of Sociocracy was birthed in 1851 by French philosopher Auguste Comte and formalized as a governance system in the mid-20th century by Kees Boeke and Beatrice Cadbury. See https://en.wikipedia.org/wiki/Sociocracy#Origins for more.
[206] https://en.wikipedia.org/wiki/Sociocracy

- **The Collaborative Operating System** (COS)—as the COS folks put it, "a framework for leading, managing, and working that enables groups and teams to make high-quality decisions, function together effectively, execute plans quickly, and create higher individual and collective commitment to shared goals."[207] The COS does so via 5 elements. Please note: while I've had valuable explorations with COS practitioners about their methodology, I don't think I can say it any better than they do. So though you'll likely figure this out on your own, I largely drew this from their website.
  - Identifying the Problem—to ensure that: 1) there is, in fact, a problem, 2) the problem is worth solving, and 3) the group believes the problem can be solved (I, of course, would offer that the problem *must* be solved)
  - Involving relevant Stakeholders—involving the right people from the very beginning
  - Designing collaborative meetings—to ensure that we don't "spend too much time in painful, unproductive meetings which lack focus, churn repeatedly around the same issues, and fail to generate productive action"
  - Forming the collaborative team—by "defining and scoping the work as well as making the necessary binding agreements that enable people to come to a high level of ownership and alignment"
  - Creating the collaborative plan—working "at the 50,000 ft level to design a master plan integrating the preceding lessons/Elements"…

…all of which is intended to explicitly answer the question "given our company's goals and purpose, which system of organization shall

---

[207] http://thecos.org/learn-to-collaborate/what-is-cos2.html

we use?" vs. simply defaulting to a hierarchy—too often governed by implicit rules largely unrelated to high performance.

- ***Reinventing Organizations***[208] by Frederick Laloux, a book by the former McKinsey consultant that:
  - Chronicles the historical relationship between emerging levels of human consciousness and radically more productive organizational models
  - Uses real-life case examples to detail how running such organizations actually works
  - Explores the conditions that ensure that such organizations thrive—i.e., how they start and/or transform and what results do they generate…

…by fundamentally questioning every aspect of management and coming up with entirely new organizational methods—many of which he summarizes and illustrates throughout the book, especially in his appendices.

Emerging Principles for Scaling

I'm attracted to the above-mentioned systems of management because they mirror the core principles (and, in some cases, similar practices and processes) that are emerging from and are embedded in the way of working laid out in this book. In the spirit of distilling, I'll encapsulate (much as Craig Reynolds' Boidian rulesets do) this mirroring by calling out the practices and processes for activating what consistently show up as the principles of:

---

[208] Formally called *Reinventing Organizations: A Guide to Creating Organizations Inspired by the Next Stage in Human Consciousness* (2014).

- *Purpose*(s)[209]—out of which we each act, which show up in this work in the goals made explicit at the Individual, Team, and Organizational Level, as well as in each strategic team's lever, and, as you'll see the at the Ecosystem/Sustainability Level, even there.

- *Free Will*—embodying that by ensuring that the overall system incorporates the legitimate purposes, concerns, and circumstances of a 360° set of leaders/stakeholders via each individual's map/worldview; engages each individual/team in graphing their goals and goal specific BOTs (behavior over time); in the mapping validation and revision; and in the systemic analysis and strategic design.

- *Reciprocity*—by making explicit, exploring, and assessing the integrated inter-dependencies across the Integrated Map; collectively designing goals at the subgroup and organizational levels; exchanging information and feedback, especially in the Strategy Summits but also in the BOT process and mapping validation; and making sure we've accounted for each individual's needs and concerns in our reality check—assessing our level(s) of confidence. Just in case Reciprocity seems less significant here, it is a fundamental biological behavior (formally called reciprocal altruism) exhibited by primates,[210] birds, fish, and even bacteria. Jordan Peterson, in his No. 1 international best seller, *12 Rules for Life*, describes how even with rats at play—if a larger rat doesn't let a smaller rat win at least 1 of 3 rounds, the smaller rat will quit playing.[211] Our human predisposition is even described by Cialdini[212] in his work on persuasion and in game theory.[213]

---

[209] For a deeper and, at the same time, pragmatic approach to Purpose, check two of my friends' books—Tim Kelley's *True Purpose: 12 Strategies for Discovering the Difference You Are Meant to Make* (2009) and Holly Woods' *Golden Thread: Where to Find Purpose in the Stages of Your Life* (2020).

[210] Jordan Peterson, *12 Rules for Life: An Antidote to Chaos* (2018).

[211] Jordan Peterson, op cit.

[212] in his book *Influence: The Psychology of Persuasion* (2006).

[213] Often described, perhaps unfairly, as "tit for tat".

- *Transparency*—is fundamental to ensuring the requisite degrees of Awareness, Alignment, and Action at the levels of the Organization, Team and Individual and is provided by each of the mechanisms described in the Flight Manual…

…principles that, if at any point we overlook them, we find ourselves, and our venture, on thin ice. On the other hand, by consciously keeping these principles front of mind at each step—much like our Starlings—we can adroitly navigate even the most challenging of courses. With practice, you'll come to develop a felt sense of when one of these is off, and even more so when it's on.

I've trained in and have a surprisingly visceral relationship with Holacracy—experiencing it as the one most akin to Life itself. By that I mean that Holacracy creates the initial conditions for autonomous sovereignty in a collaborative framework—much like the actors in a natural ecosystem—each pursuing their own goals and evolving themselves and the ecosystem over time.

That said, each of these methods has the potential to revolutionize your leadership, your organization and your "impossible" issue/opportunity in a way that alters two foundational elements—governance and engagement—by:

1. Transforming the perceived complexity of management into a finite set of rules that enables your organization/network to "flock" (to self–govern/manage) in alignment with the potential inherent in the Boidian model while, at the same time,

2. Awakening those innate human characteristics that lie at the root of our innate ability to solve our increasingly complex issues/opportunities—yet doing so in ways that evoke the felt sense of being more fully human, more fully engaged in work and in life.

So my suggestion for your own internalization—your ability to embody scalability—is similar to how I'd encourage you to explore this book:

immerse yourself in one (or more) of these systems—discovering for yourself which is the best fit for your purpose, your mission, and your values. And if you'd like to understand more about the "why" of my own preferences, feel free to reach out to me.

Internalization: Embodying scalability for Oneself

That we need to internalize both the "what" and, more specifically here, the "how" seems, in the context of what we've now explored, self-evident. It seems particularly so if we're to avoid, as we alluded to early on, our own form of "insanity"—i.e., continuing to do more of the same while expecting a different result.

In any change effort, if we're to develop the ability to scale, we need to explore—in our own real world—four simple, straightforward domains. We need to ask ourselves a series of even more practical questions—i.e., "how does this…:

1. Start?

Where will this change start? Who will start it? How will it start? We should be able to walk out into the organization or the market or the society or the constituent base and touch the person(s), place and/or object where the change begins and describe how this will start. We have a responsibility, as leaders—when positing a change effort—to think it through to this fundamentally simple level.

2. Spread?

How will this change spread? How will it move from person to person, place to place? Which people and places? Will it spread linearly, exponentially, slowly, quickly? Again, we should be able to walk this through—literally. If not, we've not thought this through clearly enough. And in an increasingly interconnected, autonomous, and transparent world, change can spread like a virus. So the change should be designed to take advantage of the increasingly viral nature of our technological, social, economic, and political environments.

3. Self-direct?

Once our healthy "virus" is released, how will we ensure that it moves in the general direction vital to effecting (not simply affecting) the needed outcome. In an organization, one way to ensure this is through the use of collaboratively developed systemic metrics coupled with increasing transparency about the state of the goal or system we're collectively concerned about. We need to consider specifically how our viral agents/actors will get feedback about the impact of their efforts so that they can adjust and re-align their efforts on behalf of the/our whole—in short, so they can continue to learn.

4. Self-sustain?

All too often, change efforts—technological, organizational, market-driven, social, political—launch, gain traction, and then die.[214] Usually, such efforts don't survive because they fail to take into account limits to growth inherent in the larger system of which they are a part—organizational, market, social, even environmental. Either that, or they've not been designed to be sustainable at the operational/executional level (referring back to Boids, Holacracy, etc.).

Asking ourselves this series of questions—insisting that we walk ourselves (even in our mind's eye) step by step through each of these phases—should help us to recognize which system to adopt—or whether we need to innovate our own. Invariably, by doing so, we'll realize the need to design our change process deliberately, consciously, thoughtfully—be it organizational, market, or social—as a viral strat-egy—one that we can then catalyze. And this is a critical distinction—that leaders need to act as catalysts. And, as with any catalyst, not get consumed in/by the process—simply trigger it—staying available to the process to address the inevitable surprises presented by the innate uncertainty of life.

---

[214] For market examples, see *Crossing the Chasm*, by Geoffrey Moore. For social examples, see Howard *Zinn's A People's History of the United States.*

Internalization: Embodying scalability at scale

Speaking of scalability, we'll now have the responsibility for enabling internalization by our larger pool of systemic actors. As they become aware of the why, what, and how of scalability, they too will seek the means for this paradigm/mindset shift to become second nature. They too have been acculturated, almost invisibly, to historical systems that no longer accord with today's (much less tomorrow's) wicked problems/ opportunities. They too will need to practice and then master this new system of self-organization/management that best matches their/our challenge. For that, there's the transitional element of...

90-day projects

The only way to truly internalize this is to do it. In our experience, there are *three significant stumbling blocks/opportunities* in launching new initiatives within an emerging, self-organizing network.

The *first* is *getting collectively clear about what to work on*, understanding where the leverage points are in one's system. The *second* is *building the relationships needed* to actually work together to shift a system over time. We've been able to achieve both of these via the strategic systemic mapping and alignment work we've done so far—this well-proven methodology for allowing the levers in any system to emerge from the network/system itself—while simultaneously building the relationship and alignment essential to causing collective impact over time.

The *third* is the *ability to quickly, with a minimum of risk, demonstrate the ability to move the needle via a self-organizing/managing network*, something that this 90-Day methodology enables. The advantages of 90-Day projects are threefold:

- *Immediately extending the momentum* typically generated in the strategic phase
- *Achieving significant impact* toward the measurable, time-specific goals that emerge from the strategic phase

- *Embedding a fundamental shift* in the way work gets done—the paradigm and mindset shift—the cultural nuts and bolts of working together both within work Teams and across the Organization/Network as a whole, in the context of the real world.

Briefly, this process includes specific protocols for:

- **Establishing a self-organizing governance and communication structure for the network including:**
  - A small set of Work Teams acting on the levers identified in the strategic phase–teams themselves intentionally small enough to ensure agile response times, including:
    - At least one "generalist" from the network
    - At least one credible, knowledgeable "expert" in the strategic domain
  - A "Coordinating Circle" made up of members from each of the lever/work Teams and any needed experts or stakeholders:
    - Each of whom are capable of helping to navigate obstacles that may arise during the 90 days.
  - A networked communication process embodied in the members of the network—a process that both gathers and disseminates the metrics and learnings across the network in real-time as they occur.
- **Successfully executing a cohesive, integrated set of high impact projects requires:**
  - A set of positive, reality-based, measurable, time-specific goals, generated in the strategic phase
  - Agile, 5-member lever Teams sufficiently aware of the domain(s) influencing their goals that they are able to impact them

- One on-call expert per Team able to respond to specific knowledge/information requests
- One overall Network Project Manager to guide self-governance across the Teams and the Network.

- **Embedding the specific behaviors essential to successful collaboration over time calls for:**
    - A 1-day launch session for all Teams orienting them to the 90-day purpose, process, and protocols
    - A 1-day session for *each* Team grounding, within the context of their specific goal, the 90-day process and protocols
    - Weekly (or another optimal frequency) calls for each Team to share results and learnings, adjusting strategies as needed
    - Brief, bi-weekly bursts of networked communications to ensure all members are aware, aligned, and in action
    - Monthly meetings of the Coordinating Circle to adjust the Teams and the overall process as needed
    - At the culmination of the 90 days, a 1-day joint Coordinating Circle/Lever Teams meeting to share achievements and learnings and, grounded in that, to evolve the network's emerging strategy
    - Authentically appreciating each contributor and thoughtfully celebrating your achievements.

The Real World: Vermont Farm -to-School (VTFTS) Network

90-day Projects: While 90-day projects have been applied with the GNSC, a major contractor to the U.S. Navy, The Nature Conservancy, and others (especially when working there with my Conversant friends), one very public one I can share is with the Vermont Farm-to-School Network which goes like this…

Working with Meagan Camp and Betsy Rosenbluth of Shelburne Farms and the VTFTS Network, we had hosted a successful 2-day strategy offsite—attended by, among others, the heads of the Department of Agriculture and Education; folks from: the Governor's office, the USDA, the Vermont Community Foundation and senators Patrick Leahy and Bernie Sanders offices; farmers, processors, and distributors across the food system; the pre-K through 12 school systems, from principals to teachers to food service directors; the National Farm-to-School Network, other NGOs and NPO's...

At the close of that 2-day event, we asked that question, "How many of you are willing to take 1 next step?". That led to the 1–day launch of their 90-day projects. Central to their 90 days was the realization of the need to ground their strategies collaboratively and systemically in a cohesive set of formal funding proposals to the Vermont Community Foundation (VCF)—in place of the often multiple and siloed requests.

The VCF responded by noting that these were the most integrated and comprehensive set of proposals they'd ever received, that they would fund them all, and, based on the potential they sensed in this process, they would also fund the Project Manager (Betsy Rosenthal) for the next 18 months. Following that cycle of work, the VCF came back to the Network conveying that this was the most successful project in their portfolio. As a result, the VCF was offering an unsolicited $200,000. While this was both a complete surprise and tremendous validation, it was also big money for such a small group. The VCF simply required that Network share their plans for the money and the funds were theirs. This unprecedented offer was accompanied, at the same time, by the State of Vermont's exploration of a similarly unprecedented $400,000 grant to the Network.

This ability to use 90-day projects to: 1) extend the momentum from the strategic design work, 2) accomplish high impact results in a remarkably short timeframe, and 3) fundamentally shift the way work gets done, has consistently created similarly surprising breakthrough results in other business, social, and environmental projects. And the VTFTS work continues today—working toward the same reality-based goal that emerged from that original process.

Now that we've begun to internalize scalability: 1) as an emergent response to our "impossible" challenge, 2) practiced it as individuals and as an organization/network, and 3) demonstrated our ability to generate high impact results, it's time to ensure our ability to self-sustain.

So how do we do *that*? How do we catalyze something that can self-sustain? Perhaps even go viral? That question naturally leads to…

Chapter 6: At the Level of the Ecosystem

Ecosystem Relationship x Ecosystem Clarity = Sustainability

We've now arrived at a new vista, if you will: a meta–viewpoint of awareness based on our path up to and through levels 1-5—one where 3 interdependent questions pertinent to Sustainability at the level of the Ecosystem now present themselves:

- First, what are we now equipped with? What assets or attributes or abilities do we now have—and what are our current _capabilities_?

- Second, where do we now find ourselves in our journey on the path to harnessing chaos & complexity? Within what _strategic landscape_ do we now find ourselves located?

- Third, as the product of these two, what is our long term, _strategic fitness_ based on the two—relative to our goal?

Our current capabilities as an Organism

As a means for immersing ourselves here, it may help to meditate on it this way…

In levels 1- 5, we have birthed (if I may) an "organism"—an entity—be it an organization, a network, or a community—made up of the 360° integration of our individual "purposes, concerns, and circumstances"[215]

---

[215] Continuing to build here on the work of my friends at Conversant, as captured in their Conversation Prep Chart (see: https://www.conversant.com/resources/tools/conversation-prep-chart/)

relative to the shared intersection of our global goal. Referring back to the beginning of our journey, we have now answered:

Our four fundamental questions, i.e.,

1. What is the *state of our Reality* (past, present & future)?
    - via our BOT and our +RBMTS Goal
2. What is the *structure causing our Reality*?
    - via our ecosystem map
3. *Where do we intervene* in our Reality?
    - via our leverage analysis of that map
4. Then (and only then), how do we *make the structural then behavioral changes*?
    - via our integrated, high-leverage, action-based, 90-day strategy acting on those levers

...now enabling action at our 3 Levels +1

- Building upon our emergent leadership, Relationship & Clarity at:
    1. The *individual* level
        - via individual interviews and individual systems maps;
    2. The *subgroup* level
        - via affinity group explorations of Reality;
    3. The *whole group* level
        - via strategic design and action;
- enabling collaborative strategic action at:
    4. The *ecosystem* level
        - via decentralized, self-managed, scalable execution/ organizational design.

More specifically, we've done so by developing a portfolio of resources, including:

- A 360° set of Individual perspectives, interviews, and maps
- An Inclusive, felt-sense experience in our Subgroups/affinity groups, each with their own unique:
  - Goals
  - Behavior over time graphs (BOTs)
  - Compelling sense of urgency
  - Integrated map deep dives
- An integrated, validated, shared map of our ecosystem
- A rigorous, multi-dimensional analysis of our Map, its Goal, and Levers
- The experience of our Strategic Summit out of which emerged Teams systemically focused on each Lever
  - Each with their own systemic Goals, Strategies, and Phases
  - A set of Immediate next steps in their DARCI charts
  - All of which generated the experience of:
    - Self-organization/management
    - Self-organizing principles and processes
    - Emergent safe-to-fail probes
    - And deepening relationships with:
      - One another
      - Reality
      - & Self
- A 90-day launch that:
  - Immediately extended our momentum
  - Achieved significant impact
  - Embedded a fundamental shift in the way work gets done;

- Our Flight Manual designed to guide our "swarm" of actors by:
  - Providing access to collective Awareness, Alignment, and Action
  - at the Network, Team, and Individual levels
- Exposing us to the principles and even practices of reality–based self– governance/management systems.

These, then, are our assets—having emerged as we've deepened Relationship & Clarity—ones that make up the heart, brain, bone, and muscle of our organism, respectively. At this stage in our development, if we're to be sustainable, we need to embed this way of working in our DNA—but DNA relative to…

Our strategic landscape

From the very inception of working in this way, we've consciously designed all of this with sustainability in mind—something our complex context has demanded—a context (one laid out in at the beginning of this conversation) sourced from an ever-deepening awareness of:

- The demands of current Reality relative to our responses
  - And the gaps in our ability to solve for that
- That something is fundamentally broken about the "what" and "how" of our response
  - Evidenced by our two diverging lines
- That Complexity demands emergent solutions
  - Captured in the modified Cynefin framework and
- That all of this demands a step-change in our mindset
  - Dana Meadows' most potent lever[216].

---

[216] Donella Meadows, op cit.

Our strategic fitness

These two determinants—the fitness of our "organism" to its strategic "landscape" (both of those relative to our +RBMTSGoal)—determine our ability to sustainably adapt and evolve going forward. Because of that, we need to be able to test our level of fitness, both initially and along the way.

And while we've used Scenario Planning in F100 efforts, there's ample guidance for that tool readily available to you[217]—guidance I find incredibly valuable and would highly recommend. Given that, we'll focus here on lesser-known approaches, either uniquely found here or uniquely applied here.

In the spirit of suggesting that you decide for yourself, you may feel that you've already embodied the principles, practices, and processes ingrained in this way of working—that, because you've embodied them, this chapter may not be needed. And for some I've worked with, that has been true—these elements were internalized enough to carry on—able to keep all of this alive as they went.

So in that spirit of optimizing your time spent here, if you feel like you've got what you need (at least for now), feel free to move on to _Chapter 7: Possible_—a brief but pivotal chapter—one I'd ask you not to skip.

That said, I have encountered times when either: 1) levels 1- 5 were in place but still more was needed to embed this in our DNA—either institutionally or culturally, or 2) the elements I'll cover in this chapter significantly amplified the impact—and further embedded this way of being, or 3) both. So with that in mind, feel free to read on...

Many years ago, when I first came back into the consulting world working with my friends at ARC International, we were engaged in organization-wide change efforts with Fortune 100 companies. We frequently heard a fairly constant and widespread refrain of, "Well, I'll be

---

[217] For more here, see the classic _Scenarios: The Art of Strategic Conversation; Kees Van der Heijden_ (1996).

glad when *this* change is over, and we can get back to normal." Contrary to that fantasy, even back then, there was no normal to return to.

That's now increasingly true in today's world—one impacted by issues like the COVID-19 pandemic, our massive protests against racial and social injustice, even our ongoing confusion about things as fundamental as Reality. Even back in my days with ARC, change was becoming—and now clearly is, ongoing—both externally in the world at large and internally within our organizations—for each of us individually as leaders and collectively as communities. And it's change at an accelerating rate—something that's clearly amplifying now—one of the key markers of a complex world. Therefore, our solutions—both their "what" and their "how"—must be consciously designed to be sustainable.

TIMEOUT: Merging Relationship & Clarity

At this point, it's likely clear that any claim that Relationship & Clarity somehow exist independent of one another is sketchy at best. At this level, especially, every Relationship act evokes greater Clarity while increasing Clarity deepens Relationship. Still, the mechanisms/tools we'll experience here tend to be weighted more to one aspect of the equation or the other—more on either the Relating or the Clarifying strand of our DNA helix. So in this last level, I'll continue our pattern of describing the level, then going deeper into additional approaches to ensuring Sustainability—approaches that will, if embarked upon with the specific intention of and attention to[218] Sustainability—flesh out/firm up the sustainability aspect of our enterprise while more deeply embedding this into the DNA of our organism.

---

[218] Michael Gerber does an excellent job of capturing the value of both *Intention* and *Attention* in his books based on *The E-Myth* (1998 & 2004).

In addition to our now well-developed initial conditions (our resources from above), there are a couple of other lessons learned that have helped to solidify our road ahead. BTW, it's still possible for us to allow this to break—to mistakenly relax into believing that things will somehow go back to normal. These two object lessons fall into one (or both) of two buckets:

- Minimizing the impacts on others in our ecosystem
- Maximizing one or more positions in our ecosystem.

In keeping with our rhythm so far, we'll still parse this out by defining Ecosystem, Ecosystem Relationship, Ecosystem Clarity and Sustainability—along the way delving into the last of our tools for solving for the "impossible", including:

- Sometimes, it *is* about the Map!
- And then again, it's not about the Map!
- The Stakeholder Assessment Grid
- The Organizational Learning Engine
- Beliefs, Purpose, and Sustainability.

So now, on with our rhythm…and deeper into Sustainability…

Ecosystem

Once solutions begin to scale—once you're successful in what you thought might be the hardest part of the job, your solution becomes of import to the larger system of which it is/you are a member. It begins to have, as you intended, an impact on your larger "host" system—usually the industry or market or society or environment writ large—that composite of customers/constituents, competitors, distributors, legislators, the media, educators, theologians, politicians, investors/donors, etc. And your impact may extend to include the regional or even global environment.

So if our solution/strategy/organism is to be sustainable, it must somehow contribute to the net mutual benefit of that larger ecosystem of which it is/you are a part. At the same time, it cannot be so alienating—to either a dominant stakeholder or a collectively powerful group of smaller stakeholders—as to ensure our/its destruction. Or—as is the case with our society, economy, political system, or environment—our self-destruction. Most of these stakeholders (with the exception of "bullies" addressed in Chapter 4) have legitimate roles in our interdependent society—roles that have now become a part of the infrastructure that sustains our system/ecosystem—and can't simply be ignored or marginalized, not without consequence.

Our failure to consider the perspectives of other major stakeholders in the system—be they allies, adversaries, or neutral parties—often results in a critical miscalculation—miscalculation that, once made, is not easily overcome. So in order to ensure that our well-developed strategies/solutions won't begin to gain traction only to be thwarted, we need to be able to anticipate their impact on each of the critical stakeholders in our system. So how do we ensure that we don't inadvertently conflict with the essential interests of a powerful, even necessary, force in the system—one either powerful or necessary today or, potentially, tomorrow?

Many leaders think like this instinctively. Yet regrettably, far too many don't. And it's not necessarily because the latter don't want to, but because we've not been taught how to. In fact, I'd make the case that we've actually been taught *not* to. Those who do think this way routinely scan their environments—often in their mind's eye—doing so innately as they make decisions.

In fact, as the scope and scale of a leader's sphere of influence increases, they must increasingly learn to satisfy a broader range of stakeholders—if their enterprises and efforts are to meet with success. Startups, in particular, now have to grapple with this consideration—anticipating well before they launch out of stealth mode—what barriers in the larger system they are likely to encounter as they scale. But rarely do we do this explicitly, systemically, rigorously, and collectively. And, as our world becomes increasingly complex, holding this in our head poses two problems.

First, the human mind is demonstrably poor at holding high levels of complexity—especially domains with incomplete, ambiguous and/or paradoxical dilemmas to be solved for—to say nothing of our implicit biases.[219]

Secondly, even if they can, transferring/communicating this level of complexity to others—those others needed to innovate, execute, and scale the solution, sustainably—is in itself, overwhelmingly complex.

My first encounter with this—actually, the genesis of realizing the need to work in this way—unfolded like this...

The Real World: An F100 Strategy process: Sometimes it is about the Map!

Though we've introduced the notion of "it's not about the Map" before in this conversation, sometimes it is. Yes, the conversation it enables is a "must have". And, in some cases, the map becomes the dominant tool—we lead with Clarity as the means for building Relationship. For example ...

Shortly after returning to consulting from the world of psychotherapy, I was coaching the executive team of an F100 company. Because of my facilitation skills, I was asked to design and lead the strategic planning effort for their largest business unit. But...

"Tom," I said with a bit of skepticism, "I've never done strategy at the Fortune 100 level before."

"Well, think about it," he responded, "and let me know how you'd handle it."

Long story short, we designed something that deviated significantly from what the global strategy consulting firms had proposed—a pathway that delighted him—and immediately got to it.

---

[219] Speaking of rigorous, see the relevant chapters of the book by Richards J. Heuer, Jr., *Psychology of Intelligence Analysis, Central Intelligence Agency* (1999).

Deep into the process we were working with Michael Porter's[220] notions of strategic positioning, strategic fit, and activity mapping— with the textbook example (at the time) of Southwest Airlines…

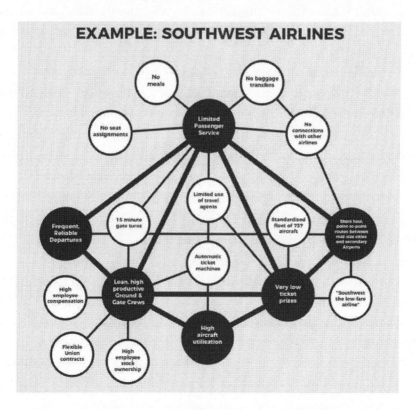

…using this to explore these issues for Tom's team. That is, we were asking the question, "How is it that the various aspects of your company fit together in such a way as to account for your position as one of the top performing companies in your industry?".

There was silence…no one had a clue! No one understood how their organization functioned as an organism, how the various parts and pieces, the different business units, fit together to create a

---

[220] Michael Porter, "What is Strategy?" *Harvard Business Review*, Nov-Dec 1996, copyright 2013, New Markets Advisors

self-reinforcing, resilient enterprise capable of continually evolving in their competitive ecosystem. Now don't get me wrong—they were best in class. But they were best in class in their silos[221] —great at marketing, distribution, finance, sales, etc. But no one had their head around the business as a whole, as a system—the interdependencies of resources and relationships that consistently, predictably outperformed their competitors.

I was incredibly naïve—ashamedly so. I actually thought that someone out there knew how things worked—be it a business or a government or…. Nope! And since then, that's only become clearer—at both local and global levels. Surprisingly few leaders actually have their heads around their enterprises in such a way that they can either: 1) simulate it accurately under a variety of conditions or, even if they can, 2) convey that succinctly and successfully to others. Hence, the need for working in this way.

This, then, was when we (Jim Ritchie-Dunham and I) first collaborated on a system-wide mapping effort. It was one that enabled leadership to get its head around their complex-adaptive system—enabling strategic alignment and action capable of overcoming the inertia embedded in the ongoing struggle—ensuring that their various perspectives were seen, heard, understood, appreciated and included. Even as we strive for Clarity, we can't do so without alluding to (even illustrating—as apparent in Porter's image above) its dependence on Relationship.

Eventually, as Tom and I got clear about the consequences of this level of complexity, Jim and I (along with our invaluable team[222]) were able to design and build a system dynamic model as a strategic decision-making platform (in this case, a working simulation). It enabled Tom and his team to literally explore, across the enterprise, the role of various decisions about pricing, competition, market share, regulator and customer satisfaction,

---

[221] I'd be foolish to ignore the role that informal social networks played here—likely one of their primary assets. Still, there was no formal, explicit understanding or structure.

[222] Including Hal Rabbino, Annabel Membrillo & Conrado Garcia Madrid

etc., and their impacts on one another—and on ROI, EBITDA and beyond. For the first time, much like with the GNSC, Tom and his team were able to get their heads around their complex world in a way that they could both comprehend and communicate.

So in this case, it actually was about the Map as a tool for "hosting" the conversations. That is, postulating changes in one or more factors, generating the results, then engaging in the conversation about "why" that result—then "what" to do about it. This way of modeling, engaging with, and interpreting our ecosystem ensures that we come into both Clarity about and then Relationship with the ecosystem level of our world, one another and our stakeholders—and, through that, the fitness of our solution/strategy with our strategic landscape—something that simply must be internalized if we are to succeed sustainably.

Ecosystem Relationship

Engaging at the level of Ecosystem involves *giving stakeholders a voice, demonstrating your understanding, and adding value*. And as we've said before, the Map is simply one vehicle for that—a very necessary vehicle, but only one. You often have to begin where you are with what/who you've got—whether or not it's ideal. Many times, you can't even get all of the stakeholders to engage in an effort or event for a variety of reasons—limits of time, money, and access in the best of cases—fear, resentment, or animosity in the worst.

But more often than not we can anticipate the goals, means, and needs of others if we really make a focused, thoughtful effort to take on their perspective. We can literally try to stand where they stand—see what they see as if we are looking out through their eyes—seeing, feeling, hearing, and experiencing the world as they do.[223]

---

[223] This is actually a practice that Ghandi employed: taking on the body posture and mannerisms of those he was to negotiate with, doing what it took to access their worldview/perspective. Again, NLP is good place to go to find tools and techniques for literally shifting perspective and experiencing the world from another's point of view (search "three perceptual positions").

As an integral part of our interrelated, holistic system, we are—our position and function is—somehow reflective of the whole, enabling us to speculate with a surprising degree of accuracy about other parts/members of the system.[224]

At this point in our work—our progress with this systemic process—we've already experienced some of this—having conversations with different stakeholders, mapping their worlds, reflecting back to them what we see and understand, listening to our market or to our constituents to understand them well enough to design a scalable solution. And doing this at the level of the larger system—our company, our market, our industry, our society, our ecosystem—is neither that different nor that difficult. Again, it requires a shift in our state of being—a shift to literally empathize (vs. sympathize) with them—understanding that, like us, they have purposes, concerns, and circumstances[225] that determine much about how they behave in the world. And if we've made a good faith effort at this, when it comes time to engage with them—to explore, modify, validate, and incorporate their perspectives—they will see, understand, and appreciate this, extending some degree of trust in response to our best efforts—that is, if there's any possibility of cooperation or collaboration at all.[226]

This, then, is the beginning of Relationship with those larger forces in our ecosystem—and, done well—the beginning of our mutually beneficial relationship. And even if such a relationship doesn't develop with every part of the ecosystem, it can at least begin with a critical mass of actors in our larger ecosystem—that leading edge of early adopters. It may take time, but that's implicit to Sustainability. One such shift in relationship was experienced here...

---

[224] All subsystems are reflective of the larger system of which they are a part.

[225] For more on thinking/being from this perspective, see my friend & colleague, Mickey Connolly's work at www.conversant.com and their Conversation Prep Chart.

[226] And, according to James Surowiecki (*The Wisdom of Crowds*, Random House, 2004), there's ample evidence that humans naturally seek to coordinate and cooperate.

The Real World: Preserving 245MM acres of Southern U.S. Forests: Then again, it's not about the Map!

Okay, in our last example with a global energy firm, it *was* about the map. Still, most aren't up for building out a system dynamics simulation. And, though incredibly and rigorously valuable, many don't need a simulation. In those cases, here's where the map is specifically deployed as a vehicle for deepening Relationship across their Ecosystem—putting them solidly on the path to Sustainability...

In 2019, a diverse group of actors came together to explore how to maintain nearly a quarter billion (yes, with a "b") acres of forest in the Southern U.S. by 2060. It was an effort they entitled Keeping Forests as Forests (KFAF). The group included representative leaders from perspectives as varied as Georgia-Pacific and The World Wildlife Federation; Coca Cola and the Wild Turkey Federation; the U.S. Forest Service and the Center for Heirs Property; investment firm managers and loggers/lumberjacks.

Some leaders represented African American landowners who had been historically marginalized—even cheated out of their land and/or the market value of their holdings since the 1800s. Others were designing innovative ways to monetize forests via an "Airbnb" approach to forest recreational use. There were sharp, rigorous investment managers for whom guaranteeing shareholders a competitive rate of return over time was absolutely crucial.

Environmentalists were concerned about the flora and fauna both supported by and supporting these forests, especially in an era of climate change. Local officials paid particular attention to the ecosystem services of water capture, retention, and filtration provided by forests, while also struggling with population growth and urban heat sinks as forests shrank. And more.

There were more than 25 stakeholder perspectives in all—each concerned about the diverse economic, social, and environmental benefits of our Southern Forests—gathering to see if we could find common ground that would ensure forests' ability to thrive in perpetuity—able to sustainably provide these benefits.

Given the range of systemic actors, there were, similarly, a range of potentially discordant purposes, concerns, and circumstances ranging from historic racism and economic inequity to economic development and timber harvest; from environmental protection to recreational use; from urban sprawl to climate change; and so on.

As you can imagine, early on there was some concern about the ability for such varied, seemingly divergent points of view to be represented at a level that ensured each perspective would be seen, heard, understood, appreciated, and included. Could we do it at an actionable level—one that would simultaneously protect what was vital to each stakeholder as they contemplated navigating through such complexity to a strategically viable, mutually beneficial path forward. So my friend from an earlier project, Scott Davis, reached out to my longtime friends at Conversant (Anne Murray Allen and Kell Delaney) and me to engage in a systemic mapping and strategy effort.

To give you a bit more context (short of encumbering you with the whole map[227]), the 6 major sectors of their map were:

- The Quality and Quantity of Scientific Understanding re: Healthy Working Forests as essential to…

- The Quality and Quantity of Healthy Working Forest Value (environmentally, socially, and economically) which underpins…

- The Ability to Monetize Healthy, Working Forests (again, environmentally, socially, and economically) as critical to…

- The Ability to Incentivize Healthy, Working Forest Landowners (of whom there were more than 80,000) which also requires…

- The Ability to Design for Healthy Working Forests and Forest Landowners, all of which must culminate in…

- The Ability to Deliver for Healthy Working Forests and Forest Landowners…

---

[227] If you are interested in their map, you'll find it at scottspann.com/impossible.

...comprising our "math" for achieving our goal of 245 million acres by 2060.

Beginning with that first section on Scientific Understanding, there were—as there should be when one is fully committed—quite spirited conversations. Each different perspective sought to make sure that their world was fairly and accurately depicted. There was even significant pushback from some about the need to emphasize—at the beginning of the map—the environmental importance of healthy forests as an essential starting point—initially worrying some that the map was already biased in favor of the environmentalists.

But as we deepened our spirited journey through the interrelated resources and relationships—and most importantly, the interdependencies and feedback loops between and among the various sectors of our Integrated Map—we were able to align, as a group, both on the need for environmentally healthy forests AND on the realization that humankind had so shaped the Southern Forest ecosystem that environmental health was now dependent upon ongoing human intervention/management to restore and maintain its well-being over time.

For example, without the underlying economic value of the forests, no sustainable management would occur through selective harvesting. The resulting overgrowth would risk massive firestorms in the case of drought. Unlike the West—with its large blocks of Federal and State Forest ownership—the Southern Forest had, over time, been parceled out among over 80,000 landowners—making meaningful intervention with a few large landowners unfeasible. Without economic value—and the attendant market mechanisms, those who chose to live on their land and/or otherwise preserve their portions of the Forest, would lose the economic opportunity of sustainable forestry. To ensure their own personal economic well-being and that of their families they might be compelled to sell their land for development—especially in light of the levels of economic inequity in the South.

The key, in addition to Scott Davis's and Conversant's early work, to bringing these disparate perspectives into alignment over the course of our 3-day meeting of 25+ leaders was threefold—designing to enable leaders to:

- *Experience the challenges*, curiosity, information exchange, and alignment that naturally grew out of our conversation
  - as we walked and worked our way through our integrated map of the social, economic, and environmental ecosystem that determines our ability to achieve our goal
  - Using the map to literally hold the conversation—vs. having it/us go "random"—i.e., jumping into the too frequent "monkey mind" of large group conversations
- *Engage in the analysis* in a step-by-step sequence, incorporating:
  - Leadership input—requiring folks, each with their own copy of the map, to seriously think through the whole ecosystem as they selected and weighted their top 20 levers, allocating their finite pool of 200 points across their chosen 20
  - Group conversation—about the overall analysis, their input coupled with the other analyses, making sense of what was and/or was not a lever, and why
  - Post-conversation reflection—making a final choice of levers via their SurveyMonkey survey, creating their rank-ordered list of levers for final decision making, so they could
- *Refine that list* to an actionable Strategy Map that:
  - reduced their 147-element integrated map…
  - to 17 high-leverage variables…
  - distilled down to 7 strategic action areas…

…simplifying their complex problem in a way that they each and all (from among the myriad perspectives from across the ecosystem) felt confident would enable them to achieve their global goal while simultaneously satisfying their own local goals.

Closing the loop here on this example of building ecosystem relationship—and tying this back to our grounding in group psychology—the KFAF group actually traversed each of the stages of the SCT SAVI grid (see the reminder graphic below), hitting at least one of the elements from each of the 9 stages—evolving to the resonating, responding, and integrating stages of group/team development by the end of the second day—carrying that flow forward into the third, and now beyond.

I offer the SAVI grid here to reinforce the realization that what we're doing aligns with—even resonates with—other approaches to evoking what's most fully, constructively, and creatively human about us—using SAVI as an arm's length, third-party source of validation, from a psychological perspective, about the value of working in this way.

SAVI° Grid

System for Analyzing Verbal Interaction
CLASSIC

PERSON		TOPIC	
Personal 🎵	**Factual** 🎵	**Orienting** 🎵
1 FIGHTING	**2 OBSCURING**	**3 COMPETING**
Attack/Blame	Mind-Reading	Yes-But
Righteous Question	Negative or Positive Prediction	Discount
Sarcasm	Gossip	Leading Question
Self Attack/Defend	Joking Around	Oughtitude
Complaint	Thinking Out Loud	Interrupt
	Social Ritual	
4 INDIVIDUALIZING	**5 FINDING FACTS**	**6 INFLUENCING**
Personal Information Current	Facts & Figures	Opinion
Personal Information Past	General Information	Proposal
Personal Opinion/Explanation	Narrow Question	Command
Personal Question	Broad Question	Social Reinforcement
7 RESONATING	**8 RESPONDING**	**9 INTEGRATING**
Inner Feeling	Answer Question	Agreement
Feeling Question	Clarify Own Answer (with data)	Positives
Answer Feeling Question	Paraphrase	Build on Other's Ideas or Experience
Mirror Inner Experience	Summarize	Work Joke
Affectionate Joke	Corrective Feedback	
Self Assertion		

(Red) AVOIDANCE · (Yellow) CONTINGENT · (Green) APPROACH

Silence, Laughter, Noise

Note: The Grid is intended to be used in conjunction with SAVI™ training.
Taken out of context, the content of the Grid may be ambiguous, confusing, or misleading.
SAVI™ is a registered trademark of Yvonne Agazarian, Claudia Byram, Frances Carter, and Anita Simon. Copyright © 2011 Simon & Agazarian.

One of the most inspiring moments of the project (as further evidence of the ability to evoke Relationship at the Ecosystem level) came as we were each sharing our individual closing thoughts and feelings. We clearly called out the shared experience that, over the course of just 3 days, we'd transitioned *from* a somewhat disordered set of individual ideas and opinions *to* a collaborative, cooperative network, deepening our understanding, appreciation, and respect for one another. And we were able to align around the creation of the enabling conditions needed to "maintain 245 million acres of Southern Forests and their inherent social, economic, and ecological values for the benefit of current and future generations by 2060" (their goal). To experience that degree of deepening in Relationship, especially in such a short time, is truly gratifying.

Ecosystem Clarity

So how does one ensure that this is done explicitly, systemically, and collectively in a way that evidences not only our good faith and best efforts, but also a decent strategic grasp of our ecosystem? How does one rigorously and reliably enter into the state of being that will ensure that, even if we don't reflect the goals, means, and needs of the larger forces in this ecosystem with *absolute* precision, we at least move most of the way there?

One way is by integrating stakeholder goals, needs, and their value exchange via a thoughtful, balanced stakeholder assessment, one that enables us to walk in their shoes to more deeply understand and appreciate their: 1) primary objective and 2) their primary problem, along with, in a reciprocity-driven system, their primary 3) deliverable, 4) expectation, and 5) shared resource(s) in a value-exchange network.

Stakeholder Assessment Grid...The Real World: 24 utilities, regulators, foundations, and NGOs

This need for value-adding reciprocity across an ecosystem lies at the root of a sustainable ecosystem. To see and understand this in action, let's turn our attention to this Stakeholder Assessment and its explanation below…

Stakeholder Assessment Grid[229] ②

Perception of Stakeholder Deliverables and Expectations with These Groups

	Utilities	Energy Policy ③	Environmental Advocates	Economic Advocates	Industrial Consumers
Utilities ①	O: Safe, reliable, profitable power P: Increasing competition, costs, complexity, aging, inflexible, underinvested infrastructure, environmental uncertainty	D: Concessions ③ E: Give & Take on issues critical to my success ④ SR: Regulators, politicians, media	D: Compliance with the law E: Work within the legislative process SR: Regulators, politicians, media	D: Jobs; taxes; reliable, economic energy E: Political support SR: economy, workforce	D: Reliable, economic energy E: Predictable demand, loyalty, revenues SR: The generation system; politicians
Energy Policy	D: Good research and alternatives ⑤ E: Serious consideration and adoption ⑥ SR: Politicians, regulators, rate-payer funds, media	O: Clean energy development P: Established dirty energy system – both physical and political	D: Environmental Improvements E: Political Support SR: Funders, politicians, regulators, utilities, media	D: Jobs, taxes, clean environment E: Political support SR: Energy system; politicians, media,	D: Energy savings E: Adoption SR: Energy system
Environmental Advocates	D: Sound research on the impact of dirty energy on life on the planet E: Responsible actions to curtail impacts SR: Politicians, regulators, media, the environment	D: Sound research on the impact of dirty energy on life on the planet; political support for change E: Sufficient levels of change SR: Utilities, politicians, media, funders	O: Save life on the planet P: A culture addicted to consumption	D: None E: None SR: Environment	D: Sound research on the impact of their activity on life on the planet E: Responsible actions to curtail impacts SR: Politicians, regulators, media, consumers
Economic Advocates	D: New customers E: Reliable, economic energy SR: the Economy, workforce, community	D: None E: None SR: Energy system	D: Taxes for environmental compliance E: Reasonable demands SR: environment	O: Jobs, taxes, economic growth P: Increased competition, globalization, economic stagnation	D: Community resources for growth and prosperity E: Loyalty, jobs, taxes SR: the community, the economy
Industrial Consumers	D: predictable demand; revenues E: reliable, economic energy SR: the energy system	D: None E: None SR: energy system	D: None E: None SR: environment	D: Jobs, taxes E: Political support SR: workforce, economy	O: contribute to society; make a profit P: increasing costs, competition and complexity.

Key: O = Objective, P = Problem, D = Deliverable, E = Expect in return, SR = Shared Resource

[229] As you know by now, you can find this at scottspann.com/impossible.

TIMEOUT: The Experience

Just to be clear, as you step into this bit, I'd ask you to keep in mind that—much like with the conversation around the BOT or the Integrated Map—*it's the experience* of working our way through this that generates the value—though the product itself is incredibly useful, too. As Moltke the Elder,[228] Churchill, and Eisenhower knew, it's not the artifact (in their case, the plan) but the thought experiment (in their case, the planning).

So before you try to construct one of these, how would you even read it? Let's take an example focusing on the Utilities. If you are the CEO of a Utility company, your world could well look like this…

"As CEO, my objective (O:) ① is to ensure the sustainable production of energy that is: *safe*—first and foremost, for my employees, my customers, and my community; *reliable*—I need the hospitals, the high-tech manufacturers and biotech companies, the elderly in their homes, and the children in their schools—especially in our Northern winters—to have an energy source they can rely on; *profitable*—I have employees to support, vendors to pay, investors to whom I owe a return.

"In my good-faith relationships with other stakeholders in a value-creating, value-exchanging system (in our economy), I deliver value and expect something of value in return—and you and I likely each impact resources that are critical to both of us."

[228] https://www.britannica.com/biography/Helmuth-von-Moltke

For example, as CEO, "I experience the following with 'Industrial Consumers' ②:

- I deliver (D:)
  - reliable, economical energy (a significant commodity for industrial consumers in an energy dependent economy)
- I expect (E:), in return,:
  - predictable demand (I can't afford to build capacity and then have it sit idle)
  - loyalty (don't leave me holding the bag on my investments on your behalf—by, say, relocating to China)
  - revenues (I need to be paid for what I deliver, just like everyone else in the economy)
- And our shared resources (SR: resources we both impact) include:
  - The generation system—very time I shut down a generator for maintenance or you turn on a major plant, we each put the system under stress and the energy supply at risk
  - Politicians—we're both trying to ensure that current and future policies don't unfairly disadvantage us relative to other parts of the system and, where possible, even provide us with advantages. Even so, sometimes our demands on them conflict."

When we first proposed this exercise to the leaders in this group, they doubted their ability to accurately and adequately populate this grid, arguing that they couldn't possibly know enough to fairly represent these various points of view—particularly those of their staunchest opponents. As a former student of *bushido*, I was reminded of Sun Tzu's *The Art of War* teaching on the importance of understanding your "enemy"—i.e., "To know your Enemy, you must become your Enemy".

I use quotes around "enemy" here as, in this way of working, I find it most useful to hold other parties in the system simply as systemic actors vs. "enemies" as a way of avoiding the emotional charge (and, therefore, clouded thinking) such labels can arouse.

As it turned out, since they'd interacted either directly or indirectly with the other positions in their ecosystem for years now, they were incredibly adept at identifying each of the critical elements for the full range of stakeholders. We had them actually stand up and reposition themselves in the room—literally reseating and imagining themselves sitting behind the desk or standing in the office of a specific leader whom they knew from each sector.

From there, they looked out at/visualized that other leader's or actor's or stakeholder's world—considering their unique purposes, concerns, and circumstances—really taking on that persona/perspective. Then from there, complete the worksheet. They were quite surprised by the face validity of their assessments—many of them citing this exercise as reshaping their long-held opinions—sparking new insights—opening new creative options for negotiating across their ecosystem.

What's fascinating about this is that, even in good-faith relationships, we can be structurally conflicted. For example, with energy policy advocates, utilities—in good faith—offer concessions ③ to the energy policy world and expect, in return (as an act of reciprocity), that the energy policy advocates will engage in give and take ④ on issues critical to the utility companies' success (as utilities try to optimize other stakeholder demands in their systems, from employees, investors, customers, etc.).

Energy policy advocates, on the other hand, offer (from their perspective) really well-thought-out, well-researched alternatives ⑤ to the current and future energy and climate needs and expect that—because they are so well thought out—the energy companies should at least give them serious consideration and, ultimately, adopt ⑥ them. Both expectations are reasonable and, all too often, in conflict.

But when we know such structural conflict exists, do we have a better or worse opportunity for entering into conversation and relationship with our partner in the system? If we acknowledge their challenges, are they more or less likely to listen to us and to consider what we are concerned about? Do we have a better or a worse chance of coming up with a mutually beneficial solution with this knowledge and relationship than without it?

All of these are (forgive me) rhetorical questions—but they make an important point. All too often, we hold—literally, in our minds and even in our nervous systems—other legitimate stakeholders as somehow thoughtless, ill-willed, even malicious participants in the system. And, sometimes, they are (that bullies bit, again). More often than not, though, they are either uninformed[230] or conflicted—trying to solve a really difficult problem affecting multiple stakeholders—and they simply don't know how.

Returning to our example in Guatemala, it was CARE's good faith effort to understand their key stakeholders in the system— even ones with whom they may have felt at odds—that opened a conversation both within CARE itself and with their society at large, about the individual and collective purpose of their work and its impact on society.

As a result of their good faith—and their skill in acting on that in a way that added value to the social conversation—CARE was both: 1) actively invited to participate in an increasing number of significant conversations, relationships, and projects and 2) responded to as a leader in Guatemalan society in domains previously unavailable to them. They themselves caused this level of engagement by willingly—and skillfully—taking on both another's perspective and the perspective of the system as a whole. They then actively reflected that understanding in their thinking, their speaking, and their behavior. As a result, they increased the likelihood that the solutions they developed would be

---

[230] For example, business and government leaders in Guatemala were largely unaware that malnutrition among indigenous children is as high as 70%, a devastating situation for each child, their families & communities and, ultimately, for the nation. When Andres Botran (a wealthy businessman—and, yes, of the Botran Rum family), did discover it, he immediately went to work increasing national awareness and working to solve the problem.

more easily integrated into the existing system—and more useful to a broader range of stakeholders.

Sustainability

In systems terms, sustainability is intrinsically about optimizing across the ecosystem—vs. maximizing for any one aspect.

> ### TIMEOUT: Maximizing breaks systems
>
> Again, let's think this through for ourselves using a few everyday examples of the harm that maximizing one aspect of the ecosystem over another does (and please feel free to call up a few of your own)...
>
> Maximizing a population: When, say, the lemming population (okay, so not quite an everyday example, but useful) grows too large and overgrazes the slow-growing moss on which they depend, they drive themselves into mass famine—accounting for the sudden sharp decline in their numbers. By the way, it's an absurd—though popular—myth that they commit the kind of mass suicide popularized in the 1958 nature documentary *White Wilderness,* when, allegedly, the cameraman had a friend tossing lemmings from the top of a cliff to simulate the suicide fallacy.[231]
>
> Maximizing a shareholder value: In another example, take the *Forbes* article "The Dumbest Idea in The World: Milton Friedman" by Steve Denning (June 01, 2011) in which Denning cites Jack Welch (no less) calling out this misconception about the pre-emptive "responsibility" for maximizing shareholder value, along with Roger Martin Dean of the Rotman School of Management at the University of Toronto.[232] Denning even cites business, leadership, and management luminary Peter Drucker as holding a very different view than that of maximizing

---

[231] John Whitfield, *"Why Cycling Lemmings Crash,"* Nature, June 01, 2000
[232] https://www.forbes.com/sites/stevedenning/2011/11/28/maximizing-shareholder-value-the-dumbest-idea-in-the-world/#2d63cc222870

shareholder value. Welch proposes, instead, the need to balance "your employees, your customers and your products." Shareholder value, then, is a byproduct, not a goal.

Any such ideologies of maximization (vs. optimization) as a solution is a version of oversimplifying complexity—something we learned about in the Cynefin Model—that simple solutions for complex problems push the system into chaos. Even the ideology of "trickle-down" economics—a failed ideology[233] that has persisted for 40 years now—is a strategy that maximizes for 1% of the population at the expense of the other 99% (see the figure below on income levels over time since 1970.)[234]

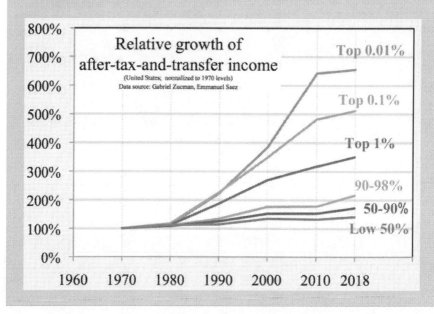

---

[233] Please, as with all of this, don't take my word for it. Check out: Warren Buffet (2019), The Guardian (2019), or Former Labor Secretary, Robert Reich (2017).

[234] Sargent, Greg. "The massive triumph of the rich, illustrated by stunning new data." *Washington Post*, December 9, 2019

If we're to get our heads around how to optimize in pursuit of sustainability, we'll need to access tools (and the perspectives they provide) like those we've been harnessing from the beginning to help us navigate and strengthen the twin strands of Relationship & Clarity— doing so while holding the intention of safeguarding sustainability.

Simultaneously holding one's own worldview, the worldviews of other key stakeholders, and that of the system as a whole affords us a unique opportunity to see and understand the system(s) within which we all live, work, love, and create. The degree to which we can navigate and internalize this holistic, ecosystem-wide perspective raises—as we open ourselves to it—our level of curiosity, communication, understanding, relationship, innovation, action, and performance—respectively. From there, our capacity to continually evolve and implement strategies and solutions that optimize for the ecosystem over time can ignite a mutually beneficial systemic response—one that the broad majority of stakeholders as a whole will want to see succeed. These systemically designed holistic solutions develop momentum such that—unless deliberately and consistently disrupted—tend to be sustainable, self-reinforcing, virtuous cycles.

Said another way, if we *don't* seek to optimize for the system as a whole—if we seek only to maximize our advantage to the detriment of others (as if we exist in a win/lose dynamic)—to the degree that we're only pursuing our "local" subsystem and its goal (especially in the absence of a mutually beneficial "global", i.e., ecosystem-wide goal), we're likely to advocate for what is (over time) our individual and collective disadvantage. (See again the "Goal" section in Chapter 4.)

Our systemic approaches for building Relationship & Clarity give us a running start on Sustainability—in keeping with the systems think-ing principle that structure determines behavior. Still, these approaches and their resultant Relationship & Clarity need to be translated into specific mechanisms if we're to ensure Sustainability beyond the initial insight they spark.

So we'll need a fuller portfolio of tools—in addition to the relationship-building Integrated Map, the conversations, and the clarifying Stakeholder Assessment workout. That is, if the reciprocating, mutually reinforcing domains of Individual and Organizational sustainability are to continue to evolve.

Organizational Sustainability: an Organizational Learning Engine

Jim Collins and Jerry Porras articulated (and, through their research, rigorously evidenced) what still stands as the exemplar of internal organizational sustainability: Vision. In their seminal 1996 *Harvard Business Review* article "Building Your Company's Vision", they relayed the results of research that revealed how it was that a select few companies had outperformed the market by a factor of 12 since 1925. Given that the average tenure of a company on the Fortune 500 list was, at the time, 20 years, 70+ years of sustainability was worthy of their curiosity—and ours.

Articulating a Vision

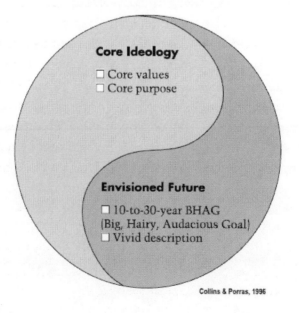

Core Ideology

☐ Core values
☐ Core purpose

Envisioned Future

☐ 10-to-30-year BHAG
(Big, Hairy, Audacious Goal)
☐ Vivid description

Collins & Porras, 1996

The way of working described in the article still relies on Collins' and Porras' framework as a broadly useful way to parse out vital aspects of organizational sustainability. While how we've deployed their wisdom is beyond the scope of this book (but will be detailed in the Practitioner's Manual), their still-valid frame includes two major components that they saw as the Yin and Yang of Vision—composed of 4 subcomponents as illustrated above.

Such organizational vision lies at the heart, literally, of organizational sustainability. Yet, when I first decided to return to the organizational world after my immersion in the humanistic worlds of Rolfing® and somatically-oriented trauma and developmental psychotherapy,[235] I was trying like mad to make sense of the rest of the field of organizational development.

I spent many long days in the Tattered Cover Bookstore in Denver, Colorado, going book by book by book through their business section—then cross-referencing it with their psychology, systems-thinking, ethology, physics, design, and other disciplines.

Initially, doing so only increased my confusion about the field of organizational design and development (OD) as I tried to get my own head around the fundamentals from a human-centric point of view. I still recall the diversity of really smart, thoughtful, insightful academicians, consultants, leaders, and other authors championing their ideas: "it's leadership"; no, "it's teamwork"; nope, it's "financial transparency"; uh-uh, "it's reward systems"; sorry, "it's communication"; you're all off, "it's personal transformation"; and so on. Pretty soon, though, a pattern began to emerge—a pattern that included and transcended any one perspective on OD—one I dubbed the "Organizational Learning Engine" (OLE')—one that looks like this:

---

[235] I feel I'd be doing you a disservice if I didn't point out that the advantage of somatically-oriented approaches to not only physical and psychological health, but even leadership—approaches that give us access to our ontology, our state of being—can't occur without a physical body. Hence, not a bad place to begin our work.

I've shared this with dozens of leaders and consultants over the years who consistently find it to be an invaluable checklist for guiding how to assess, adapt, and/or redesign organizations to optimally respond to ever-changing landscapes.

Let's briefly traverse this 10-element model to check out for ourselves what an integrated, sustainable system of OD is made up of at an elemental level—validating each of the fundamental levels separately—Individual, Team, and Organization—before summing up at the level of the Whole.

Beginning where the action actually takes place down on the ground, with the Individual, our Perceptions①—what we see, hear and otherwise sense—determine how we Think/Feel② which determines how we Act③.

Pause a moment to let that settle—to decide for ourselves whether that seems true—or not. Does it seem true that we rely on what we see, hear, and otherwise experience to help us translate reality of our situation, via our thoughts and feelings, into a response—into an action?

For everyone I've worked with so far, the answer is "Yes." Well, there is an exception. Those who operate based on ideology vs. reality consistently either ignore what they see, hear, and experience—or selectively filter it. In the clinical literature, this is known as denial—a primitive psychological defense mechanism often coupled with projection and dissociation.

At the Team level, how we ④Communicate determines how we ⑤Relate, which drives how we ⑥Perform. Again, let's play this out. If we're communicating well (authentically), the likelihood that, as a Team, we'll relate well rises—along with our ability to perform. We see this articulated more elegantly in the Align, Act, Adjust phases of Conversant's Cycle of Value model (Chapter 3).

On the other hand, poor quality communication typically damages our ability to relate, leading to poor performance which, in turn, if left unchecked, drives even worse communication (blaming, etc.)—further corroding relationship and performance.

We see both ends of this spectrum (value and waste) well-discriminated in both the Conversant model and Yvonne's SAVI model (again, Chapter 3).

At the level of the Organization—assuming that our work is aligned with our purpose—our awareness of a condition in need of attention via ⑦Transparency naturally stimulates an innate sense of ⑧Accountability to respond. When we see that something needs doing—if we're healthy—we at least feel the impulse to pitch in—whether we act on it or not. In a value-exchange network/organization/community, this in turn, prompts the expectation of ⑨Reciprocity—which, if we're to be individually and collectively aware of reciprocity across the organization/network—requires Transparency. And the cycle repeats.

We can test this Organizational loop for ourselves at two levels, micro and macro. At the micro level, when we see someone in need—an elder trying to cross the street or a pregnant mother struggling to stand in a bus or train or waiting room—I'm imagining that something within us at least recognizes the need and has the impulse to help.

And I'm guessing that we would expect (or at least hope) that others would make similar gestures if the need arose. These are inborn qualities—the product of 3.5 billion years of evolution—this response to the awareness of need, taking accountability/action, and expecting reciprocity—if not directly for you, then for and/or from others. It's common to all mammals within, and even across, their communities. An excellent way to experience this is to watch the documentary cited earlier (in Chapter 4), *Why Dogs Smile and Chimpanzees Cry*—a deep dive into the emotional, communal, and even empathetic lives of animals.

At the macro level, we're seeing this play out now—something that has been amplified exponentially by COVID-19—the rising inequity in our societies—especially, in the United States. Though you're likely aware of it, beginning in the '80s, the incomes (and, even more so, the wealth) of the lower economic quintiles have either remained relatively flat (income) or fallen (wealth)—while those of the upper quintiles have risen, with the upper 1% rising exponentially (see the graph below[236])—even more so the top 0.1%—and more so still, the top 0.01%. As experts across several disciplines have reflected in the film *Capital*[237] (based on Thomas Picketty's groundbreaking book of the same name), historically this has led, not only to increasing society-wide poverty and hardship, but also to increasing racism, xenophobia, violence and, throughout history, even revolution and war—a testament to both the demand (though it expresses in differing ways) and the need for accountability and reciprocity as transparency increases.

---

[236] Sargent, op. cit.

[237] *Capital in the Twenty-First Century*, by Thomas Picketty; https://www.imdb.com/title/tt5723056/.

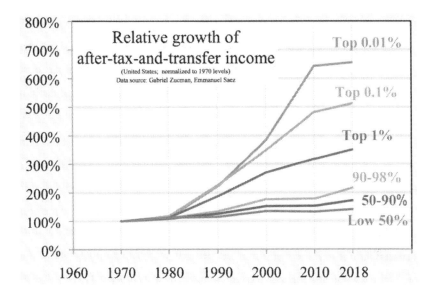

As we begin to then integrate the spheres—the Individual, Team and Organization—how these interrelate (and why there are so many differing approaches to organizational design and development) becomes clear. Following the arrows connecting the three domains: as Transparency increases, so does our ability to Perceive; eventually resulting in our Action. How we act is our ultimate Communication (actions speak louder than words). The more we Communicate, the greater the Transparency. Increasing Transparency sparks Accountability, triggering: 1) Action (if you make me accountable, I *will* Act), while also 2) increasing expectations of Reciprocity which, correspondingly, incentivizes Performance.

You can use this framework to both identify weaknesses in sustainable organizational structures and then map existing resources (books, videos, consultants, podcasts, etc.) to each domain. BTW, in over two decades of my career in Organizational Development, I've yet to come across a resource that couldn't be housed under one of the aspects of this framework—especially when we include that…

Our ⑩Beliefs lie at the root of this—as they drive our perceptions (more on this below), which then drive so much more. This may seem obvious to some. At the same time, science's ability to make sense of beliefs is in its nascent stages—still challenged to ferret this out. That said, there are recent studies that specifically target this. And I'd like us to investigate them in what I hope is a meaningful sequence, from micro levels to progressively macro levels.

But first, let's look at how the OLE' framework plays out at the internal organizational level…

The Real World: PolicyLink & OLE'

I first met Angela Blackwell[238], Founder and CEO of PolicyLink, as one of 35 leaders—mayors, agency heads, business leaders, economists, NGO leaders, academicians, and others—engaged in strategizing the implementation of California's formal response to climate change—embodied in two bills: AB32—which would reduce overall GHG's from all sources, and SB375—which would reduce vehicle miles traveled (VMT)/person while improving public health and community livability. In the process of interviewing Angela—and especially when she saw her individual map from our interview—she noted that this was the first time a consultant "got" her—actually understood the complexity of what she was seeking to cause. She then asked whether or not I did organizational development work—leading to a much deeper relationship with PolicyLink.

As a part of Barack Obama's historic 2008 presidential campaign, he cited Geoffrey Canada's Harlem Children's Zone Project (HCZ) as a model for breaking the cycle of generational poverty in the U.S. This took the form of the Promise Neighborhoods program.[239] Angela and PolicyLink were intimately familiar with the HCZ—voluntarily

---

[238] My thanks to Angela, Josh, and Policylink for allowing me to include their story here.
[239] Promise Neighborhoods is a US Dept of Education program to support students in all neighborhoods, cradle through college.

compiling a draft implementation handbook as part of helping to brief then President-elect Obama on how to actually bring his campaign promise to life. Based on PolicyLink's grasp of the HCZ, coupled with their history of advancing racial and economic equity for all by lifting up what works, Obama engaged PolicyLink to pilot the HCZ across the U.S. via the Promise Neighborhoods program.

As a result of their successful work since their founding, PolicyLink had grown from 24 employees to 74 and from $3MM+ in revenue to $10MM+ in 10 years. Along with this, both the scope and scale of their work had expanded exponentially. This placed them on the threshold of a very different, more complex staffing structure—one that called for a very different organizational structure.

In the process of exploring how to solve for this, Angela and her leadership team felt that the OLE' model was an intuitive fit for PolicyLink's challenge—that it provided a context for both examining and addressing the redesign of their organization in response to the tremendous growth in demand, size, and complexity they were experiencing.

Using the OLE' as a guide, we proposed a discovery process to staff to elicit what would actually enable PolicyLink as a whole to build an organization in which everyone can participate and prosper—to, by design, internally mirror PolicyLink's external mission in the World. That rough frame looked like this[240]:

---

[240] Again, this image is available its original color version at scottspann.com/impossible

In the spirit of Emergence, and as a means of honoring the principles of individual Purpose, Choice and Transparency, we let each individual choose which part of the frame in which they most wished to participate. We then held four half-day group model building sessions to design the system of resources and relationships that we collectively believed would literally cause the goal of participation and prosperity within PolicyLink. These were then integrated to reflect how each of these four elements— this system—created a virtuous cycle that would ensure PolicyLink's ability to create the organizational leadership and management structure needed to both meet their external commitments/challenges while ensuring organization-wide participation and prosperity.

The result was a suite of organizational design and development mechanisms. These included: a new leadership decision-making network to support Angela as she transitioned from hands-on internal management to more outward-facing strategic activities; a leading-edge leadership 360° process[241] to guide ongoing leadership and man-

---

[241] Again, relying on the statistically validated and well-tested Leadership Circle 360 system.

agement development from a set of values that arose from the members of organization itself; a project management system that highlighted the magnitude, risk/reward ratio, and condition of strategic initiatives on a single screen (vs. hosting a series of 1-on-1 weekly briefings by each project lead); a shared, accessible learnings database to fuel ongoing innovation; and systems for ensuring work/life balance in the face of ever–increasing workloads.

By seeding our organizational learning and evolution process with the simple insights captured by the OLE' framework, PolicyLink was able to emergently design a system that both the leadership team and the staff felt confident would position them for the challenges and opportunities arising out of their complex ecosystem on a daily basis.

Organizational Internalization: Your own OLE' assessment

If this simple OLE' framework resonates for you, it doesn't have to be employed at such a scale over several months. You can begin to act on it today by assessing (on, say, a scale of 1-10) each of the 10 elements—either on your own, with your team or across your organization. Your resultant score can then serve as the basis for individual, team, or organizational conversations. From there, moving on to systemic solutions for strengthening your organizational structure and behavior to further embed this way of working—and of being—into your organizational DNA. Still, I hope you'll seriously consider the next section essential to any of your conversations, that is…

While internal organizational structures can create the initial conditions requisite for Sustainability, we can magnify their impact by similarly acting to ensure…

Individual Internalization: Belief as a choice

Just as our Beliefs lie at the heart of the OLE', our internal state of Being—rooted in our Beliefs—is absolutely crucial to our Individual Sustainability. Of particular impact is the *embodied* quality of our Beliefs.

Beginning even at that first level—the Level of the Individual—our Beliefs energize and animate us up to and through the sixth level— Ecosystem Sustainability—and beyond. Given their seminal role, let's go deeper here—picking up where we left off in the OLE' model.

A deeper dive on Beliefs

As I promised before we jumped into PolicyLink, we'll now delve more deeply into Beliefs in what I hope is a meaningful sequence— from micro levels to progressively macro levels. My apologies if this seems a bit tedious but I feel an obligation—a responsibility to you—to ground the intangible, often unconscious and implicit nature of Beliefs in physical reality—just as we need to do with all of this.

This depth of focus on Belief here is both deliberate and essential. That is, if we're to truly design ourselves for the Sustainability we seek in our World, our Beliefs either limit or liberate that space, and, thereby, us.

Let's first look at the impact of our neurology on our perception, then, second, on our behavior.

Let's begin with an MIT study[242] that examines prior beliefs and their impact on perception. In this work involving animals (then, later, humans), scientists discovered how the brain encodes prior beliefs and puts those beliefs to use in the control of behavior, doing so at the synaptic level. As a result, they found that "prior beliefs bias behavioral responses by warping the neural representation."[243] Jon Lieff, MD, has shared that expectations act at the neuro-physiological level of the brain to cause the buildup of blood flow in some parts of the brain while dampening it in others.[244] So there are clear mechanisms that explain how beliefs and expectations impact the brain at a physical

---

[242] See *How expectation influences perception*, Anne Trafton | MIT News Office, July 15, 2019.
[243] ibid.
[244] Jon Lieff, M.D., *Searching for the Mind*, April 12, 2015, jonlieffmd.com/blog/how-does-expectation-affect-perception.

level—impacting even our perception, the basis of our relationship with Reality itself.

Going deeper on that second level—behavior, Kathy Dean and Jeanie Forray (in the *Journal of Management Education*) examine the achievement disparity for students of instructors who believe in a fixed (vs. growth) mindset regarding learning ability—i.e., do we believe that: a) intelligence is innate or b) it can be developed.[245]

For those who believe intelligence is fixed, the achievement disparity between the perceived lesser group (Native American, Blacks and Hispanics) and another, perceived superior group (Whites and Asians) is *double* over just a 2-year timespan. While I won't attempt to explain the subtleties here—the article is an interesting, informative read across a range of belief biases. Similar outcomes have been reported along, not just racial and ethnic dimensions, but gender and others, as well.[246]

Michael Connors and Peter Halligan (in *Frontiers in Psychology*) are even more explicit, stating that "when a belief is accepted as true and held as such, it…will contribute…to configuring the person's perception, memory, and action. As a result, the person will perceive the world in a way that is consistent with the new and congruent existing beliefs. There is…considerable evidence that beliefs can act to bias the perception and interpretation of information so that it is consistent with the beliefs."[247]

Returning to Yvonne Agazarian and *Systems Centered Therapy* (SCT), one of the theoretical foundations upon which her body of knowledge relies is on the fundamental significance of Beliefs as postulated by Alfred Korzybski, the founder of the field of general semantics.

---

[245] Kathy Lund Dean, Jeanie M. Forray, "Perception Becomes Reality: How Our Beliefs Affect Student Learning Outcomes," *Journal of Management Education*, July 11, 2019.
[246] Brookings Institute, *How our education system undermines gender equity*, April 23, 2018, brookings.edu/blog/brown-center-chalkboard/2018/04/23/how-our-education-system-undermines-genderequity.
[247] Michael H. Connors and Peter W. Halligan, "A cognitive account of belief: a tentative road map," *Frontiers in Psychology*, 13 February 2015 | https://doi.org/10.3389/fpsyg.2014.01588.

Yvonne[248] shares early on in her groundbreaking book that "Korzybski (1948) portrayed man as a map maker who is often so reluctant to revise the map [the belief system] to fit the territory [Reality] that he is apt to revise the territory to fit the map instead."[249]

Despite our best intentions, our most deeply held beliefs are beyond our conscious choice/control. This was made distressingly clear in Malcolm Gladwell's book *Blink* in which he describes our tendency toward implicit bias as evidenced by Harvard's "Project Implicit" test where, *regardless of your race*, you take microseconds longer to connect positive concepts with black faces than white ones (*even if you're Black*).

Like so much of life, the knowing about the pivotal role of Beliefs is not new. Perhaps it's best summed up by Gandhi:

**Your beliefs become your thoughts,
Your thoughts become your words,
Your words become your actions,
Your actions become your habits,
Your habits become your values,
Your values become your destiny.**

M K Gandhi

---

[248] Yvonne Agazarian, *Systems-Centered Therapy for Groups*, London, pg. 4 (1997).
[249] Yvonne Agazarian op cit.

What we choose to believe?

As you've likely derived from my early use of the question, "What are you seeking to cause?", I choose to believe that we have far more control over our contributions to Life, to Society, and even to ourselves than we currently exercise (or, especially relevant in this context, even *believe* is possible). This naturally extends to our belief in our ability to actively determine (or, at least, influence), well, our beliefs themselves.

For me, personally, I've taken the dilemma of beliefs and their impact on perception, thought, feeling, and action to heart or, at least, I'm attempting to. I say "attempting to" as this is, for me, an ongoing practice—something I aspire to by constantly reminding myself—especially when I slip—to return to what I *choose* to believe. As a way of reinforcing my intention to actively (vs. passively) manage my beliefs, I publicly declare (on my website and, whenever appropriate, in conversation) that I *choose* to believe that *most* people:

- *Want to do the right thing*—and, in complex systems, that's not always straightforward
- *Want to live lives of meaning and belonging*—and we're all trying to relearn how to do that
- *Need to be challenged and to learn*—and need the two to be closely coupled in time
- *Are designed to collaborate and succeed*—we've just been systematically taught not to
- *Value being led*—and are tired of being misled.

That "most people", by the way, is an acknowledgement that bullies do indeed exist—psychopaths, sociopaths, and narcissists—for whom an additional set of understandings and skills are needed.

Individual Internalization: Your Felt Sense of Belief

While this is not a book about Beliefs (a subject for its own books, its own body of knowledge/work), any aspiration to solve an "impossible" issue/opportunity relies, at its core, on our own deeply held Beliefs—and their intrinsic relationship with our own Purpose. Inasmuch as these two seeds are central to, not only this work, but to our very state of being, they warrant at least a bit more attention.

As for choosing and internalizing your Beliefs…

… and how you might choose to do that, there's another way of thinking about Beliefs that we might find useful—a way for us to evaluate the value of whatever beliefs we choose to hold (or, at least, to practice). For example, asking ourselves a series of questions like:

- How's that working? (I.e., what's the natural consequence of holding one set of beliefs over another?)
- How/do/are such beliefs serving us?
- What emotions or even sensations arise in your body as you reflect on those beliefs?
- Do you feel weaker or stronger? More relaxed (and ready) or more tense (and restricted)?

This is akin to the "For" vs. "Against" mindsets we've contemplated throughout our conversations in this book where an "Against" frame constrains us while a "For" mindset liberates us.

As but one example, if I choose to assume positive intent, until demonstrated otherwise, akin to our "innocent until proven guilty" ethic, I'm usually delighted at how well the interaction goes. If, conversely, I show up assuming other than positive intent, well, things don't go as well—the interaction is not nearly as creative or productive.

Or perhaps this is best summed up by Byron Katie[250] with 2 of her 4 questions:

- How do you react—what happens—when you believe that thought?
- Who would you be without the thought?

About choosing and internalizing your Purpose...

I've consciously sequenced our conversation about Purpose to follow Beliefs specifically because (too) many leaders I've worked with have such limited beliefs about what's possible that even accessing, much less actualizing, their purpose was beyond their reach. As but one example, in the work my friend Tim Kelley[251] did with me, the first thing he checked for was whether or not I had any limiting beliefs.

The principle of "purpose" scales from the purpose of an object (e.g., Heidegger's "hammer") to that of a meeting to that of your own Life. Ideally, as we become increasingly aware of and more intimately familiar with our Life's Purpose, more and more of our Life comes into alignment with our Purpose. As for deepening our Relationship with and Clarity about our Purpose...

As a part of my work and relationship with my friends/colleagues at Conversant, they offered me a slot in their transformational leadership course Credibility, Influence, and Impact,[252] hosted at the Home Ranch—a horse ranch (an elegant one) nestled in the mountains of Colorado near Steamboat Springs. As a part of that program, we probed the "shadow" side of my purpose (my inauthentic self) to create fertile ground for my authentic self, a sense of purpose that guides me to this day. Revealing my authentic self/purpose was a team effort that included questions like:

---

[250] Byron, Katie, *Loving What Is: Four Questions That Can Change Your Life Kindle*, (2002).

[251] Kelley, Tim; *True Purpose: 12 Strategies for Discovering the Difference You Are Meant to Make*, Transcendent Solutions Press (April 1, 2009).

[252] For more on their innovative and awakening approach to leadership see: https://www.conversant.com/credibility-influence-impact/

- What about you would survive any change in circumstance?
- What essential value are you to life? We need you because….
- What is the word God gave you to be?
- What problem are you the answer to?
- and others…

…along with a set of rich, deep, mutually supportive (working with my team) insights, exercises, and events that brought far more aliveness to my life than I can do justice to here. Ha! Some of the most valuable lessons came from ranch manager Johnny Fisher's "horse whisperer" approach to our relationship with our chosen horse as our teams prepared for the cattle roping event that capped off the end of our first week together.

Another approach to Purpose is that of my friend, Tim Kelley,[253] who walks you through a diverse array of strategies for accessing and illuminating your Purpose—including indirect, direct, and facilitated practices along with methods for clearing fears and living into your Purpose. My good friend, Holly Woods, also offers a rich, well-researched approach to finding Purpose as it relates to different stages of life through a blend of hard data and client stories.[254]

Whatever method you choose—whether one of these, a vision quest, silent retreat, or even plant medicine—your ability to forge an ongoing, ever-present, lived experience of your Purpose will amplify and enrich, not only your life, but that of those around you—serving as your own "divining rod" when confronted with pivotal decisions.

The Real World: Ontology and Leadership in an F100 company

Back with my good friends (and highly skilled colleagues) at ARC International, Dennis Stratton and I were leading a 3-day leadership

---

[253] Tim Kelly, op cit.
[254] Woods, Holly; *The Golden Thread: Where to Find Purpose in the Stages of Your Life*, New Degree Press (April 8, 2020).

offsite with a senior F100 team—the leadership team of one of their most significant business units. We'd spent the prior 2.5 days grappling with strategic, performance, and cultural assessments—visioning from there, then prioritizing, strategizing, and planning. Now it was time to prepare for leadership's re-entry into the day-to-day—to engaging with their next level of teams, staffs, and employees.

ARC's style of consulting evolved out of the world of ontological coaching and consulting—one that understands humans as biological, linguistic, emotional, somatic, cultural, and historical beings. We are/it is this holism that is the underlying driver of our behavior, communication, and, ultimately, performance—the source of our beliefs and perceptions, many of which limit us— even though they operate below consciousness—outside of our everyday awareness.

To access and illuminate this limited awareness, we used a practice we called a "Leadership Stand."

TIMEOUT: "Resourcing" before "stressing"

I need to acknowledge the potential for "shaming" or in some way harming those I work with—ways to make sure I "do no harm." As I learned as a trauma psychotherapist, one should never stress someone's nervous system without having first resourced it—having provided a way for the individual to deal with whatever arises from the probe employed in an effort to help them more fully discover themselves.

In the case of the Leadership Stand, it is possible—if left unchecked, untended—to literally cause someone to feel shame. So I'd put this in the "professional: do not try this at home" category until such time as one knows—with a high degree of confidence, how to help someone deal with any perceived negative consequences from "failing" this exercise—something for the Practitioner's Manual.

Near the end of our retreat, each leader spent a bit of time getting clear about what they were now committed to—deeply, consciously, even viscerally committed to—their purpose going forward. Then, with the leadership team sitting in a circle, each leader, one at a time, would stand and speak their commitment.

The ontological test of their authenticity was whether or not each (hopefully all) of the other leaders *literally* felt moved to stand up—did those seated actually sense an energetic impulse to rise based on a leader's physical and verbal presence—or not. The exercise was transformational!

For those whose stand was confirmed, their commitment deepened—fortified by the resonance with their peers. For those whose stand didn't initially resonate, we more deeply plumbed the true depths of their purpose—and even their lives—until we achieved resonance. *Repeating that caveat*: As we did here, one should only engage in practices that, when we're surfacing a *weakness*, also bring the requisite *strengthening* resource to bear to "cure" that weakness. Anything less risks causing significant harm.

To this day, I use this standard (if not this exact process) to confirm, not only the purpose and commitment of the leaders I work with, but even my own. If I can't literally sense it in my body, hear it in my voice, and express it in my mood, I know something is off—and I go looking/sensing for what's amiss.

And as a part of my own promise to you—my own commitment, I need to be sure that this Leadership Stand example doesn't somehow land as an isolated "one-off"—unrelated to this way of working. The very reason we did this on the backend of our leadership offsites was that, without the Relationship & Clarity that came out of our intense time together, this level of confidence out of which commitment arose would not have been possible.

Unlike what too many will-based leadership and personal change processes rely on—i.e., simply willing oneself into action—when properly designed and enacted, responsible commitment shows up as an emergent property. That is, if we've done our job well—working authentically, level by level, paying explicit, conscious attention to both our Beliefs and our Purpose—people naturally reach for commitment— instinctively see, even feel how, by adding their commitment, fueled by their Beliefs and Purpose, to that of the Whole, what we're each/ all seeking to cause now becomes possible.

Speaking of possible…

Chapter 7: At the Level of Possible

"Impossible" Relationship x "Impossible" Clarity = Possible

Now we're entering a very different chapter—a more reflective one—arriving at our pivotal one.

We've spent around 300 pages together, sharing what's been discovered over 20 years of working in this way—how working successfully with "whole" systems by definition compels us to conceptualize the work *first* based on what it means to be fully Human—*only then* adapting/applying systems thinking/system dynamics tools to solve the kinds of complex, wicked problems emerging today—ones arising at increasing rates—rates now shifting from linear to near exponential as, for example, COVID 19 intersects with our economy(s) intersects with our political system(s)— or as COVID 19 intersects with a white police officer's killing of George Floyd intersects with structural racism—and so on.

This way of working proposes (and I've experienced) that the ongoing practice of literally holding, simultaneously, both the people and the process in one's nervous system—internalizing, even embodying this "whole"—prepares the ground[255] out of which optimal solutions can and, if we stay present to this practice, inevitably *do* emerge.

But that's my experience and, while I have an abundance of testimonials from leaders I've worked with, I'm an "n of 1"—far too

---

[255] Robert Fritz op. cit.

small a sample size. It's been my intention all along that, in sharing this with you—given the successes I've been privileged to be a part of—that it will become yours, too. That you'll join in this ongoing exploration, discovery, evolution, and then documentation of the principles, practices, and processes—the disciplines required to reliably, productively, and even predictably replicate your own success at scale. And at a scale sufficient to close those gaps we posited early on—those gaps between what Reality says is needed and what exists today— preparing us for those gaps yet to come.

If this way of working is to become your experience…

When I'm initially consulting with leaders—helping them to think and feel through how to approach their own complex, "impossible" problem—I don't ask them questions like, "What's our next step?" or "Can I send you a proposal?" I wait for them to ask—to initiate the first move in the direction of our aligned, authentic partnership.

In my conversations with them, I've simply been seeking to add as much value as I can until such time as they "reach" for this way of working. We're not ready until that impulse to act shifts from external (me) to internal (them)—ensuring that our relationship arises organically—out of a natural, felt sense of attraction to the common-sense validity of working in this more fully human, yet more rigorous, more emergent way.

Similarly, I'm not attempting to "push" this way of working with you— seeking, instead, to be transparent with you. I'm simply sharing what has worked across industries, issues, geographies—even cultures—even in the face of predetermined beliefs/biases that this is "impossible." I'm laying this before you, asking that you apply your own common sense and judge for yourself. If, as a result, you don't feel a natural impulse to reach for this—if some new and promising insight hasn't awakening in you, then I've not (yet) done my job—not (yet) kept my promise.

At one time, I too was tempted to label as "impossible" those issues/opportunities confronting us today—this next step in our evolution—those challenges confronting us as Individuals, as Leaders, as Organizations, and as Societies—perhaps even as a Species. If I chose a state of denial, I could almost find strange comfort in using that excuse to step back from the edge of such challenges—taking the safer (in the short term), easier, more conventional, more convenient path.

I could even ascribe it to things like time, money, or skill. Yet we know from experience that it's not the amount of time involved. Working in this way has consistently been a relatively low overhead effort in every organization in which it's been applied, even in the case of a $30B technology company taking 30 days (start to finish) while involving less than 8 days of client involvement.

Even that's more than made up for in the relationships developed (again, with self, others, and Reality) and, as a result, the follow-on ease and effectiveness of implementation that this method and mindset evokes.

It's not the money—even in the short term, the depth of Relationship & Clarity, of understanding, insight, and effective, efficient execution developed recoup the cost of such processes many times over.

It's not a matter of skill. If you like, we'll even teach you and/or your staff *how* to do this. Actually, that's the only way this will scale. Doing so is in line with my own Purpose that this way of working has to scale. All of us who see and work on such issues simply have to scale such solutions.

Even if I were to choose such excuses, I'd then find myself confronted by several questions, questions I'll share with you beginning with the crux of the matter…

Can we really permit "impossible" to be true?

Like so many questions, this is a question that only causes more questions—now delving into the "why" corollary of our "what" and "how" conversations about scalability—adding "why" to the "what" and "how" of our opening "fundamentally broken" context. What I welcome about this is the seeming truth that answers divide, questions unite.[256] So in that spirit, these other questions—these other opportunities to unite—include:

- What are the consequences of allowing these challenges to be "impossible"? The consequences for:
  - Political Polarization?
  - Climate Change?
  - Income Inequity?
  - Racism?
  - ...?

... and the consequences for what's most important to you?

- What happens to
  - Our People?
  - Our Planet?
  - Our Economy?
  - Our Community(s)?
  - ...?
- What happens to our loved ones?
  - And what will we say to them?
    - To our Friends?
    - To our Partner?
    - To our Children?
    - And theirs?
- What happens to us? To you and/or to me?
  - In my Body?
  - In my Mind?
  - Even in my Heart?

---

[256] Something I first learned from the K'iche & Mam peoples of Guatemala

While each of these questions offers a richness within which to unite, I find this last one potentially the most telling in this domain of asking me or you to decide for ourselves. That is, what happens to me (or to you), even physiologically—in my nervous system, my bloodstream, my endocrine system, my immune system—to say nothing of my energy levels, my creativity, my contributions, my mood, and even my Spirit. Then from that place—that state of being (or rather, *not* being), what happens to myself and to others? Do I feel stronger or weaker? Am I more or less creative and innovative? Will I even live longer—or not?

I think you likely know the answer, but just in case, please do consider the bodies of research[257] pointing to the health consequences of our choice to side either with the "possible" or with the "impossible"— with optimism or pessimism—with "for" or "against." And as you no doubt know intuitively, choosing "possible" overwhelmingly prevails.

I intentionally used the word "choosing" just now because, as we explored earlier, either perspective (impossible or possible) is a choice—a chosen Belief—something over which, should we so decide, we have (or can achieve) dominion. I find the words of Mohammed Ali somehow fitting in such a context:

"Impossible is just a word thrown around by small men
who find it easier to live in the world they've been given than
to explore the power they have to change it. Impossible is not
a fact. It's an opinion. Impossible is potential.
Impossible is temporary.

Impossible is nothing."

Our ability to overcome the "impossible" in the real-world cases I've shared here has been the result of our conscious, deliberate, and

[257] To see it from both sides, check out: *Optimism and your health*, Harvard Health Publishing, Harvard Medical School, May, 2008 and "IS PESSIMISM BAD FOR YOUR HEALTH?", Marcia Angell, Executive editor, *The New England Journal of Medicine*; *The Washington Post*, May 14, 1996.

committed choice for "possible"—that same state of being that enabled our species to do "impossible" things like create the airplane, eradicate polio, put a Man on the Moon, birth the internet and the Apple Watch (something that was once a fantasy of the old Dick Tracy comics first birthed in 1931)… And there's so much more yet to come—but only if we *choose*.

There was something that I shared early on that may have even greater meaning now: that quote (by way of Robert Dilts) from Gilles Pajou (CEO of the French Pharmaceutical company Pharmacia), "In order to grow as a leader a person must feel a strong will to modify the environment to make it better, then create challenging situations that (he or she) can't get out of except by changing."[258] For me, this is a change I seek to embody—even in my bones.

What now will change?

So we've/you've covered a lot of ground. We've gone from assuming that resolving complex, multi-stakeholder issues was impossible to creating relationship & clarity both individually and collectively through a nested set of relationships from the individual through to the ecosystem—and beyond. With ourselves, our partners, our team, our organization, our constituents/markets, and our society/ecosystem—ultimately with Reality—the Reality of being fully human existing in the Reality of Nature and Life itself. We've done so in a way that evokes certain abilities—leadership, trust, innovation, execution, scalability, and sustainability. These are essential to causing a positive, collective change in our world—something that, without such a set of principles, practices, and processes—ultimately, perspectives—would seem impossible, but now, isn't.

And these changes *must* become possible—not so much because these principles and practices are *the* answers (which, by the way, they're not—simply our preferred approach), but because we, as a species,

---

[258] Robert Dilts, *Visionary Leadership* (1996).

must create such solutions. The complex, multi-stakeholder/multi-sectoral issues now emerging *must* be solvable. Too much is at stake for us—individually and collectively—for this and future generations—for our children and grandchildren and beyond—even for our past generations, if we are to authentically respect and build upon their struggles, their solutions, their contributions. And as we've covered this ground—my clients and colleagues and I—we've re-experienced what, to us at the time, seemed impossible—and was, until it wasn't.

Now, through our stories, I hope you've experienced a bit of it—at least enough of it to decide for yourself whether the issues and opportunities now confronting you are impossible—or not!

In asking you to decide for yourself, authentically posing such a question requires that I, too, thoughtfully, truthfully answer it. My answer lives in my not forgetting what's possible—not forgetting, even for a moment, that others do, by and large operate with good intentions. My answer lives in not forgetting, for even an instant, that the broad majority of people want to live lives of meaning and belonging, rarely ever setting out to do the wrong thing—almost always seeking to do the right thing. It's simply that we live in a complex world where making such decisions isn't as straightforward as we would hope.

Inherent in my own answer is the acknowledgement that this has become, not my work, but my practice—to borrow from our OLE' model, a way of perceiving, thinking, feeling, acting, communicating, relating, and performing to the best of my ability—practicing transparency, accountability, and reciprocity wherever possible—in service to our whole. Ultimately, it's a way of Being rooted in choosing to believe that what's good for us individually and what's good for the Whole can be explicitly and simultaneously named, understood, and included in whatever solutions emerge. We simply can't continue to play a finite, "win/lose" game.[259]

---

[259] In the spirit of James Carse's *Finite and Infinite Games* (2011).

So now, a final question…

Early on in our conversation—way back near the beginning, I posed what may be _the_ question:

> "Now that I know what's possible,
> what's stopping me? What's stopping us? What's stopping you?"

I think you know my answer. I look forward to yours. In the meantime …

I sincerely hope this finds you & yours thriving,

R. Scott Spann, Founder & Strategist
Innate Strategies, Inc.
May 30th, 2020
Aboard _Vivant Pleinement_
Sausalito, CA, USA

Acknowledgements

This was almost the toughest part of the book for the following reason…

I'm thoroughly convinced that there exists information, ideas, and innovations seeking to manifest in physical Reality that only become apparent "whenever two or more shall gather in [its] name." It's from that context that I've approached the acknowledgements section– wanting to give credit to the thousands of individuals, groups, and conversations that have contributed to this Work.

I quickly realized that, even if I could list each of the individual clients, teachers, friends, family, authors, and others (both living and departed) scattered across diverse disciplines, geographies, and cultures to whom I am indebted, I could never adequately acknowledge their contribution. With some, I studied for years. With others, it was a single significant word, phrase, or idea that contributed volumes to the work.

Worst of all was the fact that, inevitably, I would leave out someone deeply deserving.

Of course, all of this only compounds the acknowledgements problem.

So, I quickly realized that the acknowledgement section could well do more harm than good.

With that in mind, I've chosen to do two things…

First, name those whose contributions appear in the book as they arise in context—either explicitly or in the footnotes.

Second, knowing that such an approach omits far too many (and recognizes far too few), I've chosen to keep a running list on my website at scottspann.com/impossible.

So, if perchance I've omitted you (or someone I should have acknowledged), *please* let me know and I'll immediately: 1) apologize and 2) amend the list.

With apologies (and appreciation) in advance,

Bibliography

Agazarian, Yvonne, *Systems-centered Therapy for Groups*; Guilford Press, 1997.

Alexander, Christopher, *A Pattern Language*, Oxford University Press (January 1, 1977.

Allen, David, *Getting Things Done*, Penguin Books, 2001.

Andrea, Steve, *The New Technology of Achievement*, William Morrow Paperbacks (February 19, 1996).

Angell, Marcia, Executive editor, "IS PESSIMISM BAD FOR YOUR HEALTH?", *The New England Journal of Medicine*; *The Washington Post*, May 14, 1996.

Axelrod, Robert, *The Complexity of Cooperation: Agent-Based Models of Competition and Collaboration*, Princeton University Press (August 18, 1997).

Block, Peter, *The Answer to `How' is `Yes!'*, Berrett-Koehler, 2003.

Box, G. E. P., "Robustness in the strategy of scientific model building", in Launer, R. L.; Wilkinson, G. N. (eds.), *Robustness in Statistics*, Academic Press, pp. 201–236, (1979).

Brookings Institute, "How our education system undermines gender equity", April 23, 2018.

Capra, Fritjof, *The Turning Point,* Random House Publishing Group, (1984).

Carse, James, *Finite and Infinite Games: A Vision of Life as Play and Possibility*, Free Press (September 15, 1986).

Castenada, Carlos, *A Separate Reality: Further Conversations with Don Juan*, Simon & Schuster (1971).

Cialdini, Robert, *Influence: The Psychology of Persuasion*, Quill; Revised edition (January 1, 1993).

Collins, Jim & Porras, Jerry, *Built to Last: Successful Habits of Visionary Companies,* Harper Business; 10th Revised edition (November 1, 2004).

Collins, Jim & Porras, Jerry, "Building Your Company's Vision", *Harvard Business Review*, 1996.

Collins, Jim, "Turning Goals into Results: The Power of Catalytic Mechanisms", *Harvard Business Review* (July-August, 1999).

Connolly, Mickey; Rianoshek, Richard, *The Communication Catalyst,* Kaplan Publishing (August 20, 2002).

Connors, Michael H. and Halligan, Peter W., "A cognitive account of belief: a tentative road map," *Frontiers in Psychology*, 13 February 2015.

Cooperrider, David & Whitney, Diana D., *Appreciative Inquiry: A Positive Revolution in Change*, Berrett-Koehler Publishers; 1st edition (October 31, 2005).

de Waal, Frans cited in *Bonobos: Unique in Mind, Brain and Behavior*, edited by Brian Hare, Shinya Yamamoto, (2017), p.119.

de Waal, Frans, *Chimpanzee Politics: Power and Sex Among Apes*, HarperCollins; 1st U.S. edition (January 1, 1983).

Dean, Kathy Lund & Forray, Jeanie M., "Perception Becomes Reality: How Our Beliefs Affect Student Learning Outcomes," *Journal of Management Education,* July 11, 2019.

Denning, Steve, "The Origin of 'The World's Dumbest Idea': Milton Friedman", *Forbes*, Jun 26, 2013.

Diamond, Jared, *Collapse: How Societies Choose to Fail or Succeed*, Penguin Group USA Inc.; 1st edition (December 31, 2004).

Dilts, Robert, *Visionary Leadership*, Meta Publications, (1996).

Doerr, John, *Measure What Matters: How Google, Bono, and the Gates Foundation Rock the World with OKRs,* (Portfolio, 2018).

Eva Wong, *Taoism: An Essential Guide*, Shambala, 2011.

Ferris, Tim *Tools of Titans,* Mariner Books (2016).

Fleisher, Carol & Deats, Paula, *Why Dogs Smile & Chimpanzees Cry* (1999).

Forrester, Jay; *Industrial Dynamics*; Martino Fine Books (December 2, 2013).

Fox, Justin, "From 'Economic Man' to Behavioral Economics", Harvard Business Review, (May 2015).

Fritz, Robert, "The Power of Structural Creative Tension", blogpost, (2013).

Fritz, Robert, *The Path of Least Resistance,* Ballantine Books; Rev edition (April 22, 1989).

Galloway, Timothy, *The Inner Game of Tennis* (1972), Macmillan; Main Market edition (December 1, 2014).

Gerber, Michael, *The E-Myth Revisited: Why Most Small Businesses Don't Work and What to Do About It*, Harper Business; Updated, Subsequent edition (October 14, 2004).

Ghonim, Wael, *Revolution 2.0: The Power of the People Is Greater Than the People in Power*, Fourth Estate (January 19, 2012).

Gladwell, Malcolm, *The Tipping Point: How Little Things Can Make a Big Difference*, Little, Brown; 1st edition (February 29, 2000).

Gleick, James, *Chaos: The Making of a New Science*; Viking Adult, 1987.

Harvard Health Publishing, "Optimism and your health", Harvard Medical School, May, 2008.

Heuer, Richards J., Jr., *Psychology of Intelligence Analysis*, Central Intelligence Agency (1999).

Holle, Britta, *Motor Development in Children: Normal and Retarded,* Blackwell Science Ltd (December 31, 1977).

Katie, Byron, *Loving What Is: Four Questions That Can Change Your Life*, Crown Archetype; 1st edition (March 19, 2002).

Kauffman, Stuart, *At Home in the Universe: The Search for the Laws of Self-Organization and Complexity*, Oxford University Press; 1st edition (September 7, 1995).

Kelley, Tim; *True Purpose: 12 Strategies for Discovering the Difference You Are Meant to Make*, Transcendent Solutions Press (April 1, 2009).

Koestenbaum, Peter & Block, Peter, *Freedom and Accountability at Work,* Pfeiffer; 1st edition (August 1, 2001).

Laloux, Fredric, *Reinventing Organizations: A Guide to Creating Organizations Inspired by the Next Stage in Human Consciousness*, Nelson Parker; Illustrated edition (February 20, 2014).

Lieff, Jon, M.D., *Searching for the Mind*, blogpost, April 12, 2015.

McChrystal, General Stanley*, Team of Teams: New Rules of Engagement for a Complex World*, Portfolio, (2015).

Meadows, Donella H., *Places to Intervene in a System*, Whole Earth Winter 1997.

Meadows, Donella, *Thinking in Systems: A Primer*, Chelsea Green Publishing; Illustrated edition (December 3, 2008).

Moore, Geoffrey, *Crossing the Chasm: Marketing and Selling Disruptive Products to Mainstream Customers*, Harper Business; 3rd edition (January 28, 2014).

Murphy, Michael, *The Psychic Side of Sports* Addison Wesley Publishing Company; 1st edition (January 1, 1978).

Pascale, Richard; Sternin, Jerry, Sternin, Monique, *The Power of Positive Deviance: How Unlikely Innovators Solve the World's Toughest Problems,* Harvard Business Review Press; American First edition (June 16, 2010).

Peterson, Jordan, *12 Rules for Life: An Antidote to Chaos*, Random House Canada; Later prt. edition (January 23, 2018).

Picketty, Thomas, *Capital in the Twenty-First Century*, Belknap Press: An Imprint of Harvard University Press (January 1, 2014).

Porter, Michael, "What is Strategy?" *Harvard Business Review*, Nov-Dec 1996.

Pratchett, Terry, *Guards! Guards!: A Novel of Discworld*, HarperCollins e-books; Reprint edition (March 17, 2009).

Richardson, George P., "Problems with Causal Loop Diagrams", *System Dynamics Review*, (1986).

Ritchie-Dunham, James & Rabbino, Hal, *Managing from Clarity: Identifying, Aligning and Leveraging Strategic Resources*, Wiley; 1st edition (September 12, 2001).

Robertson, Brian, *Holacracy*, Henry Holt and Co. (June 2, 2015).

Senge , Peter; Hamilton, Hal, & Kania, John, "The Dawn of System Leadership", *Stanford Social Innovation Review*, Winter 2015.

Snowden, David J. & Boone, Mary E., "A Leaders Framework for Decision Making", *Harvard Business Review*, November 2007.

Sterman, John, *Business Dynamics*, McGraw-Hill Education; HAR/CDR edition (February 23, 2000).

Surowiecki, James, *The Wisdom of Crowds*, Random House, 2004.

Tolle, Eckhart, *The Power of Now*, New World Library (October 6, 2010).

Trafton, Anne, "How expectation influences perception," *MIT News* Office, July 15, 2019.

Van der Heijden, Kees, *Scenarios: The Art of Strategic Conversation* Wiley; (1996).

Watts, Alan, *Out of Your Mind 03: The Web of Life (Part 1)*, 19:10.

Wolfram, Stephen *A New Kind of Science,* Wolfram Media (May 14, 2002).

Woods, Holly, *Golden Thread: Where to Find Purpose in the Stages of Your Life*, New Degree Press (April 9, 2020).

Zinn, Howard, *A People's History of the United States.* Harper Perennial (August 2nd 2005).

Index?

Hi there,

Yes, I know, an index would have been ideal. At the same time, I'd delayed publication quite a while already—and my publishing consultants had delivered a well-advised ultimatum—now or never!

So, instead, I generated a fairly detailed Table of Contents, one that should enable you to find what you're looking for.

Still, if that really doesn't do it for you, reach out and let me know. And, if enough folks insist on one—well, then I'll know for sure that I need to generate one—and will—and I'll send it out to those who've requested it. In the meantime…

Thanks for making it this far and please stay in touch.

About the Author

Scott solves seemingly "impossible" problems in Business and Society. His work is inspired by his experience with business leaders – trying to do the right thing in complex, competitive situations; with Social leaders in NGO's and government – seeking to satisfy diverse stakeholders in ways that benefit the whole; as a Rolfer and trauma psychotherapist – witnessing people recover from the injuries that life and humanity too often deal us; his time in nature as a cowboy, hunter, and sailor; and his training as an internationally competitive athlete.

Born and raised in South Texas working on ranches and fishing boats, Scott's work experiences range from consulting with Arthur Andersen & Co. to launching the Texas office of The Nature Conservancy; Managing Vice President of RPC, a small national consulting firm, to leading the Rolf Institute; Vice President for ARC, International, a global leadership development & cultural change group, to Stone Yamashita Partners, a global branding & strategy firm; CEO for VC firms to working with former guerrilla and indigenous leaders in Guatemala. And he continues to learn by working with Business and Social leaders today.

Scott has applied his unique strategic methodology successfully in businesses like Apple, HPE, and Humana; on social issues like Climate Change, Affordable Housing, and Social Justice with foundations and NGOs; and on complex projects for the U.S. Navy and the White House.

To learn more about Scott and his work, visit www.scottspann.com.

Made in the USA
Las Vegas, NV
08 June 2023

73128686R00187